REASONABLE
SERVICE

A RATION OF
MY PASSION

KWETE QUAYNOR

Reasonable Service

A Ration Of My Passion

Kwete Quaynor

authorHOUSE®

AuthorHouse™
1663 Liberty Drive
Bloomington, IN 47403
www.authorhouse.com
Phone: 1-800-839-8640

© *2012 by Kwete Quaynor. All rights reserved.*
e-mail: ekq30@hotmail.com
Mobile Phone Number: +233 (0) 20 421 0 421

No part of this book may be reproduced, stored in a retrieval system, or transmitted by any means without the written permission of the author.

Published by AuthorHouse   08/14/2012

ISBN: 978-1-4772-1252-3 (sc)
ISBN: 978-1-4772-1251-6 (hc)
ISBN: 978-1-4772-1253-0 (e)

Library of Congress Control Number: 2012909880

Any people depicted in stock imagery provided by Thinkstock are models, and such images are being used for illustrative purposes only.
Certain stock imagery © Thinkstock.

This book is printed on acid-free paper.

Because of the dynamic nature of the Internet, any web addresses or links contained in this book may have changed since publication and may no longer be valid. The views expressed in this work are solely those of the author and do not necessarily reflect the views of the publisher, and the publisher hereby disclaims any responsibility for them.

CONTENTS

I offer this book to the Almighty God.

For all things were made and came into existence through You. As I stepped into the unknown, from the onset of writing this book, I felt insufficient yet You freely caused Your Holy Spirit to lead me into all the truths You revealed through Your Word.

You provided strength, understanding, wisdom and preserved my life and that of this book up until this time.

It amazes me that You would choose me and honor me with the privilege of being the vessel through which this book was to be written when I least expected. Just the thought of this honor more than humbles me, considering the fact that I am no authority or expert in Praise and Worship and that many others could have been chosen in my stead.

All I know is that You are deserving of all Glory, Power, Honor, Praise and Worship and I trust that I have obediently been able to express clearly all that You have revealed through Your Word to me with regards to the Ministry of Praise and Worship which is my passion.

It is my prayer that this book will effectively communicate and convey your very will in heaven concerning this Ministry to your children in this contemporary world.

I dedicate this book with deepest reverence to You; Father, Son and Holy Spirit.

Love always,
Kwete.

ACKNOWLEDGMENTS

I would like to express my deepest appreciation to my earthly parents—Dr. and Mrs. Quaynor. You are the epitome of love, strength, inspiration and all that is good to and for a son. No one could have ever been what you have been and still are to me. I couldn't have done this without you and I am grateful for all the support (financially and otherwise) and sacrifices you have made to make this project see the light of day.

I am indebted to my spiritual father, Rev Dr Lawrence Tetteh, whose God-given ministry has been of great help to me. Daddy, the anointing of God upon your life has honed my gift and I am grateful to God for your life and the ministry He has given you. Thank you for all the love, prayers, teaching, support and encouragement.

I owe my sincere and special gratitude:
To Rev. Victor Osei, for all the direction and support you have offered. You generously agreed to write the foreword for this book and your candid opinion and input have been an enormous blessing to this book. God richly bless you.

To Rev Joseph Asmah (Ashco), who discovered this God-given Ministry (in praise and worship) in me several years ago, even before I could understand what it fully meant. You encouraged, mentored and inspired me through the changing scenes of my humble beginnings when I could have easily quit.

To Rev Fitzgerald Odonkor, (General Overseer HMI) and the amazing international family of Pastors and members of Harvest Ministries (Worldwide) not forgetting my wonderful 'siblings in Christ' and 'colleagues in Ministry': I am grateful to God for your lives and for how much I have benefitted from you.

To Flowers Gay Schools (Cape Coast), Worldwide Miracle Outreach, Coconut Grove Regency Hotel, COMBERT IMPRESSIONS, Floral Favors and Design House Projects: for all the assistance and varied favors you so freely afforded me.

To Kwaku Baah Acheamfuor, Eben Dodoo and Henry Louis Danso (Combert Impressions), Nana Aba Quaynor, Maame Araba Arhin, Gloria Folson and Araba Brown: for your meticulous editing and all the extra help that you generously offered. Truly, the amount of pressure you withstood and the effort you put into making this book live could have driven lesser persons barmy. You rock!!!

To all of you who helped in diverse ways to make this book a reality: May God richly bless you.

Finally, to you my precious reader: for affording me the opportunity to visit you in your privacy to share with you a ration of my passion. This wouldn't have been if you were not. Thank you and God richly bless you.

Our service to God is so important and very beneficial to our personal lives. Many people in the church today are busy doing the 'King's business' but in actual fact have neglected the King.

Our Lord requires us to give Him our sacrifice of praise, which is what brings His presence to us, as we lift up our hands and voices to His honor.

It is quite clear from this book that the author, Kwete, has had a personal relationship with God and has documented this basic truth that portrays his personal convictions and relationship with God.

Having read through the original manuscript, I can say beyond every shadow of doubt that in this day and age, we need to understand the purpose of our reasonable service to God as never before, for there is a reasonable standard we need to live up to or better still a reasonable service we need to render and anything short of that pronounces guilt upon us.

'I APPEAL to you therefore, brethren, and beg of you in view of [all] the mercies of God, to make a decisive dedication of your bodies [presenting all your members and faculties] as a living sacrifice, holy (devoted, consecrated) and well pleasing to God, which is YOUR REASONABLE (RATIONAL, INTELLIGENT) SERVICE AND SPIRITUAL WORSHIP.'-*Romans 12:1*.

It is therefore our REASONABLE SERVICE AND SPIRITUAL WORSHIP to present ourselves as a living sacrifice, holy and acceptable to God."

I highly recommend this book to the body of Christ first, and to all those who want to stay focused in the service of God.

I also personally wish the author, whom I refer to as my spiritual son and an up and coming seasoned minister who has effected a change in this generation in a very unique manner, God's blessing and speed and all the best from the depth of my heart.

DR. LAWRENCE TETTEH
General Overseer
Worldwide Miracle Outreach (UK)

Enter into His gates with thanksgiving, and into His courts with praise. Be thankful unto Him, and bless His name. For the LORD is good; His mercy is everlasting; and His truth endureth to all generations.

Cultivating an attitude of praise and worship is a great asset any Christian can have. Worship is a relationship builder. It connects us to the Most High and it releases the thought of God, the plans of God and the blessings of God and His power upon our lives, as we mere mortals, begin to walk in the Supernatural.

It is a love relationship with God that leads to brokenness. A broken spirit is a usable spirit, for God dwells in a place with those who have a broken and contrite heart.

Brokenness cultivates humility and submission to God and when we resist the enemy he flees from us.

Worship brings upon us, the covering of God and we are therefore protected. *Ps 91:1-2* 'He that dwelleth in the secret place of the Most High shall abide under the shadow of the Almighty.

Psalms 91:1-2—*I will say of the LORD, He is my refuge and my fortress: my God; in Him will I trust'*.

As you read this timely book, may the presence of God come upon you and may it develop a deeper relationship with the King of kings and the Lord of lords.

Happy reading!

REV. DR. VICTOR OSEI
General Overseer
Family Chapel International (Ghana)

The subject of worship is one that is vital to the heart of God, and will always be needed by the body of Christ. Jesus said "the time is coming and has now come when the true worshippers will worship the father in Spirit and in Truth". This makes an in-depth knowledge on the subject so crucial to every worshipper.

Breaking out of traditions and practices and seeing worship as a lifestyle is the only way to fully touch the heart of God. Therefore, reading the pages of this wonderful book, *"Reasonable Service: A ration of my passion"*, lays out most of the basics or fundamentals to a true life of worship. No one book can fully exhaust the subject of Praise and Worship, and for that reason I applaud Kwete for such a good writing, and for detailing out many of the areas that are mentioned here, and even to the extent of giving worship leaders guidelines to making their calling effective.

Kwete is a son in the Lord, and I thank God for raising him up to be a blessing to many lives. I am very proud of him, and bless God for the things the Lord has taken him through over the years to bring him to where he is. A spiritual father of mine made this statement, "A determined person is one that picks up the stones that have been thrown at him and uses that to build a strong foundation for his life." Kwete is a living testimony to this truth.

I recommend this book to every believer, especially Praise and Worship leaders. I suggest that as you read the book, you use it as a guide to build yourself up and allow the Holy Spirit to be your teacher. You also have to pluck yourself into the vision of your local Pastor and work as a team to bring your local church to that place of experiencing the power of God in worship.
God Bless.

Rev. Joseph Asmah
Senior Pastor
All Nations Church (NJ)

- -

Kwete Quaynor and I grew up in the same town at a time when there was a definite move of God stirring in the land of Ghana. Some of us, as little children, were caught up in the wind that blew over our land. We were blessed to have interacted with young zealous men and women who are now spearheading God's work in the nation of Ghana.

As we have grown older and watched as other generations come after us, a question I ask myself is what impact our generation will have on those to come after.

This book is timely not just for its splendid content but also for what it stands for: The dawn of God's next generation of Christian writers.

I wish him all the best.

Rev Oko Bortei-Doku
Overseer, SAVED,
Lighthouse Chapel International

- -

Kwete Quaynor's life is characterized by a passion for everything he does. This unwavering commitment is reflected in the pages of his maiden book, Reasonable Service, which seeks to draw each of us into a stronger personal relationship with God through the medium of worship. The importance of this book is underscored by the fact that the secret or private victory is always a prerequisite for consistent public victory.

Albert Ocran,
Bestselling Author, Speaker and
CEO of Combert Impressions

- -

This is a full study material for almost all the vital ingredients found in the Bible about Praise and Worship.

Pastor David Ocansey
Head Pastor
Harvest Chapel Int. (Cape Coast, Gh.)

- -

In this book 'Reasonable Service', Kwete highlights some insightful truths about worship that leaves one with a refreshing and a rewarding experience of a new devotion to God and His Kingdom. Its evergreen message is both timely and relevant. Generations shall surely benefit from this book.

Rev Tetteh Djangmah
Senior Pastor
True Vine Charismatic Ch. Int.

INTRODUCTION

Sometime ago, Ghana played host to the first ever Black-American President of the USA, Barack Obama, on his first visit to sub—Saharan Africa. The Obama family visited the Cape Coast Castle, in Cape Coast (a small town where I grew up), and I witnessed the visit. Truly, the spectacle was festive and jubilant, as people from all walks of life poured onto the streets of Cape Coast and to say the least, Cape Coast was busting at her seams. The ecstatic crowd gathered awaiting the arrival of this great man and when his 'birds' (helicopters) touched down eventually at the Sewdu Park, the excitement reached a crescendo. Queues which had formed for hours waiting to catch a glimpse of Obama could hardly hold as people shoved and pushed in anticipation.

Eventually, some of us were able to get just a peep—trust me—that was only a little peep because he was virtually obscured as he was whisked away in his vehicle. Later, I had almost the same glance at Michelle and the kids. And that was it. That was all!!! Really, hundreds of thousands of people who had stood for hours waiting to see him saw nothing of him because the roads and venues he visited were cordoned off for security purposes. Again, the crowd that gathered was so thick; one could hardly see anything from a distance. Those who for some reason could not step out unto the choked streets stayed home and watched a live telecast of the visit.

I remember trying to convince some friends of mine to stay at home to watch the live telecast, but Patrick and Veronica nearly ate me alive. Even though some people knew that they didn't have the slightest chance of seeing anything—considering the multitude that had gathered—they were still prepared to go and somehow be a part of the occasion. People were still prepared to park their cars far from the cordoned areas and walk for hours just to be part of the occasion. What struck me even more was the fact that, people who knew even from the time they set off from home, that they did not stand a chance of seeing Obama, were still disappointed when they did not get to see him and were so tetchy about how upset they were at their not getting to see him. But really considering it all (no disrespects), Barack Obama is just a mortal like us. If our attitude towards a fellow man could be as hitherto described, how much more should we behave when it comes to things pertaining to the presence of the Most High God?

Queues formed way before the Obamas' anticipated arrival yet how often do we act in eagerness to meet with the Most High God? Even though we must prepare ourselves daily in anticipation of meeting God, how many times have we been in church early enough in expectancy of meeting with God? Interestingly, people were prepared to endure the scorching sun and the tiring walk and all other inconveniences just to see Obama but how much are we as Christians voluntarily prepared to be 'inconvenienced' for the sake of meeting the King of kings?

Many knew they were not going to get to see Barack Obama let alone meet him yet they were anxious to be part of the celebration. Even when some were being persuaded to stay home and watch the live telecast, they would not have any of it. On the contrary, how often have we as Christians not stayed at home, making silly excuses and trying to convince ourselves (for whatever reason) that there is no point in going to church. Most of the time, all we need is an excuse to stay at home, so we just need to hear 'jump' and our immediate response is 'how high?'

Again, people were highly disappointed because they could not even catch a glimpse of Obama yet how often in our daily lives or even after church services, have we expressed disappointment or grumbled at the fact that for some reason we did not experience or encounter God in ways we would have wanted to or should have?

Though no one directed the crowds to cheer and celebrate as Obama passed by them, they still went absolutely euphoric. That was as a result of encountering a fellow man and I could not help but wonder how many times our praises to God have reached such a spontaneous, involuntary, uncontrolled and non-stage managed crescendo with the true understanding of the One we have been called to meet in praise and worship.

There are rituals we perform, songs we sing and gestures we make so repeatedly, which have lost their true meaning because we have become too conversant and familiar with them and as a result, they have become just empty practice. I believe that the real reason why we are unable to experience God the way we are supposed to is because we hardly understand what we do when we do them in the house of God. For many, if there could be a way of better understanding certain actions or inactions, they would stand a good chance of experiencing the power and might of His glory.

The fact that someone tends to like or love something in particular does not necessarily mean that anything labeled as such will satisfy him or her. As a matter of fact, a container might not necessarily contain what the label depicts. So it is spiritually in our Christian walk. At times, the supposedly, Spirit-filled, tongues-speaking, Blood-washed, demon-chasing Christians, unfortunately are the very ones who fall victim to 'packing just anything', labeling it 'praise and worship' and presenting it to God as a sacrifice. We need to come to the realization that, even though we are called to praise and worship God, we cannot label just anything 'praise' and, or 'worship' and present it to God Almighty as a sacrifice.

Just like Abel, we need to do the 'right thing' if not (as mentioned in Scripture), even our fat sacrifices will be abominable in the sight of God and what we may label 'praise' might even be noise in His ears. The only reason why Cain's sacrifice was rejected whilst that of Abel was accepted must have been because, as Scripture says, Abel did 'the right thing'. The time has come for believers to attach the required seriousness to the praise we render to God and our worship too. We need to rise above treating our meetings and services as 'just some other occasional social gatherings' to the level where we thoroughly understand the essence of sacrificing praise and rendering worship to God.

These love notes from God take us on an indispensable expedition of spiritual awakening and awareness—back to the very basics which have so long been forgotten and neglected. Even though it seems in this present day that many have become spiritually sophisticated, we cannot afford to get so spiritually advanced to the extent of neglecting or forgetting the fundamental truths.

This is not another wonderful academic or theoretical script in theology intended to add-on to your impressive collection, warming your book shelf. This is a dose of Biblically based spiritual ministration to be administered daily in order to enhance our understanding of Praise and Worship and ultimately, enable us render a 'Reasonable Service' to the Most High God.

As God ministers to you through this book, may He also minister to your unique needs and add unto your spiritual attainment. May He make you an exceptional praise giant and a true Spirit lead worshipper, willing and able to render a *'Reasonable Service'* the way He requires of you. AMEN.

Enjoy the read.

CHAPTER 1

GOD'S HOUSE & HIS PRESENCE

IT is good to be in the HOUSE of God, for David acknowledges that in *Psalms 122:1* by saying, *'I was glad when they said to me, Let us go to the house of the Lord!'*—Yet knowing the difference between being in God's house and being in His **presence** is even better BUT best of all is choosing to be in His Presence. This opening chapter will explore the difference therein and further lead us into what it takes to access the presence of God which we all so desperately need.

GOD'S PRESENCE

So often we hear people claiming to have been in 'the presence of God' when in actual fact they have only been in the house of God and not necessarily in **'His presence'**.

We seem to take so many things for granted in our Christian walk, thereby mixing up what should have been our basic principles and as a result, inevitably confusing ourselves. However, in this book, God compassionately teaches us some fundamental yet essential truths that should alter our approach towards praising and worshipping Him. In this book, I will by the Grace of God, share what He Himself will have you learn as regards praise and worship.

Primarily, it is significant to establish that being in the 'House of God' is not the same as being in the 'Presence of God', and to distinguish clearly between the two.

It is important to note that, one may enter a house and yet not be granted recognition or audience by the occupants of the house for various reasons. If for instance you decided some time ago, to pay me a visit at 103 Pennan Road, Tillydrone, Aberdeen, AB 24 2UA, you would have gotten the address to my residence right and may have even found your way there (in person) without any difficulty, considering the brilliant planning and house numbering system of Aberdeen, not to mention the admirable technology of navigators now on the market. Yet, having discovered 103 Pennan Road, and probably, having met or fellowshipped with others who might have been there looking for me, would not have necessarily implied that you had met with me or been in my presence for that matter. Others might have seen you there and shared fellowship with you, but then it could well have been that you might not have been in my presence. You may not have met my presence and may not have shared fellowship with me.

In like manner, I dare to say that, *being in the house of God is not the same as being in His presence*. Let's face it—many find their way to different 'places of worship'—(which may generally be churches) yet never really get to enjoy the presence of God.

For this group of people, church turns out to be nothing more than just another public gathering.

Sometime ago, the son of a prominent ex-president visited my country, Ghana. The visit had to do with some charity work of some sort and together with his entourage; he decided to visit one of the well known kings in Ghana. It must have been on their itinerary and I believe the necessary preparations had been made to receive them at the palace. To the best of my knowledge, they got the address and directions to the palace right and found their way there but upon arrival, some of them were turned away to dress properly before the king could grant them audience since some of these visitors were considered inappropriately dressed and hence could not be permitted into the presence of the king.

Initially, I presume the visitors might have been excited to have reached the palace and in that light might have taken it for granted that they were going to meet with the monarch or better still, be in the presence of the king of that land. You can imagine how embarrassed or disappointed they were as the news broke that they were not going to be allowed to see the king because of the way some of them were dressed. Apparently, none of them could have sincerely claimed to have been in the presence of the king despite the fact that they entered the palace. I believe this scenario reinforces the point that, simply finding our way into someone's house does not automatically mean we would have had the honor of seeing that person or of enjoying the person's presence.

You could be in someone's estate or even in their building and still not be in their presence even though the person may be in that estate or even the same building with you.

Imagine you going to Buckingham Palace to see the queen on an occasion when she was absent. Your being there would not imply that you were in the Queen's presence, regardless of who you met there and what hospitality was accorded you. In the recent past, an ex-president of the Republic of Ghana, whilst still serving as president, was in London on a state visit at the Queen's invitation. Amidst the glitter and pageantry and all the colorful setting which included an inspection of the guard and a state banquet amongst other functions, the Queen was there with him. She had granted him audience and actually communicated and shared fellowship with him. In this instance and in no uncertain terms, it can be said that, that ex-president was in the presence of the Queen. If the Queen had not shown up at the function, the opposite would have held true.

In the previous illustration (that is, the ex-president's son's visit to one of the palaces in Ghana), it was the guests' dress code that disqualified them from seeing the king, but there are quite a few more things that may debar us from being granted access into certain people's presence.

Another important matter to establish is the fact that, though God is everywhere, He does not manifest or reveal Himself everywhere. Let us consider this scenario:

Pastor Reuben Obeng is a powerful man of God who had been invited to preach at a service. Apparently, most of the members of the assembly did not know him in person and when he arrived (humble as he is); he had decided to sit at the back of the auditorium, without the leadership of the ministry noticing him. As the time for him to minister approached, people became very anxious, questioning the whereabouts of the invited preacher man and how long it was going to take for him to show up. Not until he had been called upon or his identity revealed, did those around him know who he was.

The scenario also demonstrates how God manifests Himself. God being everywhere doesn't necessarily mean He manifests or reveals Himself everywhere.

THE DRESS CODE

If earthly kings demand a certain dress code before one can come into their presence, how about the King of kings? Of course, He deserves the best.

It is imperative to know that there is a 'dress-code' one must adhere to when approaching the presence of our God and until we get that 'dress code' right, we are bound to encounter challenges in accessing God's presence or at worst we could even be barred from entering into His presence all together.

Questioning who will debar us from God's Holy presence? Do you remember when Adam and Eve were driven out of God's presence (in the garden)? Scripture says God set an angel guard over the garden to prevent them from entering into it again. I believe it is clear to you now that the presence of God is guarded hence impossible to enter anyhow.

You don't just wake up one day and automatically find yourself in His presence. No! Things don't just happen that way. In the days of old, the High Priest's leg had to be tied as he went into God's presence. This was done so that, if for some reason, his standing was not right with God and he incurred His wrath and was struck dead, he could be pulled out, which affirms the fact that the presence of God was not a place anybody could meddle with anyhow.

In our present day, we may not have often heard about people being physically put to death by God's presence as a result of their wrong standing with Him as was feared in the olden days. But who can tell why peoples' health, prosperity, ministry, wisdom and other virtues and gifts die off so suddenly especially when they claim to have been into the very presence of God? Could it probably be as a result of our entering into His presence anyhow and thereby incurring His fury?

If we respect our earthly kings by honoring dress codes, conducting and comporting ourselves in a certain 'acceptable' manner whilst in their presence, then isn't it prudent that we honor God even the more?

What then will be the right garment or dress code we need to adhere to when going into God's presence?

According to *Isaiah 61:1-3,*

> *1 'The Spirit of the Lord God is upon me, because the Lord has anointed and qualified me to preach the Gospel of good tidings to the meek, the poor, and afflicted; He has sent me to bind up and heal the broken-hearted, to proclaim liberty to the [physical and spiritual] captives and the opening of the prison*

and of the eyes to those who are bound, 2 To proclaim the acceptable year of the Lord [the year of His favor] and the day of vengeance of our God, to comfort all who mourn, 3 To grant [consolation and joy] to those who mourn in Zion—to give them an ornament (a garland or diadem) of beauty instead of ashes, the oil of joy instead of mourning, the garment [expressive] of praise instead of a heavy, burdened, and failing spirit-that they may be called oaks of righteousness [lofty, strong, and magnificent, distinguished for uprightness, justice, and right standing with God], the planting of the Lord, that He may be glorified.'

Did you realize that praise is referred to as A GARMENT?

In a moment we will consider what garments are for, for which reason the Bible speaks of a garment of praise but before then note that:

▶ The wearing of garments takes an effort since garments obviously don't exactly jump onto people all by themselves. Again, I suppose a garment to be worn is chosen carefully—if not, the purpose for wearing it will be defeated. For example, if the weather is cold, it will not be particularly sensible to wear a sleeveless top nor would it be fashionably sensible to wear a nightgown to a cocktail dinner. I remember a good number of people criticizing an ex-president of Ghana for wearing a suit on the occasion of the 50th Independence Day celebrations. Their reason being that, the president could have done better by wearing something traditional to portray the rich culture of his nation and for that matter Africa. Well, that was their opinion and I refuse to comment on it, yet the point I am bringing to the fore is the fact that there are different garments that are considered ideal for certain occasions and not for others. As a general perspective or as a matter of principle, reasonable people are expected to adhere to such dress codes. Note that in like manner, there are different types and forms of expressions of praise, suitable for different occasions.

▶ A garment may turn out to be of no good if it was just kept in a closet and admired from a distance without actually wearing it.

Just don't forget these three points we have discussed because they will soon come in handy in explaining some further points.

Now a few reasons readily come to mind in considering why we would choose to wear a particular garment over another and I wouldn't be surprised if they strike you as well. I reckon, we wear garments so that they probably:

▶ protect us from the elements of the weather
▶ enhance our beauty
▶ make us look presentable for certain occasions
▶ demonstrate modesty
▶ reveal our identity

Now, when God promises a garment of praise in *Isaiah 61:3,* He contrasts it with heaviness:

3 'To grant [consolation and joy] to those who mourn in Zion-

> *-to give them an ornament (a garland or diadem) of beauty instead of ashes, the oil of joy instead of mourning, **the garment [expressive] of praise instead of a heavy, burdened, and***

failing spirit—that they may be called oaks of righteousness [lofty, strong, and magnificent, distinguished for uprightness, justice, and right standing with God], the planting of the Lord, that He may be glorified.'

I suppose heaviness mentioned here refers to despair as some other versions have it. It also indicates faintness, feebleness, or weakness. This means that, should we accept to wear the garment of praise, which God has provided and which He contrasts with despair, (then just as we physically wear our garments for protection from harsh elements of the weather), praise will spiritually afford us protection against the negative spiritual elements of faintness, feebleness, weakness, heaviness and despair. For this reason, it is important that we wrap up protected in praise.

Praise again enhances our beauty and makes us presentable as we come into the courts of the Almighty God.

We need not be prophets to be able to make out the profession of a nurse in uniform. Again, should we meet a soldier in full military uniform or a chief in his full traditional regalia, there won't be the need for the former to pull out a gun or the latter to show us round his kingdom for us to know their respective professions. What I am driving at is that, people's garments or attires usually reveal their identity.

In the same manner, it shouldn't take much effort to identify Christians by their garments of praise. I believe one reason why some demons may have ventured (with or without success) to treat you with so much disrespect or to play silly pranks on you is because they didn't see what was supposed to identify you as a Christian—your garment of praise.

Can you imagine yourself tired and already frustrated, in traffic and the driver right in front of you driving recklessly? I suppose your first reaction, if you had the chance to overtake him, would be to give him a piece of your mind or maybe make a gesture to register your disgust. (Can I have some honest drivers standing up to be counted?) But now, imagine that just before you uttered that word or made that gesture you noticed that the man was dressed in full military regalia. I can bet that a good number of us would have either had a second thought and to be on the safe side, swallowed our words and forgotten about whatever gesture we would have imagined making.

Maybe you would save that for another driver someday! Why? The uniform alone would have made you think twice. On the other hand, imagine he was still a military man of the same rank but in mufti. I am sure you would have had a go at him without even thinking twice. Now, do you understand why sometimes, even as Christians, demons easily use us with such impunity when we are not dressed up in our garment of praise?

One day at my work place in London, my line manager walked up to me and asked, 'You are a Christian, aren't you?' For a moment I thought that was a very strange question to ask especially when I didn't have the slightest idea about what necessitated it. But I came to understand later that she had gathered it from the way I would go about praising God even as I discharge my daily duties.

Initially, she thought I just loved music—the 'music type' or the 'singing type' as she put it, since most of the praise songs I sang were in my local dialect which she obviously could not understand.

Eventually, she came to realize that there was more to it than just singing, so she became very curious.

Praising God had identified me as a Christian!!!

CHAPTER 2

GOD'S DESIRE TO COMMUNICATE & SHARE HIS POWER & AUTHORITY

I believe the ultimate reason for the act of creation was as a corollary of God's longing to have a family, a friend, someone to live with, fellowship with and even share His authority and power with.

THE CRUCIAL 'RAISON D'ÊTRE' FOR CREATION

There may be many reasons attributed to the purpose of man or why man was created. I am not by this book, seeking to side with or dispute any of those reasons though I have no regrets in quickly hinting that some of them do not 'hold water'.

What I intend to do now is just to mention a few reasons why I believe God must have created me or mankind in general:

1. TO SHARE AUTHORITY AND POWER

According to **Revelation 19:16:**

'And on His garment (robe) and on His thigh He has a name (title) inscribed, KING OF KINGS AND LORD OF LORDS.'

It is interesting that He was not referred to as the 'Ruler of subjects' but rather as KING OF KINGS AND LORD OF LORDS, which at least points out one certainty, doesn't it? We are supposed to be kings and nothing less. He is our King, though we are kings ourselves (or supposed to be for that matter). That is the reason for the title—KING OF KINGS which is written on His vesture and on His thigh.

Now, as far as I know, every king has some authority and power. If He is my King and I have been made king by Him, then I can confidently say that He has also delegated to me some of His power and authority so I can execute my duties as a king.

I can therefore conveniently say that one reason why God created me is to share with me, His authority and power. Again in speaking about the man and woman, Bible says in **Genesis 1:28-30:**

28 And God blessed them and said to them, be fruitful, multiply, and fill the earth, and subdue it [using all its vast resources in the service of God and man]; and have dominion over the fish of the sea, the birds of the air, and over every living creature that moves upon the earth. 29 And God said, See, I have given you every plant yielding seed that is on the face of all the land and every tree with seed in its fruit; you shall have them for food. 30 And to all the animals on the earth and to every bird of the air and to everything that creeps on the ground-to everything in which there is the breath of life—I have given every green plant for food. And it was so.'

If this is not a share of God's power and authority then I don't know what else it is.

2. TO ENHANCE COMMUNICATION

In *Genesis 1:26,* we are privileged to discover that, so strong was God's desire for communication that the very first thing He thought of giving man even before creating him was His Image—His exact resemblance or real likeness. Even before thinking of giving man and woman dominion over the fish of the sea, the fowl of the air, the cattle, all the earth, and every creeping thing that creepeth upon the earth. (Power and authority as mentioned before) He had thought of giving us His own image. Isn't that grand!

26 God said, Let Us [Father, Son, and Holy Spirit] make mankind in Our image, after Our likeness, and let them have complete authority over the fish of the sea, the birds of the air, the [tame] beasts, and over all of the earth, and over everything that creeps upon the earth. 27 So God created man in His own image, in the image and likeness of God He created him; male and female He created them.'
Genesis 1:26-27

I used to be stunned about why God would choose to create us in His own likeness, until He gave me understanding via His Spirit. I thought to myself for a while and then repeated the question almost audibly.

Why do we sometimes get scared when we watch horror films? Or why are we scared when we see 'strange creatures'.

Then God gave me an answer: 'Because we are unable to identify with them.' As a result of our inability to relate to them there is a shaking of the very basis of communication and relationship. I have jokingly said on a couple of occasions that, if God had created Adam any different than in His own image, Adam might have, upon seeing Him, run away and never returned. The reason is simple; he wouldn't have had the luxury of identifying with God, let alone relating to or communicating with Him. Likewise, I have jokingly mentioned in the past that, had the woman not been like Adam I don't think he would have said, *"This is 'bone of my bone' and 'flesh of my flesh"* upon waking up from his deep sleep. Actually, they would have run in opposite directions. God in His own divine wisdom created us in His own image I suppose to facilitate effective communication.

According to Genesis *2:8*, '*And the Lord God planted a garden* toward the east, in Eden [delight]; and there *He put the man whom He had formed (framed, constituted).*'

Adam had absolutely nothing to do with the planting of the Garden of Eden. In reality, it was God Himself who planted the Garden of Eden which translates from the root Hebrew word meaning, 'Place of God's Presence' and placed him right in there. That was where God's presence touched the earth and God must have placed Adam there for a reason.

Seriously, have you thought about the fact that by the time Adam was created, God had created the whole world and could have decided to place Adam and Eve anywhere else on this earth yet He preferred the

Garden of Eden—in His presence. The reason, I strongly believe, was to establish a relationship and fellowship with man—An environment where He would have an uninterrupted relationship with man to ensure that man lived his life with the ability of attaining his full potential.

In other words, the garden was supposed to be a **Perfect or Model Environment** of an endless relationship with God. This is the crucial environment that every man needs in order to attain his full potential—an environment of an unbroken relationship with God, where God's presence is constantly manifest.

If you walked into Curry's Digital (UK) today and asked to buy a camcorder for instance, you will receive as part of your purchase a manual containing a set of instructions. Now you may be surprised to read an instruction that may probably warn you against immersing the product in water. I am sure if you have read something of the sort before, it would have sounded a bit crazy at that instant. I mean, who would think of doing such a thing? But truly, such instructions are given for a reason. Trust me, there are some recalcitrant kids around who are capable of doing just that, and it is such people that the manufacturers set out to warn since the gadget would either malfunction or not function at all if it were taken out of its ideal or perfect environment, and introduced into a foreign environment (water in this case).

In the same way, as human beings created in the likeness of God, our perfect or faultless environment is that which can be likened to the Garden of Eden where God's presence touched the earth—The environment of a continual bond with our creator; one that enhances or facilitates communication and fellowship with God Himself. Outside this environment, man is bound to malfunction. We originally had this environment until sin breached it and Adam was driven away from it. The good news however is that a price has been paid on our behalf that has reconciled us to God, so now, we can seek, find and remain in this ideal milieu in order to please God and serve Him as expected of us.

Just as a manual contains instructions for operating a new gadget, so is the Bible a manual for Christians. The Bible is a 'manual containing our set of instructions to be obeyed'. Sounds a bit crude or simplistic but that's the truth. The Bible cautions us daily not to leave the presence of God, because if we do we will be abandoning our 'perfect environment' which will result in our malfunctioning as Christians.

JUDAH *(THE SYMBOL OF GOD'S AUTHORITY)*
*In **Psalms 108:8** the Bible records that:*
> *'8 Gilead is Mine, Manasseh is Mine; Ephraim also is My stronghold and the defense of My head; Judah is My scepter and lawgiver.'*

Once again, we learn about God's intention to share His authority with man as a result of His intention to have His authority represented on earth.

A scepter is an instrument which symbolizes authority and power. In modern day lingo we may call it a sword of office. Now, since Judah means praise, can I suggest then that, Praise is God's scepter which is His symbol of authority. In other words, praise is the representation or symbol of God's authority on earth. Halleluiah! In as much as we have so much to jubilate about as regards praise being the symbol of authority, we need to realize also that we are required to approach this symbol as it were with respect and reverence. After all, even in our everyday life, we dare not mark around with the sword of office of say the president or any other monarch.

If we will dare not mess around with the (human) insignia of the authority of our earthly kings, presidents or heads of states, then we

must approach praise with an even greater intensity of reverence; in view of the fact that it is the representation of the authority of the Lord God Almighty. More so, when this version makes us understand that Judah is God's lawgiver, I am not messing around with the LAWGIVER.

CHAPTER 3

THE TRUE MEANING OF PRAISE

MANY people participate in praises to God for various reasons (some right, others wrong). Unfortunately however, there are many who have a wrong understanding of what praise sessions are all about. This chapter will hopefully establish the fact that our praises to God and the expressions that accompany them are not meaningless and should not be viewed as worthless routines. Praises (to God) is powerful.

1. PRAISE IS THE HUB

Psalms 114:1 &2 says:

'1 WHEN ISRAEL came forth out of Egypt, the house of Jacob from a people of strange language, 2 Judah became [God's] sanctuary (the Holy Place of His habitation), and Israel His dominion.'

The Hebrew translation of Sanctuary is a sacred, hallowed or a dedicated place—the Holy Place of His habitation as explained by this version. Hence, the Scripture suggests to me that, God's power is evident in all Israel but Judah is the nerve centre. That's to say that God's power and authority is manifest in many ways and places but praise is the command center. After all, Bible speaks of Judah (Praise) as being God's sacred or dedicated place.

2. PRAISE STOMACHS EXCEPTIONAL GOODWILL

Genesis 29:35 narrates Leah's bearing and naming of her son.

Genesis 29:35

"35 Again she conceived and bore a son, and she said, now will I praise the Lord! So she called his name Judah [praise]; then [for a time] she ceased bearing. '

You will recall that she was miserable and saw herself as the despicable wife. To make things worse, even after giving birth to three sons and trying to gain the love and favor of her husband Jacob, he loved her sister yet when she bore a fourth son she began to praise the Lord. She decided to call him Judah, saying, *"Now will I praise the Lord"*.

We may never know whether Jacob eventually fell in love with her, but it is evident from the names she gave her children that she loved and honored God.

It is important that we refocus our attention towards praising God rather than finding the favor and attention of men. There are times when we (just like Leah) sometimes think that our purpose is to please men, thereby neglecting the greater purpose and plan God has for our lives.

Leah continued to look to God in the midst of her hurt and disappointment, and He chose her to establish Judah (praise) as the avenue through which He would manifest the fullness of His glory.

Regardless of her perception of the way things seemed to work against her, she still found it in her heart to say 'Now will I praise the Lord' and it comes as no surprise to me that God was pleased. He honored her by allowing the lineage of the Messiah to flow through her womb as is revealed in the pronouncements of Jacob upon Judah with regard to what was yet to happen in the last days.

'1 And Jacob called for his sons and said, Gather yourselves together [around me], that I may tell you what shall befall you in the latter or last days.'

Of Judah he says in **verses 9-12**
'9 Judah, a lion's cub! With the prey, my son, you have gone high up [the mountain]. He stooped down, he crouched like a lion, and like a lioness—who dares provoke and rouse him? 10 The scepter or leadership shall not depart from Judah, nor the ruler's staff from between his feet, until Shiloh [the Messiah, the Peaceful One] comes to whom it belongs, and to Him shall be the obedience of the people. 11 Binding His foal to the vine and His donkey's colt to the choice vine; He washes His garments in wine and His clothes in the blood of grapes. 12 His eyes

are darker and more sparkling than wine, and His teeth whiter than milk.'
Genesis 49:1

I believe this is no rocket science. It should be easy to perceive that Judah attracted some special goodwill. The kind that none of his siblings had nor were to ever have.

The point is, there is a special kind of favor that only praise can attract and it comes with a commensurate level of blessing.

In **Psalms 78:67-69** the Psalmist says of the Lord:
'67 Moreover, He rejected the tent of Joseph and chose not the tribe of Ephraim [in which the tabernacle had been accustomed to stand]. 68 But He chose the tribe of Judah [as Israel's leader], Mount Zion, which He loved [to replace Shiloh as His capital]. 69 And He built His sanctuary [exalted] like the heights [of the heavens] and like the earth which He established forever'.

This is my prayer—that we will all find it within ourselves to praise God, regardless of the circumstances and in so doing; attract God's love, favor and blessings.

Isaiah 43:20-21 reveals the fact that we have been formed for God Himself, to set forth His praise.

'20 The beasts of the field honor Me, the jackals and the ostriches, because I give waters in the wilderness and rivers in the desert, to give drink to My people, My chosen, 21 The

people I formed for Myself, that they may set forth My praise
[and they shall do it].'
Isaiah 43: 20&21

3. PRAISE INVOLVES ADORING AND EXTOLLING

It is vital to mention that there are two aspects of PRAISE namely: *ADORING AND EXTOLLING.*

▶ Adoring

This is to reflect upon or think about the goodness of God. This entails meditating on (pondering on, contemplating, thinking about, considering or deliberating upon) God. Usually in times of adoration, we are flooded by a quiet, reassurance that fills and fortifies us. There are times when I have made time to sit in a park or on the beach, and all I have done was to think about God's greatness, His creation, and may I propose that you do same, for the result is exceptional. I am sure someone reading this book will now understand why there are times (especially when faced with challenges) when I would just escape to the beach.

Some examples of praise songs of adoration are:

'THINK ABOUT HIS LOVE'
'Think about His love; Think about His goodness Think about His grace; that's brought us through For as high as the heavens above
So great is the measure, of our Father's love
Great is the measure of our Father's love'

'WHEN I LOOK AT THE MOUNTAINS'

'When I look at the mountain, look at the valleys,
Look at the seas,
Oh my Lord You are God, You are Lord.

▶ Extolling

This form of praise is characterized by telling others about the goodness of God.

> *'4 One generation shall laud Your works to another and shall declare Your mighty acts.',*
> *'6 Men shall speak of the might of Your tremendous and terrible acts, and I will declare Your greatness.'*
> **Psalms 145:4 &6**

> *'10 All Your works shall praise You, O Lord, and Your loving ones shall bless You [affectionately and gratefully shall Your saints confess and praise You]! 11 They shall speak of the glory of Your kingdom and talk of Your power, 12 To make known to the sons of men God's mighty deeds and the glorious majesty of His kingdom.'*
> **Psalms 145:10-12**

Extolling has to be done genuinely without any element of exaggeration. God doesn't need you to help Him look and feel big with your exaggeration.

It is also possible to extol God for future expectations of what He will do. This aspect of praise can even cause the unsaved, to celebrate and confess the goodness of God as well.

'2 Then were our mouths filled with laughter, and our tongues with singing: **Then they said among the nations, The Lord has done great things for them.** *'*
Psalms 126:2

Even the Gentiles, as a result of the intensity of the Extolling of God by His people, declared the goodness of the Almighty God.

TRUTHS PERTAINING TO PRAISE

It is profitable to mention some facts about praise so that we can ascertain what praise is and what it is not.

First of all, praise is neither repetitions of empty words nor manipulation of God to obtain things from Him. Rather, praise is a means by which we position ourselves to see God's character—who He is.

NOT MIMICKING OF OTHERS

Secondly, praise does not entail mimicking certain styles or traditions, such that somebody's way of praising God becomes more of a tradition which everyone else in the church ends up mimicking. I remember at a particular time in my Christian walk when there was this dance supposed to be called the 'Holy Ghost dance'. Not that I have anything against dancing, nor even against that particular dance, especially if it is genuinely the best one can do in praising God, but when, as it was at the times, it becomes a craze or tradition which people mimic and it's as though any other dance aside that one makes you less spiritual before God, then I think there is a problem.

A FRUIT OF OUR LIPS

Now let us see how **Hebrews 13:15** defines praise as 'the fruit of our lips'

> **'15** *Through Him, therefore, let us constantly and at all times offer up to God a sacrifice of praise, which is the fruit of lips that thankfully acknowledge and confess and glorify His name.*
> **Hebrews 13:15**

> *'8 When you bear (produce) much fruit, My Father is honored and glorified, and you show and prove yourselves to be true followers of Mine.'*
> **John 15:8**

There may truly be several ways of bearing fruit but it is my understanding from *Hebrews 13:15* that one clear way to bear fruit is to praise God. Therefore each time we give thanks and praise to God we bear fruits and more so, according to *John 15:8* it is the type of fruit which glorifies the Father; and I trust that as the Father is glorified, more of His power is made available. My question now is—Who wants to glorify the Lord? If you are willing, then this is a good time to praise Him.

A MEANS OF GLORIFYING GOD

If all that cross-referencing was a bit confusing, I believe the Psalmist has made it even clearer in order to put the issue to rest. To lay it blunt, the Psalmist says in **Psalms 50:23:**

> *'23 He who brings an offering of praise and thanksgiving honors and glorifies Me; and he who orders his way aright*

[who prepares the way that I may show him], to him I will demonstrate the salvation of God.'

Really, this could not have been expressed any simpler. It's just what it is—SIMPLE AND STRAIGHT FORWARD—PRAISING GOD GLORIFIES HIM!!!

NOT EMOTION DRAWN YET INVITES EMOTIONS

Again, it is significant to note that, though praise has a strong emotional element, it should not be driven by emotions. Praising God should be by will and should never be dependent on sentiments and our bodies. Let me explain this a little more.

We need to have a free will to praise God rather than depend on our mind-set to praise God, because there are times when naturally the flesh or the body, may not really 'feel like' praising God aptly but in such rough and tough times, there is an even greater need to make a conscious effort to praise Him.

I have encountered people in churches, sitting down almost unconcerned during times of dancing and praising God and when I approached them and enquired why they were not participating in the praises, their only response had been—*'I don't feel like'*. Really, I might not have had a problem if there was a tangible excuse, knowing that dancing and clapping may not be the only ways by which we praise God. As mentioned earlier in this chapter, adoration as a way of praising God entails meditation. So I would have understood if they were probably praising God in other ways, though it's also good to dance and clap and all that—which are all expressions of praise. David I guess would bear testimony to this. But excuse me to say that, such a flimsy excuse as 'I don't feel like' is disgraceful.

It is important here to note that man is made up of body, soul and spirit. Actually the body remains the body as we all know—that which was formed out of clay. This may sound a bit too simplistic, but the soul is more of the personality aspect of man. The attribute that says *'I will'* or *'I will not'* or *'I think'* or *'I do not think'*, the personality that says *'I feel'* or *'I do not feel'*. The soul actually comprises of a man's will, intellect and emotions. Notice in **Psalms 103:1** *where* David says: *'Bless the Lord Oh my soul'*, it was obviously his spirit speaking to his soul. You see, it's the soul that makes decisions and then orders the body to act but it is the spirit that deals with the soul which in turn deals with the body.

So there may even be times when one's spirit is willing and seeking to commune with or for that matter praise God but the soul may feel the opposite. It is in such times that you are confronted with a choice to make—whether to lend your soul to the demand placed on it by your spirit by responding and in turn causing your body to act appropriately or on the other hand to imprison the spirit that seeks to praise God.

I might not have had time enough in the past to address this *'I don't feel like'* attitude but since I now have the means to, I will take my time to do so, subjecting rebuke to the guidance of the Spirit of God, who leads us into all truths, and I hope many will have the opportunity to change the rotten attitude wherever and whenever it shows up.

CHAPTER 4

CHARACTERISTICS OF PRAISE

THE characteristics of true praise are copious yet in this chapter we will consider a few pertinent ones that I trust, when well heeded to, will enhance drastically our praises to God.

PRAISE AS A PERSONAL STATEMENT

Praise at its best is supposed to be a personal statement and not a rehearsal of what someone said or did. I am not only referring to the verbal aspect of praise but praise as a whole. Do you know that even your dressing can speak for you or make a statement of some sort on your behalf? If you saw a king in full regalia, I believe even without being told you would know from his dressing, his charisma and all that he was a king. Even your dance can make a statement, and in my country for instance, in some cultural settings, the way you wear your cloth, the steps you take during particular dances and even the beating of the drums all communicate messages. Praise is supposed to be a personal statement; with all these expressions of communication being inclusive.

When Jesus cursed the fig tree, the Bible says that He spoke back to the tree, or for that matter answered the fig tree. Now the question is: Did the fig tree speak to Him for Him to have spoken back to it? Well, as to verbal (audible) speech—no I don't think so but I believe the fig tree must have spoken to Him in some other sense—it must have communicated something to Him probably through its leaves for instance, which must have provoked a response from Jesus. The issue I am bringing to the fore is that, at its best, praises (at times) do not allow for generalizations. Praise is a personal statement.

Let me share this profound truth before we progress. Note that Jesus cursed the fig tree because He could not find fruit on it, when everything around and about it communicated to the Lord that there should have been fruit on the tree. Now consider the things that God has done for and with you, and then consider the length of time you have been saved and enjoyed His mercy and see whether all these things and many more have not communicated to God that you should be producing fruits. Then ask yourself whether upon approaching you, the Lord will find your fruit ready to be enjoyed. Will He find at least the fruit of your lips, which should be your reasonable service? You cannot deceive the

Lord. You cannot afford to have everything around you (your life and the blessings of God amongst others) show that you are ready to produce fruits and yet refuse to produce that fruit. That will be like inviting the Lord over only to provoke Him to curse you rather than to bless you.

MOSES IN EXODUS

*Moses in **Exodus 15:1-13** lifts up praise to God*

'*1 THEN MOSES and the Israelites sang this song to the Lord, saying, I will sing to the Lord, for He has triumphed gloriously; the horse and his rider or its chariot has He thrown into the sea. 2 The Lord is my Strength and my Song, and He has become my Salvation; this is my God, and I will praise Him, my father's God, and I will exalt Him. 3 The Lord is a Man of War; the Lord is His name. 4 Pharaoh's chariots and his host has He cast into the sea; his chosen captains also are sunk in the Red Sea. 5 The floods cover them; they sank in the depths [clad in mail] like a stone. 6 Your right hand, O Lord, is glorious in power; Your right hand, O Lord, shatters the enemy. 7 In the greatness of Your majesty You overthrow those rising against You. You send forth Your fury; it consumes them like stubble. 8 With the blast of Your nostrils the waters piled up, the floods stood fixed in a heap, the deeps congealed in the heart of the sea. 9 The enemy said, I will pursue, I will overtake, I will divide the spoil; my desire shall be satisfied upon them; I will draw my sword, my hand shall destroy them.*

10 You [Lord] blew with Your wind, the sea covered them; [clad in mail] they sank as lead in the mighty waters. 11 Who is like You, O Lord, among the gods? Who is like You, glorious in holiness, awesome in splendor, doing wonders? 12 You stretched out Your right hand, the earth's [sea] swallowed them.

13 You in Your mercy and loving-kindness have led forth the people whom You have redeemed; You have guided them in Your strength to Your holy habitation.'

Hannah's song in 1 Samuel 2:1-10

'*1 HANNAH PRAYED, and said, My heart exults and triumphs in the Lord; my horn (my strength) is lifted up in the Lord. My mouth is no longer silent, for it is opened wide over my enemies, because I rejoice in Your salvation.*
2 There is none holy like the Lord, there is none besides You; there is no Rock like our God. 3 Talk no more so very proudly; let not arrogance go forth from your mouth, for the Lord is a God of knowledge, and by Him actions are weighed.
4 The bows of the mighty are broken, and those who stumbled are girded with strength. 5 Those who were full have hired themselves out for bread, but those who were hungry have ceased to hunger. The barren has borne seven, but she who has many children languishes and is forlorn. 6 The Lord slays and makes alive; He brings down to Sheol and raises up. 7 The Lord makes poor and makes rich; He brings low and He lifts up. 8 He raises up the poor out of the dust and lifts up the needy from the ash heap, to make them sit with nobles and inherit the throne of glory. For the pillars of the earth are the Lord's, and He has set the world upon them. 9 He will guard the feet of His godly ones, but the wicked shall be silenced and perish in darkness; for by strength shall no man prevail. 10 The adversaries of the Lord shall be broken to pieces; against them will He thunder in heaven. The Lord will judge [all peoples] to the ends of the earth; and He will give strength to His king (King) and exalt the power of His anointed (Anointed His Christ).'

Now let us check what **2.***Samuel 22: 2-51* says with particular emphasis on the *verses 2, 3, 7* which show no generalizations. Again we see in *verses 17, 18, 29, 33*, and *49* that David, in the day that the LORD had delivered him out of the hand of all his enemies and out of the hand of Saul was convinced of God's presence, and power as well as God's answer to his prayer for deliverance.

Our praises should also reflect confidence in the miracle working God, and in this regard, we should understand the importance of praising God ourselves. God deals with us differently. So what I would render praise for personally may differ from what God has done for you and for which you would render praise. Praise therefore should have an element of personal rather than general expressions. Yes, there are times when as a church or as a group we may come together in corporate praise which may be general but on our own (privately), we should be able to praise God for our personal experiences and with our personal statements.

> '2 He said: The Lord is my Rock [of escape from Saul] and
> my Fortress [in the wilderness] and my Deliverer; 3 My God,
> my Rock, in Him will I take refuge; my Shield and the Horn of
> my salvation; my Stronghold and my Refuge, my Saviour—You
> save me from violence. 4 I call on the Lord, Who is worthy to
> be praised, and I am saved from my enemies. 5 For the waves
> of death enveloped me; the torrents of destruction made me
> afraid. 6 The cords of Sheol were entangling me; I encountered
> the snares of death. 7 In my distress I called upon the Lord; I
> cried to my God, and He heard my voice from His temple; my
> cry came into His ears. 8 Then the earth reeled and quaked, the
> foundations of the heavens trembled and shook because He was
> angry. 9 Smoke went up from His nostrils, and devouring fire
> from His mouth; coals were kindled by it.

*10 He bowed the heavens and came down; thick darkness was under His feet. 11 He rode on a cherub and flew; He was seen upon the wings of the wind. 12 He made darkness His canopy around Him, gathering of waters, thick clouds of the skies. 13 Out of the brightness before Him coals of fire flamed forth. 14 The Lord thundered from heaven, and the Most High uttered His voice. 15 He sent out arrows and scattered them; lightning confused and troubled them. 16 The channels of the sea were visible; the foundations of the world were uncovered at the rebuke of the Lord, at the blast of the breath of His nostrils. 17 He sent from above, He took me; He drew me out of great waters. 18 He delivered me from my strong enemy, from those who hated me, for they were too mighty for me. 19 They came upon me in the day of my calamity, but the Lord was my stay. 20 He brought me forth into a large place; He delivered me because He delighted in me. 21 **The** Lord rewarded me according to my uprightness with Him; He compensated and benefited me according to the cleanness of my hands. 22 For I have kept the ways of the Lord, and have not wickedly departed from my God. 23 For all His ordinances were before me; and from His statutes I did not turn aside. 24 I was also blameless before Him and kept myself from guilt and iniquity. 25 Therefore the Lord has recompensed me according to my righteousness, according to my cleanness in His [holy] sight. 26 Toward the loving and loyal You will show Yourself loving and loyal, and with the upright and blameless You will show Yourself upright and blameless. 27 To the pure You will show Yourself pure, and to the willful You will show Yourself willful. 28 And the afflicted people You will deliver, but Your eyes are upon the haughty, whom You will bring down. 29 For You, O Lord, are my Lamp;*

*the Lord lightens my darkness. 30 For by You I run through a troop; by my God I leap over a wall. 31 As for God, His way is perfect; the word of the Lord is tried. He is a Shield to all those who trust and take refuge in Him. 32 For who is God but the Lord? And who is a Rock except our God? 33 **God** is my strong Fortress; He guides the blameless in His way and sets him free. 34 He makes my feet like the hinds' [firm and able]; He sets me secure and confident upon the heights. 35 He trains my hands for war, so that my arms can bend a bow of bronze. 36 You have also given me the shield of Your salvation; and Your condescension and gentleness have made me great. 37 You have enlarged my steps under me, so that my feet have not slipped. 38 I have pursued my enemies and destroyed them; and I did not turn back until they were consumed. 39 I consumed them and thrust them through, so that they did not arise; they fell at my feet. 40 For You girded me with strength for the battle; those who rose up against me You subdued under me. 41 You have made my enemies turn their backs to me that I might cut off those who hate me. 42 They looked, but there was none to save—even to the Lord, but He did not answer them. 43 Then I beat them small as the dust of the earth; I crushed them as the mire of the street and scattered them abroad. 44 You also have delivered me from strife with my people; You kept me as the head of the nations. People whom I had not known served me. 45 Foreigners yielded feigned obedience to me; as soon as they heard of me, they became obedient to me. 46 Foreigners faded away; they came limping and trembling from their strongholds. 47 The Lord lives; blessed be my Rock, and exalted be God, the Rock of my salvation. 48 It is God Who executes vengeance for me and Who brought down [and disciplined] the peoples under*

me, 49 Who brought me out from my enemies. You also lifted me up above those who rose up against me; You delivered me from the violent man. 50 For this I will give thanks and extol You, O Lord, among the nations; I will sing praises to Your name. 51 He is a Tower of salvation and great deliverance to His king, and shows loving-kindness to His anointed, to David and his offspring forever.'
2 Samuel 22:2-51

PRAISE IS A SACRIFICE

'6 And now shall my head be lifted up above my enemies round about me; in His tent I will offer sacrifices and shouting of joy; I will sing, yes, I will sing praises to the Lord.'
Psalms 27:6

'17 I will offer to You the sacrifice of thanksgiving and will call on the name of the Lord.'
Psalms 116:17

'15 Through Him, therefore, let us constantly and at all times offer up to God a sacrifice of praise, which is the fruit of lips that thankfully acknowledge and confess and glorify His name.'
Hebrews 13:15

All the above references to Scripture go to prove that praise is a sacrifice but then one may ask what it is that we sacrifice? In praise we sacrifice or surrender our pride. We sacrifice by making the effort to overcome situations around us that are not 'too pleasant' so as to rise up and still praise God. This endorses the fact that even when things seem humanly 'bad' we still need to praise God in those circumstances. That is sacrifice. We praise continually in spite of a certain feeling or the lack of it. Actually, the Bible says, for us to praise God even in those difficult situations and circumstances. Even in those hard times, we should be able to individually sing:

> *'I'll say yes Lord, yes—To Your will and to your way*
> *I'll say yes Lord, yes—I will trust you and obey*
> *When Your Spirit speaks to me; with my whole heart I'll agree*
> *And my answer will be yes, Lord yes'.*

In praise we sacrifice or surrender our all in all—including any pride within us, and it is important that a sacrifice stays on the altar until it is ultimately consumed. A sacrifice does not jump off an altar even when the fire burns hottest. Truly, it is not an easy feeling when some areas of our lives begin to get consumed on the altar of sacrifice.

It is not easy at times when we are called to offer praise under certain circumstances—especially when we are confronted with options that seem to offer easy ways out. Yet it is even in those hard times that we need to offer our sacrifice (of praise)—when it costs us most. In fact, it is when it costs us most that it passes for a true sacrifice.

Read 2 Samuel 24 and 1 Chronicles 21

After David had grieved and repented for his sin against God, God responded to David, commanding him to offer a sacrifice in a specific place and in a specific way.

Ornan in turn presented David with a tempting offer to accept all that he needed to offer the sacrifice which God had demanded of him. But

David was quick to realize that all that Ornan had offered were Ornan's property and not his (David's) and that the sacrifice had been asked of him (David) and not Ornan. Apparently, it would have been such an easy way to satisfy the demands of God but it would not have cost David anything. In other words it would not have touched his life. Actually it would not have been a sacrifice at all if he had accepted Ornan's offer. We need to realize that, one important thing about rendering a sacrifice is the element of personal involvement. In fact, it is actually an insult to God when we try to play smart by attempting to pull the wool over His eyes by offering things to Him just to satisfy His demands without paying the price for anything. In other words, what we tell God by doing that is that we are 'smatter' than Him—and that we can find ways to trick Him. David understood that in sacrifice there was the need to offer what would touch and cost the one sacrificing.

How many times do we not entertain and give in to the temptation of preferring that the pastor, or the music director, or the choir makes the sacrifice of praise or worship on our behalf.

There is a cost we need to pay even in offering praise, yet many times, when we are offered with our peculiar 'Ornan's offer', we are quick to jump at it, only proving how myopic our understanding of praise as a sacrifice is. With the offer of great choir music or an excellent message from the pastor we are quick to take the easy option of settling in the back seats or pews and just enjoying the efforts of others. After all, we think our 'Ornan' has offered all we need to satisfy the demands of God and then we shamefully (at times) blame it on our tiredness as a result of the same blessings (good jobs, children, sweethearts, etc) we once upon a time prayed to God so fervently for. Standing on your feet, dancing and singing even in the midst of difficulty, pain, hurt, depression, tiredness, heaviness and all the challenges could be the cost that you may have to foot to make your praise a sacrifice. Will you stand up and like David say to your 'Ornan' that, you will not offer anything that does not cost you or will you just sit back and take the easy way out by settling for your 'Ornan's offer' and depend on the efforts of others. Remember that there is always an 'Ornan's offer' and God is watching with rapt attention. What are you going to do with it?

PRAISE IS A PERSONAL COMMAND DECISION

Praise as explained earlier is a sacrifice and to sacrifice anything, more so praise, demands that the person sacrificing makes a personal decision. There are even times when it's advisable to keep these decisions to yourself. In making these decisions however, allow the Spirit of God to lead you as to what to do. Abraham for instance needed to take a personal decision to sacrifice Isaac without consulting anyone else. Not even Sarah.

Can you imagine what Sarah's response would have been had Abraham told her about sacrificing Isaac? After waiting so long and going through all the challenges associated with her supposed 'barrenness' can you imagine Abraham telling her that he had taken a decision to sacrifice their 'only child'. I am almost certain that it would have been the perfect recipe for marital problems and even worse. I can just imagine how some might have seen it as a weird, illogical and probably silly decision. I am sure that some physicians of their time might have probably attributed Abraham's decision to possible dementia as a result of his old age? I am sure that in our present day some people would have had him arrested for 'sakawa'.

Most often than not, we allow ourselves to be discouraged by others when they get to know what we intend to sacrifice. Some may even start making fun of you and probably start calling you names to ridicule you. In any case, it is up to you to stand up and be counted. There are times you may have to make a personal decision and to carry it through, even if it means keeping that decision to yourself. When in the opening chapters we discovered that praise was a garment, I mentioned that if we had a garment tucked away in a closet, it would be of no use to us. I further mentioned that it beholds on one to make a decision as to which garment to wear and to then make the effort to actually wear it, since it would not literally jump unto you. Now it comes to light again that, just like the garments in your closet, you need to make a personal decision today to wear praise and make the effort to wear it in place of the despair you may be wearing. Will you decline making the personal decision to wear the garment of praise God has given you in place of the despair that the evil one has clothed you in?

PRAISE RECOGNISES GOD'S WORK IN OTHERS

From *2 Samuel 22:2-51* as discussed earlier under praise as a personal statement, we realize that aside praise being a personal statement; it was not exclusive of what God had done for others. David also recognizes that God did for him what He would do for others and lists the mighty works of God on behalf of others.

In *2 Samuel 22 Verses 26-28; 31,* the Bible says:
> '*26 Toward the loving and loyal You will show Yourself loving and loyal, and with the upright and blameless You will show Yourself upright and blameless. 27 To the pure You will show Yourself pure, and to the willful You will show Yourself willful.*

28 And the afflicted people You will deliver, but Your eyes are upon the haughty, whom You will bring down.'
'31 As for God, His way is perfect; the word of the Lord is tried. He is a Shield to all those who trust and take refuge in Him.'

In praising God therefore, we can also acknowledge what God has done in the lives of others as well. Note however that should I praise God for something He has done or something I believe He will do in your life, it is still my praise to God—it is not and will never be your praise. It still goes to my account. You need to praise God yourself if you want to benefit from the rewards of praising Him. Indeed we can both praise God for the same thing(s), but if I praise God for something(s) He has accomplished or I believe He will accomplish in your life or your situation it doesn't seize to be MY PRAISE TO GOD.

CHAPTER 5

BIBLICAL REASONS FOR PRAISING GOD

EVERY moment of our lives, we are presented with a new motivation to praise God so I may never be able to exhaust these reasons, but it is my prayer that these few reasons will have a mighty impact as the Spirit of God ministers to you as you read on.

PRAISE AS AN INSTRUCTION

The Bible admonishes us to offer praise as a sacrifice not only once or once in a while but constantly.

> '15 Through Him, therefore, let us constantly and at all times offer up to God a sacrifice of praise, which is the fruit of lips that thankfully acknowledge and confess and glorify His name.'
> **Hebrews 13:5**

To make it even clearer, David, the man after God's own heart, buttresses the point that we need to praise God relentlessly.

> *In **Psalms 34:1** David says:*
> *'I WILL bless the Lord at all times; His praise shall continually be in my mouth.'*

In both Scriptures (quoted from Hebrews and Psalms) it is Biblically clear that there is the need to praise God at all times and 'constantly' is the operating word here.

> ***Psalms 113:3** says:*
> *'From the rising of the sun to the going down of it and from east to west, the name of the Lord is to be praised!'*

That is more like constantly isn't it? Once more, in accordance with the practice of the early church I believe we, in our present day, should find reason to render praise to God continually.

> ***Luke 24:53** says:*
> *'53 And they were continually in the temple celebrating with praises and blessing and extolling God. Amen (so be it).'*

▶ An Instruction From God's Own Throne Room

It is worth mentioning that praising God is a message to be adhered to from the throne of God Himself as discovered in.

Revelations 19:5:

'Then from the throne there came a voice, saying, Praise our God, all you servants of His, you who reverence Him, both small and great!'

As though the above scripture was not emphatic enough to let us know that God calls us to Praise Him, **Psalms 150:6** indicates that Praise is not optional. Actually it is an obligation for you and I who have breath.

'Let everything that hath breath praise the LORD.
Praise ye the LORD'

THE WILL OF GOD CONCERNING OUR LIVES

One of the main priorities of a Christian is to do the will of God. If the whole purpose of man is to know God and to please Him then one of the sure ways to please Him is to do His will. Imagine you living with a child who always does things contrary to your will. Obviously this child would not please you, however the reverse will also hold true. In order to please God, we need to find out what His will is and do it. I am not disputing the many other ways some have discovered to please God. All I am saying is that, praising God is one sure way of pleasing Him.

1 Thessalonians 5:18 urges us to give thanks in everything and in every circumstance since it is the will of God for us through Christ Jesus.

Therefore if we choose to praise God in everything then that will amount to pleasing God (by doing His will). In other words, to do the will of God, we surely have to praise him continually. I am not in any

47

case implying that in times of difficulty we should thank and praise God with the view that it is His will for us to suffer such mishaps. In fact, more often than not, such situations might have arisen due to a domino effect of our own wrong doing though sometimes this may also be as a result of the works of the devil.

> *In **1 John 3:8b** Bible says:*
> *'[But] he who commits sin [who practices evildoing] is of the devil [takes his character from the evil one], for the devil has sinned (violated the divine law) from the beginning. **The reason the Son of God was made manifest (visible) was to undo (destroy, loosen, and dissolve) the works the devil [has done].***'*

This means that the devil has been busy working (stealing, killing and destroying according to **John 10:10)**. Yet the Bible mentions thereafter that **'I am come that they might have life, and that they might have it abundantly.'**

From the foregoing Scripture, it is therefore unacceptable to attribute everything that happens to God. We do not thank God for everything or for that matter give Him praise for everything. What we do is to rather give Him praise in all things and in all situations for what His word says He has done and will do for us.

Hence we Praise God for His stake over the power of the devil, for the fact that He is still God and for the fact that He will come through for us since He is supreme.

When the three Hebrew children praised God in the middle of the fiery furnace, I don't think it was their understanding that God had brought them into the furnace to burn, nor do I think they were praising God for the fire but I believe *they were thanking God for His presence with them in their situation*. This means that, regardless of our predicaments we can still thank God for His presence with us.

EVIDENCE OF BEING SPIRIT FILLED

It is crucial to recognize that offering genuine praise is proof of a true spirit filled life.

> *18 And do not get drunk with wine, for that is debauchery; but ever be filled and stimulated with the [Holy] Spirit. 19 Speak out to one another in Psalms and hymns and spiritual songs, **offering praise with voices [and instruments] and making melody with all your heart to the Lord, 20 At all times and for everything giving thanks** in the name of our Lord Jesus Christ to God the Father.;*
> ***Ephesians 5:18-20***

Other versions have it as 'giving praise always . . .' Once again, the call is for us to give praise always, continually or at all times. Halleluiah!

THE CHRISTIAN'S MAIN BUSINESS

Bible teaches us that we are a chosen generation and a royal priesthood and frankly, as a royal priesthood our main occupation should include rendering praise to God.

> *'9 But you are a chosen race, a royal priesthood, a dedicated nation, [God's] own purchased, special people, that you may*

set forth the wonderful deeds and display the virtues and
perfections of Him Who called you out of darkness into His
marvelous light'
1Peter 2:9

We can show forth the wonderful deeds and display the virtues and perfections of God by **praising Him constantly.** In any case that is what we will be doing for all eternity—that is if we truly want to make it to heaven. So the earlier we get used to this, the better. Spurgeon puts it—'Praise is the rehearsal of our eternal song.'

And the Psalmist calls us to enter into His courts with praise:

'4 Enter into His gates with thanksgiving and a thank offering
and into His courts with praise! Be thankful and say so to Him,
bless and affectionately praise His name!'
Psalms 100:4

A FRUIT OF OUR LIPS

In refreshing our memory concerning the fact that Praise is the fruit of our lips. The Bible says in ***Proverbs 12:14*** that:

'From the fruit of his words a man shall be satisfied with good, and
the work of a man's hands shall come back to him [as a harvest].'

If the fruit of your lips is praise and of that same fruit we are to be satisfied or fulfilled then by inference, we are promised by God Almighty to be satisfied with good things by the offering of our praise!!! The day God revealed this to me, my attitude towards praise changed, and by that understanding I came to appreciate the fact that my satisfaction is tied to my resolution to render praise.

CHAPTER 6

PRAISING GOD IN DIFFICULT TIMES

THE truth is that it is not always easy to praise God. That I can understand and identify with, yet it is no excuse to exempt us from praising Him. Beloved, there are records of others who might have seemingly, had *'genuine'* reasons to have pulled the brakes on praising God or for that matter had seemingly 'good reasons' for saying they 'did not feel like' praising Him considering some peculiar situations they might have at one time or the other encountered, yet they still praised God. ***Let us look at some Biblical examples:***

JOB

Take the story of Job for instance. In one day, according to ***Job 1:13-19*** total disaster struck:

> *'13 And there was a day when [Job's] sons and his daughters were eating and drinking wine in their eldest brother's house*

[on his birthday], 14 And there came a messenger to Job and said, The oxen were plowing and the donkeys feeding beside them, 15 And the Sabeans swooped down upon them and took away [the animals]. Indeed, they have slain the servants with the edge of the sword, and I alone have escaped to tell you. 16 While he was yet speaking, there came also another and said, The fire of God (lightning) has fallen from the heavens and has burned up the sheep and the servants and consumed them, and I alone have escaped to tell you. 17 While he was yet speaking, there came also another and said, The Chaldeans divided into three bands and made a raid upon the camels and have taken them away, yes, and have slain the servants with the edge of the sword, and I alone have escaped to tell you. 18 While he was yet speaking, there came also another and said, Your sons and your daughters were eating and drinking wine in their eldest brother's house, 19 And behold, there came a great [whirlwind] from the desert, and smote the four corners of the house, and it fell upon the young people and they are dead, and I alone have escaped to tell you.'

In such a situation and under such circumstances I am sure it was not easy to praise or worship God yet after hearing all the news, the very next thing Bible says he did according to *verse 20* was to worship the Lord.

*'20 Then Job arose and rent his robe and shaved his head **and fell down upon the ground and worshipped.**'*

If even under such circumstances Job could worship God then I tend to ask myself in those 'I don't feel like' times whether I really have an excuse.

Surely there is no qualm about the fact that there are times when things rub us on the wrong side, making it quite difficult for us to rise up above certain circumstances to offer praise yet it is even in such times that the Bible calls on us to offer praise the more. When we are faced with challenges, our first reaction should be to rise above the challenge to a level of praise where we will encounter the solutions and answers, rather than to sink to the level of the problem where the enemy awaits the opportunity to imprison us the more.

PAUL AND SILAS

Remember that in the Acts of the Apostles, Paul and Silas probably might have had cause to grumble and complain. Their situation could not have been described as favorable yet they did not allow it to get the best of them. They had been unjustly arrested, flogged severely and as though that was not enough, they had been thrown into prison and again put in chains.

In spite of all these, they did not waste their remaining energies on questioning their predicament but rather found it within themselves to render praise.

They turned their prison sentence into a praise service. The result being their freedom, and even more, an evangelical success story where the magistrate who had thrown them into prison's heart turned to God and many more were saved. I cannot speak for you but I might have done otherwise if I found myself in such a situation yet these unwavering men of praise knew just the right thing to do and I believe there is a lot to learn from them.

HABAKKUK

Habakkuk resolved to recognize God's worth regardless of the austerity of the season he found himself in.

> *'17 Though the fig tree does not blossom and there is no fruit on the vines, [though] the product of the olive fails and the fields yield no food, though the flock is cut off from the fold and there are no cattle in the stalls, 18 Yet I will rejoice in the Lord; I will exult in the [victorious] God of my salvation! 19 The Lord God is my Strength, my personal bravery, and my invincible army; He makes my feet like hinds' feet and will make me to walk [not to stand still in terror, but to walk] and make [spiritual] progress upon my high places [of trouble, suffering, or responsibility]! For the Chief Musician; with my stringed instruments.'*
> ***Habakkuk 3:17-19***

Situations and circumstances are dynamic, swinging like a pendulum between what we may see as 'good and bad' yet the worth of God never changes and hence our praise and worship must also remain steadfast, after all the Bible teaches us that if we claim to love God and are called according to His purposes, then all of these circumstances around us are working together for our good. Don't you think that's one more reason to thank and praise God for?

DAVID

I have come to understand that it is not impossible for man to praise God in difficult times—in those 'night seasons' as the Psalmist calls them in Psalms 22:2 & 3 where he says:

> '2 O my God, I cry in the daytime, but You answer not; and by night I am not silent or find no rest. **3 But You are holy, O You Who dwell in [the holy place where] the praises of Israel [are offered].**'

David teaches us that it is possible to praise God regardless of how difficult the situations might be. The Bible admonishes us to give thanks or as other versions say give praise in all things not for some things. The operating word here is **'in'**. This means that you don't have to wait till you are out of the situation in order to decide whether or not it was *'good and worth'* praising God for. The Bible says whilst you are still **in** the situation, give thanks.

> '18 Thank [God] in everything [no matter what the circumstances may be, be thankful and give thanks], for this is the will of God for you [who are] in Christ Jesus [the Revealer and Mediator of that will].'
> **1 Thessalonians 5:18**

So we give thanks when we are going through sickness by claiming his promise that by His wounds we have been healed—*1 Peter 2:24* ('He personally bore our sins in His [own] body on the tree [as on an altar and offered Himself on it], that we might die (cease to exist) to sin and live to righteousness. By His wounds you have been healed')—and we thank God also that He took up all our infirmities and sicknesses.

Whilst still in the situation what we do is to give God thanks for His answers to the attacks of the evil one. *We give thanks for God's word concerning every situation we find ourselves in.* Note that we are not asked to give thanks 'for' the situation. We are required to give thanks in the situation.

JESUS

In the week prior to His crucifixion, Jesus and His disciples were just concluding their last evening meal and as in accordance with the tradition at the time, a number of songs were sang.

> '26 *And when they had sung a hymn, they went out to the Mount of Olives.'*
> **Mark 14:26**

The last which most probably was *Psalms 136:1-6*—The Great Hallal.

> '1 *O GIVE thanks to the Lord, for He is good; for His mercy and loving-kindness endure forever. 2 O give thanks to the God of gods, for His mercy and loving-kindness endure forever. 3 O give thanks to the Lord of lords, for His mercy and loving-kindness endure forever—4 To Him Who alone does great wonders, for His mercy and loving-kindness endure forever; 5 To Him Who by wisdom and understanding made the heavens, for His mercy and loving—kindness endure forever; 6 To Him Who stretched out the earth upon the waters, for His mercy and loving-kindness endure forever; 7 To Him Who made the great lights, for His mercy and loving-kindness endure forever—8 The sun to rule over the day, for His mercy and loving-kindness endure forever; 9 The moon and stars*

*to rule by night, **for His mercy and loving-kindness endure forever;** 10 To Him Who smote Egypt in their firstborn, **for His mercy and loving-kindness endure forever;** 11 And brought out Israel from among them, **for His mercy and loving-kindness endure forever;** 12 With a strong hand and with an outstretched arm, **for His mercy and loving-kindness endure forever;** 13 To Him Who divided the Red Sea into parts, **for His mercy and loving-kindness endure forever;** 14 And made Israel to pass through the midst of it, **for His mercy and loving-kindness endure forever;** 15 But shook off and overthrew Pharaoh and his host into the Red Sea, **for His mercy and loving-kindness endure forever;** 16 To Him Who led His people through the wilderness, **for His mercy and loving-kindness endure forever;** 17 To Him Who smote great kings, **for His mercy and loving-kindness endure forever;** 18 And slew famous kings, **for His mercy and loving-kindness endure forever—**19 Sihon king of the Amorites, **for His mercy and loving-kindness endure forever;** 20 And Og king of Bashan, **for His mercy and loving-kindness endure forever;** 21 And gave their land as a heritage, **for His mercy and loving-kindness endure forever;** 22 Even a heritage to Israel His servant, **for His mercy and loving-kindness endure forever;** 23 To Him Who [earnestly] remembered us in our low estate and imprinted us [on His heart], **for His mercy and loving—kindness endure forever;** 24 And rescued us from our enemies, **for His mercy and loving-kindness endure forever;** 25 To Him Who gives food to all flesh, **for His mercy and loving-kindness endure forever;** 26 O give thanks to the God of heaven, **for His mercy and loving-kindness endure forever!.** '*

Psalms 136:1-26

'For his mercy endureth for ever' **appears 26 times** even though in all this Jesus had on His mind His betrayal, the garden of Gethsemane and the cross, amongst other agonizing thoughts. Yet he could find reasons to declare 26 times that God's mercy endureth forever.

Even in His darkest hours, His commitment to the Lord was not broken. His heart refused to be intimidated by His feelings—and trust me—He must have had feelings (as He had a body and a soul) like any one of us yet He found it in Himself to give praise to God. He was made man with passions just like you and I. The Bible says:

> *'15 For we do not have a High Priest Who is unable to understand and sympathize and have a shared feeling with our weaknesses and infirmities and liability to the assaults of temptation, but One Who has been tempted in every respect as we are, yet without sinning. '-*
> **Hebrews 4:15**

Jesus Christ, with passions like ours, foresaw the agony ahead and could still dig from deep within Himself, a praise song to God in affirming that His mercies endureth forever.

I believe therefore that in spite of the fact that our minds and the circumstances around us may see danger, torture, disgrace, hurt and all the 'negatives', our souls should be able to declare God's lasting and eternal mercies.

Looking back to all these examples aforementioned and the fact that even under hostile conditions all these great personalities still persisted in praising God, the question now is—do we still have room to accommodate the *'I don't feel like praising God'* syndrome without feeling the pinch of guilt and shame? The last time I checked I still had not found a good enough reason for not praising God. We should be awake to the fact that praise is not a ritual or custom by which we refresh God's memory about His greatness and we do not praise God to tickle or excite His pride either.

CHAPTER 7

THE IMPORTANCE
OF PRAISE

Praise is of major importance since it:

- ▶ Exposes our beliefs
- ▶ Amends our philosophy and thoughts
- ▶ Serves as a conduit for deep friendship with God
- ▶ Institutes God's rule in our lives
- ▶ Reveals the truth about who we are in relation to God

Now let us take a more critical look at the aforementioned.

PRAISE EXPOSES OUR BELIEFS

Permit me to mention that it is impracticable to divorce what we say publicly from what we believe and think, and consequently, what we do.

'34 You offspring of vipers! How can you speak good things when you are evil (wicked)? For out of the fullness (the overflow, the superabundance) of the heart the mouth speaks. 35 The good man from his inner good treasure flings forth good things, and the evil man out of his inner evil storehouse flings forth evil things.'
Matthew 12:34 & 35

Abundance here depicts a filling and overflowing or superabundance. Again,

Matthew 6:19-21 says:
'19 Do not gather and heap up and store up for yourselves treasures on earth, where moth and rust and worm consume and destroy, and where thieves break through and steal. 20 But gather and heap up and store for yourselves treasures in heaven, where neither moth nor rust nor worm consume and destroy, and where thieves do not break through and steal; 21 For where your treasure is, there will your heart be also.'

The above Scriptures show therefore that one can only bring out good things out of the treasure of a good heart. Scripture further declares that where a man's treasure is, there also his heart will be. Isn't it amazing to realize therefore the link between what men declare with their mouths and the state of their heart and for that matter what their beliefs are? As a matter of fact if your belief is in God then your heart will be filled with His praise which will eventually overflow and cause your mouth to declare His praise.

Praise will in this sense therefore unveil your belief. Praise is thus proportional to our belief.

The figure below illustrates that it is our belief that holds our good treasure where our heart is, since the Bible says that where a man's treasure is, there his heart will be also. Now out of the abundance of the good heart the mouth speaks praise.

Essentially, Believing and Praising build upon each other and from the illustration below we discover that from our belief we render Praise which consequently results in our beholding His Power and Glorious Hand which in turn ushers us into High praise, which ultimately increases our faith and brings us to a greater level of belief. It therefore goes without question that our view of God determines our praise, which really is a disclosure of our belief.

ILLUSTRATION

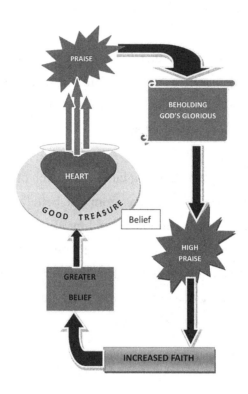

PRAISE AMENDS PHILOSOPHIES AND THOUGHTS

Human as we are, we face problems, pressures, stress, sickness and death and even when we try ignoring these, there are still problems associated with relationships; paying of bills, dealing with cantankerous people, demands from authority, and many more. The truth is that our hearts get hauled in so many different directions with all these issues of life competing for our attention. These are the things that usually succeed in averting our time, energies, attention and mind-set from God, causing the spiritual realms to become unclear for us and, ultimately causing a loss of spiritual focus. Praising God even in such times redirects our minds from what men and situations do to us to what God can do for us. The Psalmist teaches us to seek God's direction in such times:

*'11 Teach me Your way, O Lord, that I may walk and live in Your truth; direct and unite my heart [solely, reverently] to fear and honor Your name. **12** I will confess and praise You, O Lord my God, with my whole (united) heart; and I will glorify Your name forevermore. **13** For great is Your mercy and loving-kindness toward me; and You have delivered me from the depths of Sheol [from the exceeding depths of affliction].'*
Psalms 86:11-13

Praising God also serves as a reminder of the fact that we are called to live in the spirit, and thus the need to refocus our minds on the spiritual realities of life as a solution to our problems. You need to deal with your problems if not, as is said, they will deal with you.

When we believe that God is bigger than our problems and capable of dealing with them, it reflects in our praise which in turn comforts, empowers and heals us and further changes our attitude and attention positively.

Again, in praising God we set our priorities right by focusing on His love, blessings, and our responsibilities towards others, instead of the temporary feelings of depression that weigh us down. With such attention focused on God rather than any other thing or person, we are bound to break through.

PRAISE SERVES AS A CONDUIT FOR DEEP COMPANIONSHIP WITH GOD

Praise causes us to experience God's presence both within and around us. This is because as we sing praises to God, the atmosphere gets saturated with His presence (since via our praises we literally build a throne for

Him to sit on) resulting in us experiencing His tangible presence in and around us which fosters a better companionship or relationship with Him. Bible says He inhabits the praise of His people—***Psalms 22:3*** *'But You are holy, O You Who dwell in [the holy place where] the praises of Israel [are offered].'* No wonder we experience Him in our times of Praise so strongly. The word 'inhabits or dwell in' in Hebrew translates into actual sitting on or residing. Another translation of the same verse has it as 'thou are enthroned upon the praise of Israel' which means that each time we offer praise to Him we offer Him a throne to sit on in our presence.

PRAISE INSTITUTES GOD'S RULE IN OUR LIVES

I can say without any iota of doubt that where ever God dwells and manifests Himself, He reigns. God cannot cohabit with any other power or spirit that is not of Him. Provided His presence is needed and accepted, any other spirit or power contrary to The Spirit of God will have to make way. Since the Bible says that He inhabits the praise of His people, it means that He literally sits upon the praise, dwells upon it—more like takes residence in the praise of His people. Now, since He is sovereign and praise is our means of inviting God to take residence and establish His power and authority in our lives, it goes without saying that in whatever aspect of our life that we invite God into via praise, He comes in and He reigns there, kicking out any negative powers or spirits that might have previously taken residence. So for instance, if regardless of an uncomfortable financial challenge, I wake up in the morning and praise Him for being in and sorting my finances, He is then invited into my financial situation—an invitation He then honors which automatically causes the negative influence of poverty, for instance, to make way.

When I praise God for being in and sorting out my health condition (again an invitation He is more than willing to honor), He institutes His rule in my health condition upon arrival and after being enthroned, sickness must make way. When I start praising God for my academic prospects, He comes in, takes residence and academic failure has no choice but to push over. Halleluiah! When I praise Him for my marriage, immediately He comes into my marital life, takes residence whereupon divorce and other marital problems have no choice but to stand aside. What then are you going to start praising God for? I know, for I have tried and tested it in my own life and I can say that it works. There are times when I have had the honor of counseling some people (who were at the time) being tormented by frustrating events which the evil one was bombarding them with. In such times when I was unable to reach them personally to encourage them (one-on-one) I asked (especially because they were unable in such circumstances to do anything other than to worry), that they played some praise music and God knows how effective it had been. You can try it in times that the evil one tries to get at you. It works effectively. Why?

Simply because as soon as you fill your environment or atmosphere with praises to God, He takes residence and institutes His sovereignty and as a result any other negative element in the atmosphere certainly has to make way for the King of kings.

PRAISE EXPOSES THE REALITY OF OURSELVES
When we praise God we become more conscious of whom we are vis-à-vis who He is. Can you imagine Job, who God Himself had testified about as being a righteous man, saying:

'5 I had heard of You [only] by the hearing of the ear, but now my [spiritual] eye sees You. 6 Therefore I loathe [my words] and abhor myself and repent in dust and ashes.'
Job 42:5-6

This is after extolling God by faith in **Job 42:2:**

'2 I know that You can do all things, and that no thought or purpose of Yours can be restrained or thwarted.'

Here the prophet Isaiah himself in **Isaiah 66:1&2:**

'1 THUS SAYS the Lord: Heaven is My throne, and the earth is My footstool. What kind of house would you build for Me? And what kind can be My resting-place? 2 For all these things My hand has made, and so all these things have come into being [by and for Me], says the Lord. But this is the man to whom I will look and have regard: he who is humble and of a broken or wounded spirit, and who trembles at My word and reveres My commands.'

Isaiah is broken and stunned, more so shaken at the presence of God but this is not disparaging. Actually, God strips him with the purpose of putting him back together as a stronger and more powerful worshipper.

This is what happens to us when we go to God in true praise. We are 'unclothed' so that we realize who we really are in respect to God. Obviously, there have been times when we have become too familiar with God that we take things (especially His leniency) for granted thinking it's alright to treat Him as an equal or even less. Praising Him as shown in the life of these great men of God, puts us in check by stripping us of all such folly and revealing our real position in relation to who He is. As in the case of the prophet, we should also (whilst still praising God) realize God's greatness and subsequently our own weakness since it is a time when God puts us under the shimmering spotlight of His holiness for us to see who we actually are in relation to who He is.

CHAPTER 8

SOME BENEFITS OF PRAISE

WHEN we praise God, we must understand that it is not a **waste** of time. In fact we **spend** time praising God and therefore always stand to gain certain benefits each time we offer true praise with the right heart and understanding. Understanding the benefits of praise I trust will change your whole perspective of praise as well as your attitude towards it. In this section, we will discover a number of benefits we stand to gain whenever we offer genuine praise to God.

PRAISE IS A THERAPY FOR SADNESS AND DRYNESS

'3 To grant [consolation and joy] to those who mourn in Zion--to give them an ornament (a garland or diadem) of beauty instead of ashes, the oil of joy instead of mourning, the garment [expressive] of praise instead of a heavy, burdened, and failing spirit—that they may be called oaks of righteousness [lofty,

strong, and magnificent, distinguished for uprightness, justice, and right standing with God], the planting of the Lord, that He may be glorified . . . '
Isaiah 61:3

As explained earlier in this book, the garment of praise in this Scripture is mentioned in contrast to heaviness or depression and for that matter despair, faintness, feebleness and sadness; which means that this garment of praise will be exchanged for all the aforementioned negative feelings and emotions. As a matter of fact, God says He will offer a garment of praise in place of all these demonic works of the devil which attack and challenge our lives. One of the benefits of praising God therefore is the therapeutic result it has on us as Christians in times of depression or despair.

PRAISE CREATES AN ENABLING ENVIRONMENT FOR GOD'S MINISTERING ANGELS

During sessions of intense praise, an environment or atmosphere of faith is created as has been explained earlier on when we discovered that praise and belief build on each other. When we express belief the result is our rendering Praise which consequently results in our beholding His Power and His glorious hand which ushers us into high praise, and thereby increases our faith. This then brings us to an even greater level of belief. Actually praise creates joy and thankfulness through which our belief in the goodness and greatness of God is whipped up, thereby increasing our faith. If you really have faith in the word of God I suppose you will sing and praise God for what His promises say about you, being assured that they will come to pass. Now, with such an atmosphere of increased faith, our desires and requests are usually met and challenges which previously might have been hard to overcome receive solutions. Such an enabling atmosphere, affords ministering angels the convenience to minister effectively to us since the spiritual environment becomes so strongly saturated with positive faith that solutions that were naturally hard to imagine, tend to manifest easily.

PRAISE ENSURES SPIRITUAL GROWTH

The Bible says that without faith it is impossible to please God. Again, the means by which we can grow spiritually is to please God by doing His will which causes us to mature in our spiritual life. Praise creates joy and thankfulness through which we believe in the goodness and greatness of God which consequently increases our faith. Yet, as previously established, in the process of belief and praise building upon each other, greater faith is released. Now, knowing that our whole Christian walk is based on faith, may I suggest that, if our faith can be increased by praising God then our spiritual lives can and will subsequently grow thereby.

PRAISE BRINGS REVELATION

Psalms 49:4 says:

> *'4 I will submit and consent to a parable or proverb; to the music of a lyre I will unfold my riddle (my problem).'*

This is usually evident when the prophetic anointing falls on us during praise. As was in the case of David on many occasions, he operated in the prophetic ministry whilst in praise. Scripture makes us to know that, it was during times of praise (such as when David played on his harp) that these dark sayings were opened or revealed. God truly brings us revelation in times of praise. Praise actually prepares us to receive the 'Rhema' of God. It takes us back to the part of scripture which says that we should enter His courts with praise. Thereafter we progress into the Holy place and then the Most Holy place where we meet with His presence and you can be sure that in His presence there are revelations of His power and His Word. It is therefore not surprising what a close link there is between the prophetic unction and praise.

PRAISE BRINGS EMPOWERMENT

Praise entails declaring the goodness of God—what He has done and what He is yet to do. This in itself is unbearable for the enemy. It's actually so embarrassing for him. The word of God is the greatest weapon we have as Christians and praise involves declaring just that. Praising God reveals how much we are empowered. So much has already been said about how praising God increases our faith. Now, who can overemphasize how empowered a Christian with great faith is.

The Bible says that when we speak in tongues we utter mysteries. The evil one cannot even understand what we utter. So when we sing in the spirit as a form of praise as described in *1Corinthians 14:2* you can imagine how weak and frustrated the devil must feel. Praise surely empowers us.

> '2 For one who speaks in an [unknown] tongue speaks not to men but to God, for no one understands or catches his meaning, because in the [Holy] Spirit he utters secret truths and hidden things [not obvious to the understanding].'
> *1Corinthians 14:2*

PRAISE SILENCES THE DEVIL

In *1 Samuel 17,* we realize how much Goliath; the Champion of the **Philistines** defied the people of God in *verses 43 & 44*

*'43 . . . Am I a dog that you should come to me with sticks? And the Philistine cursed David by his gods. **44** The Philistine said to David, Come to me, and I will give your flesh to the birds of the air and the beasts of the field.'*

To which David who eventually turned out to be the Champion of Israel, in verses *46* and *47* remarkably responds by extolling God by faith:

*'**46** This day the Lord will deliver you into my hand, and I will smite you and cut off your head. And I will give the corpses of the army of the Philistines this day to the birds of the air and the wild beasts of the earth, that all the earth may know that there is a God in Israel. **47** And all this assembly shall know that the Lord saves not with sword and spear; for the battle is the Lord's, and He will give you into our hands.'*
1Samuel 17:46 &47

Earlier in ***verse 37 David*** had said,
*'**36** Your servant killed both the lion and the bear; and this uncircumcised Philistine shall be like one of them, for he has defied the armies of the living God! **37** David said, The Lord Who delivered me out of the paw of the lion and out of the paw of the bear, He will deliver me out of the hand of this Philistine. And Saul said to David, Go, and the Lord be with you!'*

That was extolling God—A form of praise to God. As a result, the enemy's army was silenced. Halleluiah!

One of the ways to hush the enemy is via praise. In praising God, David says in ***Psalms 8:1-2:***

*'1 O LORD, our Lord, how excellent (majestic and glorious) is Your name in all the earth! You have set Your glory on [or above] the heavens. 2 **Out** of the mouths of babes and unweaned infants **You have established strength because of Your foes, that You might silence the enemy and the avenger.'***

It is obvious that in the first verse, David used praise to launch the name of the Lord, which is a weapon for spiritual warfare. The verse says that thou might silence the avenger, which in other words means that *thou mightiest shut the enemy up.*

It is interesting to note that the battle between David and Goliath was settled spiritually by their utterances before the physical event took place. The spiritual weapon (praise that David used) won him the battle even before he had physically engaged Goliath.

Now in the account of the triumphant entry in *Mathew 21:15-16*, it is interesting to note how, when the chief priest and the scribes were upset with the children who had followed and praised Jesus and had questioned Him as to whether He had heard what the children were saying, Jesus quotes form *Psalms 8:2*, and yet with what at first sight may seem as a slight 'alteration' to the verses:

'15 But when the chief priests and the scribes saw the wonderful things that He did and the boys and the girls and the youths and the maidens crying out in the porches and courts of the temple, Hosanna (O be propitious, graciously inclined) to the Son of David! they were indignant. 16 And they said to Him, Do You hear what these are saying? And Jesus replied to them,

Yes; have you never read, Out of the mouths of babes and unweaned infants You have made (provided) perfect praise?'

Jesus did not misquote David, in case that is what you are thinking. In fact, that is impossible since He Himself is the Word of God. What He did was rather interpret what David had said.

The two parts that seemingly differ are the part of David's Psalms which says 'hast thou established strength' and that which Jesus says—**'made (provided) perfect praise.'**

If both scriptures mean the same and one thing and Jesus was only interpreting what David said, then it should mean that these two statements, though 'seemingly' different, mean the same thing.

Hence, 'ordained or established strength' must then be equivalent or the same as 'perfect praise' therefore perfected praise is ordained strength!!! And this ordained strength is what ultimately silences the devil.

PRAISE COMMANDS THE BLESSINGS AND FEAR OF GOD

'5 Let the peoples praise You [turn away from their idols] and give thanks to You, O God; let all the peoples praise and give thanks to You! 6 The earth has yielded its harvest [in evidence of God's approval]; God, even our own God, will bless us. 7 God will bless us, and all the ends of the earth shall reverently fear Him.'
Psalms 67:5-7

Praise commands God's blessings and causes the earth to fear Him. Blessings are actually built into our praise and worship. That is to say, blessings are more of an inbuilt consequence of our praising God. I once heard someone say that it is as though there is such a great reservoir of blessings in heaven for us and as we praise God, our praises serve as arrows which 'puncture' the reservoir of heavenly blessings, causing it to rain on us.

You can then imagine what happens when we 'puncture' it just a few times with our occasional praise.

If we would however praise God continually as Bible entreats us to, then for a fact we will be 'drowned' in His blessings. Then we can truly sing:

> *'It is raining, all around me, I can feel it the latter rain; Right now Jesus give us more rain; until we are filled, and we are soaked with the latter rain'*

By that it means that the more we 'puncture' the heavenly reservoir of blessings with our 'praise arrows', the more blessings we will in turn receive.

PRAISE BRINGS CONTENTMENT TO OUR SOULS

Psalms 63:1-5 teaches us that with the right attitude and approach towards praise, (with the right desire and passion for God) our soul is sure to be contented.

> *'1 O GOD, You are my God, **earnestly will I seek You; my inner self thirsts for You, my flesh longs and is faint for You,***

in a dry and weary land where no water is. 2 So I have looked upon You in the sanctuary to see Your power and Your glory. 3 Because Your loving-kindness is better than life, my lips shall praise You. 4 So will I bless You while I live; I will lift up my hands in Your name. 5 My whole being shall be satisfied as with marrow and fatness; and my mouth shall praise You with joyful lips'

This scripture portrays the need for:

URGENCY
'*Earnestly will I seek You,* indicates the urgency with which David approaches praise. The promptness if you like, with which he approached praise is worth emulating.

DESIRE AND ENTHUSIASM
'*My inner self thirsts for You* shows the desire or enthusiasm with which David longs after God. He said—'as the dear panteth after the water brooks, so my soul panteth after thee', which further depicts an element of intensity.

DETERMINATION
'*My flesh longs and is faint for You, in a dry and weary land where no water is'* portrays the determination to praise God:

HUMILITY
'*Because Your loving-kindness is better than life, my lips shall praise You'* tells of David's humility which is also extremely important and worthy of mention.

All the above ingredients are elements of gratitude which in itself is paramount in our praise to God. So then what we are being told here is that if all these above mentioned elements which are the embodiment of gratitude are found in our praise, then as in *verse 5* our whole being shall be satisfied. Later on in this book we will by the Grace of God get to learn about the attitude of gratitude.

PRAISE CAUSES REVOLUTIONARY TRIUMPH AND OPENS PRISON GATES

When Jehoshaphat tried to turn the Israelites back to God three groups mounted an attack on him yet the account of events that occurred indicates the radical victory that praise holds.

> '15 He said, Hearken, all Judah, you inhabitants of Jerusalem, and you King Jehoshaphat. The Lord says this to you: Be not afraid or dismayed at this great multitude; for the battle is not yours, but God's. **16** Tomorrow go down to them. Behold, they will come up by the Ascent of Ziz, and you will find them at the end of the ravine before the Wilderness of Jeruel. **17** You shall not need to fight in this battle; take your positions, stand still, and see the deliverance of the Lord [Who is] with you, O Judah and Jerusalem. Fear not nor be dismayed. Tomorrow go out against them, for the Lord is with you. **18** And Jehoshaphat bowed his head with his face to the ground, and all Judah and the inhabitants of Jerusalem fell down before the Lord, worshiping Him. **19** And some Levites of the Kohathites and Korahites stood up to praise the Lord, the God of Israel, with a very loud voice. **20** And they rose early in the morning and went out into the Wilderness of Tekoa; and as they went out, Jehoshaphat stood and said, Hear me, O Judah, and you

inhabitants of Jerusalem! Believe in the Lord your God and you shall be established; believe and remain steadfast to His prophets and you shall prosper. **21 When he had consulted with the people, he appointed singers to sing to the Lord and praise Him in their holy [priestly] garments as they went out before the army, saying, Give thanks to the Lord, for His mercy and loving-kindness endure forever!**

22 And when they began to sing and to praise, the Lord set ambushments against the men of Ammon, Moab, and Mount Seir who had come against Judah, and they were [self-] slaughtered; 23 *For [suspecting betrayal] the men of Ammon and Moab rose against those of Mount Seir, utterly destroying them. And when they had made an end of the men of Seir, they all helped to destroy one another.'*

2 Chronicles 20:15-23

Despite their mortal enemies, the Levites responded to God's commandment by raising their voices loud in praises. Revolutionary triumph was the outcome. In our days too, the God who changes not will bring us radical conquest when in obedience, we lift our voices in praise continually.

Paul says in *2 Corinthians 10:4:*

'*4 For the weapons of our warfare are not physical [weapons of flesh and blood], but they are mighty before God for the overthrow and destruction of strongholds,'*

Instead of moaning and complaining, Paul and Silas turned their prison sentence into a praise service and as a result we have an extraordinary chronicle of events—the prison doors were opened, the magistrate was converted overnight, a household was saved and more importantly, satanic incarceration was ousted. Praise God!

'18 And she did this for many days. Then Paul, being sorely annoyed and worn out, turned and said to the spirit within her, I charge you in the name of Jesus Christ to come out of her! And it came out that very moment. 19 But when her owners discovered that their hope of profit was gone, they caught hold of Paul and Silas and dragged them before the authorities in the forum (marketplace), [where trials are held]. 20 And when they had brought them before the magistrates, they declared, These fellows are Jews and they are throwing our city into great confusion. 21 They encourage the practice of customs which it is unlawful for us Romans to accept or observe! 22 The crowd [also] joined in the attack upon them, and the rulers tore the clothes off of them and commanded that they be beaten with rods. 23 And when they had struck them with many blows, they threw them into prison, charging the jailer to keep them safely. 24 He, having received [so strict a] charge, put them into the inner prison (the dungeon) and fastened their feet in the stocks. 25 But about midnight, as Paul and Silas were praying and singing hymns of praise to God, and the [other] prisoners were listening to them, 26 Suddenly there was a great earthquake, so that the very foundations of the prison were shaken; and at once all the doors were opened and everyone's shackles were unfastened. 27 When the jailer, startled out of his sleep, saw that the prison doors were open, he drew his sword and was on the point of killing himself, because he supposed that the prisoners had escaped. 28 But Paul shouted; Do not harm yourself, for we are all here!'—Acts 16:18-28

PRAISING GOD DRAWS SOULS TO THE
SOVEREIGNTY OF GOD

It is said of the early church in the Acts of the Apostles that amongst other things, as they praised God, He added to the church daily. I remember when the Charismatic movements started to become vibrant and evident in Ghana, one of the churches that was identified with it was the Church of Pentecost, and I remember a couple of people who attended one of the assemblies. Not that I had anything against them at the time, but I just didn't feel led to join in. At the time, my entire family was Orthodox—Anglican and I don't think at my age I would have been allowed to go my way into a different church (Well, not that I even tried to). I was a mass server in the Anglican Church and I felt that was enough. In any case I can vividly remember, (even as young as I was at the time) some people—some saved now, others not, who just could not bring themselves to understand let alone accept this 'new move'. They claimed they were older than these supposedly new churches and thus could not see themselves joining 'churches', younger than them. Then there was the 'speaking in tongues' issue which was just too much for them to take in and what they could not stand the most was the 'excessive' loud singing and dancing (which I eventually have come to make out as Praise)—and the accusation was that, all these *new churches*' knew was to make noise and dance throughout their services. To them church had to be pious, sanctimonious, quiet and all that. They questioned why *'these people'* were taking it overboard and spoiling the whole great idea of church? It seemed all so disorderly in their eyes. I am not denying that in its path the charismatic move must have had its own challenges and mistakes which saw some people doing some unacceptable things but you know what? On the positive side I believe some have through this *'new move'* come to discover the true meaning of praising God. I believe the most intimidating thing for these frustrated people who had problems with the singing and dancing was the rate at which this move was growing—it was so rapid and literally people were just flocking into the charismatic churches daily. I remember people at the time blaming it on the inherent instincts of youthful exuberance with extra zeal and no knowledge. Ok so how do you explain the oldies in the charismatic churches now? I suppose that is oldie knowledge and wisdom encapsulated within a new unstoppable spiritual awakening. For all those who did not understand or unfortunately may still not understand how this *'singing and dancing'* was and still is winning more souls into the Kingdom, here it is—tucked away in *Acts 2:47*. Speaking of the early church, the Bible says that they were:

> *'47 constantly praising God and being in favor and goodwill with all the people; and the Lord kept adding [to their number] daily those who were being saved [from spiritual death].'*

PRAISING GOD KEEPS US IN TUNE WITH HEAVEN Worth mentioning again is the fact that praising God keeps us in tune with Heaven. We are privileged to have a glimpse of how the heavenly host praised God in heaven when we consider *Revelation Chapters 4-5.*

PRAISE CAUSES US TO TRIUMPH WITH CHRIST

According to *Psalms 106:47:*

> *'Save us, O LORD our God, and gather us from among the heathen, to give thanks unto thy holy name, and to triumph in thy praise'. (KJV)*

We need to understand that there is a difference between victory and triumph; we often tend to mix the two. As Christians, victory is the accomplishment of defeat over the devil, whilst triumph is the festivity of the victory already won.

Colossians 2: 8-15 says that:

'8 See to it that no one carries you off as spoil or makes you yourselves captive by his so-called philosophy and intellectualism and vain deceit (idle fancies and plain nonsense), following human tradition (men's ideas of the material rather than the spiritual world), just crude notions following the rudimentary and elemental teachings of the universe and disregarding [the teachings of] Christ (the Messiah). 9 For in Him the whole fullness of Deity (the Godhead) continues to dwell in bodily form [giving complete expression of the divine nature]. 10 And you are in Him, made full and having come to fullness of life [in Christ you too are filled with the Godhead—Father, Son and Holy Spirit—and reach full spiritual stature]. And He is the Head of all rule and authority [of every angelic principality and power]. 11 In Him also you were circumcised with a circumcision not made with hands, but in a [spiritual] circumcision [performed by] Christ by stripping off the body of the flesh (the whole corrupt, carnal nature with its passions and lusts). 12 [Thus you were circumcised when] you were buried with Him in [your] baptism, in which you were also raised with Him [to a new life] through [your] faith in the working of God [as displayed] when He raised Him up from the dead.

13 And you who were dead in trespasses and in the uncircumcision of your flesh (your sensuality, your sinful carnal nature), [God] brought to life together with [Christ], having [freely] forgiven us all our transgressions, 14 Having cancelled and blotted out and wiped away the handwriting of the note (bond) with its legal decrees and demands which was in force and stood against us (hostile to us). This [note with its regulations, decrees, and demands] He set aside and cleared completely out of our way by nailing it to [His] cross. 15 [God] **disarmed the principalities and powers that were ranged against us and made a bold display and public example of them, in triumphing over them in Him and in it [the cross].'**

With special emphasis on *verse 15* we notice that the principalities and powers have been rendered powerless by the VICTORY that was won by God through the work of Jesus on the cross. So the victory has already been won. That is not what we are called as Christians to do, rather we are called to give thanks unto God's Holy name and to TRIUMPH in His praise.

2 Corinthians 2:14 says:
'14 But thanks be to God, Who in Christ always leads us in triumph [as trophies of Christ's victory] and through us spreads and makes evident the fragrance of the knowledge of God everywhere.'

In Christ, we celebrate the victory, thus causing us to be in a continual pageant of the celebration of victory in Christ.

Hence, as evidence of Christ defeating the enemy and for that matter His victory, the triumph (celebration of victory) organized has Christ in the chariot, leading the defeated enemy (satan) in chains, spoiled and stripped of his armor, followed by all his principalities and powers, his rulers of darkness and spiritual wickedness—all of them are being dragged along and being made a public show off. Now just by offering praise to God, *Colossians 2:15* says, we jump into the chariot with Jesus and join in the ongoing celebration of the victory, which is the triumph.

CHAPTER 9

SOME ELEMENTS OF PRAISE

IN *Psalms 100* which is a Psalms of praise, God reveals certain basic truths about certain elements which are necessary for enhancing our daily praise in order to make it meaningful and authentic.

'*1 MAKE A joyful noise to the Lord, all you lands! 2 Serve the Lord with gladness! Come before His presence with singing! 3 Know (perceive, recognize, and understand with approval) that the Lord is God! It is He Who has made us, not we ourselves [and we are His]! We are His people and the sheep of His pasture. 4 Enter into His gates with thanksgiving and a thank offering and into His courts with praise! Be thankful and say so to Him, bless and affectionately praise His name! 5 For the Lord is good; His mercy and loving-kindness are everlasting, His faithfulness and truth endure to all generations.' Psalms 100:1-5*

BONA FIDE PRAISE PROCEEDS FROM A THANKFUL HEART

In the Middle East, the house setting or lay out was and probably still is pretty much comparable to what is predominantly seen in my home country Ghana (and I believe in most African countries as well). More often than not, they were built along streets, were walled and had a gate for security. One entered the courtyard or the compound via the gates of the house and from there proceeded to enter the main house.

Now consider a scenario where someone entered a compound through the gates to a house, let's say, as they escape from an enemy. I suppose that upon entering, (as was the case in those days in the Middle East), this person would be assured of some level of security or protection because the person chasing them would not dare follow them right in and harm them. Therefore having entered the house, there is an assurance (at least) of some level of protection.

Again (at least in those days), in the Middle East, as can be said of the well known Ghanaian hospitality, you could anticipate even as a stranger, some level of hospitality, the minute you entered through someone's gates. At least, there would be some water to drink, to refresh yourself and a comfortable chair to sit on then a question about your mission.

Both protection and hospitality are accorded you right from the moment you enter the gates to a house. Now, with this setting in mind we can understand better, the mindset of the Psalmist. Whenever we enter the gates which lead into God's presence, we are at least assured of protection and hospitality.

Later on in this book we shall take a walk through the tabernacle but allow me to quickly mention that in the olden days, within the tabernacle stood the altar upon which sacrifices were made and at the corners of the altar were carved horns that were overlaid with bronze. These horns were used to help tie up animals about to be sacrificed and they were also symbolic. For protection, a person in Israel could go to the altar and cling to these horns, and as long as he held onto the horns of this altar, he could not be harmed. In our modern setting though we still seek protection in the house of God—people who feel threatened still seek "refuge" in the church when they realize that there is no protection or justice for them in the world.

This must have caused the Psalmist to say in **Psalms 42:1:**
> *'1 AS THE hart pants and longs for the water brooks, so I pant and long for You, O God . . . .'*

Bible scholars have attributed this comparison of the Psalmist's soul's search for God to the hart panting after water brooks to two main things.

First, is the real thirst showing the zeal with which his soul pants after God. It is said to be known that a thirsty hart or deer will stop at nothing until it has found water to quench its thirst.

The second leans towards what I mentioned earlier as regards protection. It is also known that harts have strong scents, which preying animals smell and follow to track them down and the only way to conceal their odor is to immerse themselves in water. That is to say, when escaping from its preying enemies, the deer would pant after water brooks to immerse itself in, in order to cut off its odor to ensure its own safety and protection.

Hence, it can be inferred from the Psalmist that his soul pants after God for protection as well, which buttresses the fact that when we come to God we are afforded protection.

Now, when someone grants you warmth and protection, ideally what's about the first thing you render? Thanksgiving of course! So that element of thanksgiving is paramount as we go before God. Gratitude is however an attitude.

THE GRATITUDE ATTITUDE

You may better understand this if you have been in a relationship of some sort and all that you do is just give and give and give and never get anything in return. I trust that in the least, you will feel used. I remember once when in my life someone promised to give me a job. Honestly all the terms looked good and I felt convinced that I had gotten the right job. Because I felt so strongly about this job I just based my commitment to this relationship on trust and gave my all to it. I would just give and give and not once can I remember letting this partner down. I would just give off my best, because all I saw was this project becoming a reality. Not even once did I ever demand any remuneration for all the effort I was putting into the project—not that I had been offered anything anyway—but I did not ask either. At a point in time I noticed that almost all my life had been put on hold just because of this person and the project from which I was getting nothing, not even a written contract that I had eventually asked for at the advice of my lawyer, at least to feel some commitment on this persons' part. I cannot just explain how I felt when I was rudely awakened to the fact that this person was taking me for granted and was just using me.

It is no different a feeling when it comes to love relationships—when you love with all your heart and all you get in return is being taken for granted; and so I believe it is with any other relationship, but you need to understand that even Jesus experienced it and in *Luke 17* we are told about it.

In those days, being leprous was no small issue. You would get examined by the priest, and if whatever skin disease suspected to be leprosy was still evident, you would be isolated or quarantined for seven days. Then you would be examined by the priest again. If there is no improvement you would be quarantined again for a further seven days and if there was still no improvement, you would be cast behind the city wall where people would have no contact with you anymore and all you would get to see would be those who were in the same situation like you or even worse.

It was such a disgraceful disease in those days, that those suffering from it were to wear bells around their feet and as though that was not enough embarrassment, they were to shout to announce their presence when passing by so that the 'clean' would step aside for the 'unclean' to pass lest they get infected. That was how bad it was!

You might have been isolated and labeled unclean or unworthy in some aspect of your life. Academically, financially, socially or health wise, you might have been treated as though you have a stigma of some sort and might have been cut off from others, such that probably all those you see in your company behind your 'city wall' are just like you, worse off or just slightly better than you yet suffering similar predicaments. Such company cannot help you even if they wanted to and those who on the other side might have wanted to provide for you still cannot afford to get close to you. You might have found yourself in such a situation where, even before you show your face, as though there were 'bells around your feet', your presence is announced ahead of you—but very soon Jesus is going to heal your situation and when He does you will need to show him an attitude of gratitude.

Jesus asked the lepers to go and show themselves to the High priest and the Bible says that as they went they were cleansed. I believe that it was not only a matter of Jesus cleansing them physically because it actually, went beyond that. He had given them another opportunity to live a full rewarding life. These were people who had been cut off from their families, friends, work and you name it. Do you not realize that their physical cleansing was tied to many other things and as a result meant they had been given back all that they had lost? Unfortunately nine were caught up in what was going on around them but thank God one had a heart of gratitude and saw beyond just the physical cleansing of leprosy and decided to return to express gratitude.

> '15 Then one of them, upon seeing that he was cured, turned back, recognizing and thanking and praising God with a loud voice; 16 And he fell prostrate at Jesus' feet, thanking Him [over and over]. And he was a Samaritan.'
> **Luke 17:15-16**

I can almost hear Jesus throttle in disappointment at the fact that nine had not returned to show gratitude and so in *verse 17 and 18*

'17 . . . Jesus asked, were not [all] ten cleansed? Where are the nine? 18 Was there no one found to return and to recognize and give thanks and praise to God except this alien?'

Now I was so excited when God revealed something unique to me concerning this Samaritan man—alien as Christ describes him. The one who returned to give praise to God with the element of gratitude got something the other nine could have gotten too but lost out on as a result of their ingratitude.

Stick with me and let's hear again what Jesus' response to this stranger was.

All tucked away in *verse 19*, it is almost negligible.

'19 And He said to him, Get up and go on your way. Your faith (your trust and confidence that spring from your belief in God) has restored you to health.'
Luke 17:19

Or as in the KJV

And he said unto him, Arise, go thy way: thy faith hath made thee whole.

Got it? *Jesus said to him: Arise, go thy way: thy faith hath made thee whole.*

What? *Arise, go thy way: thy faith hath made thee whole.*

Do you get it now? **Whole!!!! (RESTORED HEALTH).** Can you remember what Jesus had previously said?

Then Jesus asked, were not [all] ten cleansed? Where are the nine? This says to me the nine were **cleansed or healed of leprosy** but of the one that gave praise to God, He said, he had been made whole. Dear one, *whole is whole—restored is restored—*and more so if God Himself said he was whole then he was whole.

You see there was the possibility of the other nine encountering some other problems or afflictions. Not necessarily leprosy related but in other aspects of their life but the one that came back with gratitude to praise God was made **WHOLE**—his health had been restored, which barred or exempted him from any other health related problem. The man was whole (restored), which means everything about the man's health was **complete, intact and in one piece.** Beloved, regardless of the fact that you may have been referred to as a stranger or an alien, I am convinced that with the right attitude of gratitude, you will be restored and for that matter made whole.

Do you now understand why some people never feel fulfilled or complete in life and are always faced with one problem or the other? If you are such a person I believe this may be a very good time to pause and reflect to see whether you have done the right thing by showing appropriate gratitude to God in all areas of your life that God has previously come through for you. If not then the time to act is now.

You know what? I would rather be made whole than just get cleansed or healed. In that regard, I will not stop praising Him with a heart filled with gratitude. Gratitude is an attitude and the earlier we all cultivate and nurture it the better. I would not allow myself to be like the people described in *Romans 1:21:*

'21 Because when they knew and recognized Him as God, they did not honor and glorify Him as God or give Him thanks. But instead they became futile and godless in their thinking [with vain imaginings, foolish reasoning, and stupid speculations] and their senseless minds were darkened.'

Rather I guess a better attitude is for you and I to join David and with like attitude say:

'1 I WILL bless the Lord at all times; His praise shall continually be in my mouth. 2 My life makes its boast in the Lord; let the humble and afflicted hear and be glad. 3 O magnify the Lord with me, and let us exalt His name together . . .' **Psalms 34:1-3**

It is very easy to be caught up in a present blessing and forget or neglect the necessary attitude of gratitude. Beware, lest you miss out on an even greater blessing of being made whole!!!

CHARACTERISTICS OF GRATITUDE:

► Determination

Supposing you got home one day very hungry and tired to find the key to a brand new state of the art luxury saloon car on your dining table and was told that a friend of yours had parked the car in your garage as a gift. I can say with all certainty that regardless of the meal that may be set on your table, your first reaction if you really had an attitude of gratitude would be to get in touch with the person to say thank you. If possible you might even get out of your home to meet up with your friend to show gratitude.

I suppose our real and acceptable attitude towards God and all He does for us should be that of intense determination to seek Him no matter what and regardless of the cost (be it our meal or rest) to show Him appreciation by praising Him with a heart and attitude of gratitude.

Yet today, whilst praises are sang in church, church folk can afford to sit unconcerned citing childish excuses such as tiredness or sometimes hunger as reasons for their actions or inactions. The question is: Do we not realize what God has done for us at all or is it just that we do not have the determined attitude of gratitude?

► Alacrity

As in the above described scenario, I guess the ideal reaction of getting in touch with the person who gave the gift would have been instantaneous. You would have been prompt in reacting if you really had an attitude of gratitude. In like manner I suppose we need to show promptness in our approach to praising God for all that He has done on our behalf. You see how weird it is to say 'oh let me wait, I will go and thank and praise God in church on Sunday', when God has done something say on Monday. If you really have some gratitude in you, where is the promptness? I believe we don't only have to wait for Sunday services to give praise to God for stuff He does for us on a daily basis. If our attitude is that of gratitude, then I guess praising and thanking God should be prompt.

► Intensity

I can vividly remember an occasion when I gave to support a friend in need. I must confess that I was embarrassed at the manner in which he thanked me. It was with such intensity, it almost drew tears to my eyes. It was as though I had bought his life for him anew and truly I had even felt that I hadn't done enough, just that I did not have the means to do more; yet the intensity with which he showed gratitude touched me so much. The intensity of his expression revealed true gratitude. How do we express our gratitude to God in our praise? With what level of intensity or passion do we praise God? Do we praise God anyhow or we do it with a true depth of intensity that portrays the element of gratitude?

▶ Humility

Expressing gratitude also has the rare quality of humility. Indeed if the reason for your thanksgiving means that much to you, you are bound to be humbled and it will reflect in your attitude. True praise in gratitude humbles us before God, causing us to completely depend upon Him. This comes when we recognize and acknowledge that all that we are and have come from Him. Need I say more about the level of humility that should be echoed in our praise to God if we really have an attitude of gratitude when we go before Him in Praise?

Our view of His ability to meet our needs reflects in the intensity with which we praise God.

Again, the extent to which we see God intimately involved in the details of our life is reflected in the frequency with which we praise God.

More so, the amount of time we spend in praising God is a reflection of the depth of our personal relationship with Him.

It is important to note that our praise further mirrors our relationship with, trust in and perspective of God.

If we would spiritually self examine ourselves, just like our ladies are advised to frequently examine themselves for lumps in their breasts, which could reveal early signs of cancer, we may just notice some 'spiritual lumps' which if not attended to early can lead to *'spiritually terminal diseases'*.

I am sure by now you know how well you are doing, as regards your relationship with, your view of and your trust in God just by the measure of praise you offer to God. Although praise is not a means of manipulating God to get things from Him, He graciously loads us with benefits when our praises please Him. In praise, we position ourselves in such a manner as to see God for who He really is and in the process receive abundant benefits.

A doctor friend of mine once made a remark in awe during my pastor's fifth anniversary thanksgiving breakfast meeting. She said "Isn't it amazing that we came to thank God and in turn we get to be blessed so much?" Doc, I fully agree with you—it's so amazing!! Praise God!

My dear pastor David usually says that your location will determine your allocation, and of a truth if we will learn to locate ourselves in the right place in praise continually, we can rest assure that we will definitely obtain our generous ration of benefits.

CHAPTER 10

SOME BIBLICAL
EXPRESSIONS OF PRAISE

THERE are several expressions of praise and this chapter by no means exhausts them all but just explores a few which are commonly used, in order for us to have a clear understanding of what we do when we do them.

10.0 *PRAISE—ACCOMPANIED BY LOUDNESS*
Shabach, as found in ***Psalms 117:1***

> '1 O **PRAISE** *the Lord, all you nations!* **Praise Him,** *all you people!'*

Praise as used here, translates into speaking loudly of in a high and befitting way or to shout with a loud voice about the greatness and goodness of God. It further means to address in a loud tone and to command triumph (the celebration of victory), glory and to shout.

It is the same translation of Shabach used for praise as seen in the following scriptures:

'35 And say, Save us, O God of our salvation; gather us together and deliver us from the nations, that we may **give thanks to Your holy name and glory in Your praise.***'*
1 Chronicles 16:35

'3 Because Your loving-kindness is better than life, my lips shall **praise** *You. 4 So will I bless You while I live; I will lift up my hands in Your name.'*
Psalms 63:3-4

Articulation or verbalization of praise is Biblical and should be encouraged in our lives as Christians, even though that is not the only manner by which we can express praise to God. In articulating our praise to God however it is also permissible to be noisy at times.

'1 MAKE A joyful noise unto God, all the earth; 2 Sing forth the honor and glory of His name; make His praise glorious!'

'8 Bless our God, O peoples, give Him **grateful thanks and make the voice of His praise be heard,***'*
Psalms 66: 1,2,8

Again, ***Psalms 47:1*** *says:*
1 O CLAP your hands, all you peoples! Shout to God with the voice of triumph and songs of joy!'

*And again **Psalms 100:1** says:*

'1 MAKE A joyful noise to the Lord, all you lands!'

The Bible usually describes praise as an active voice, spoken, voiced and sometimes loud. It is important to mention however that not all noise is praise. If a person is after God's own heart then that person must have an excellent Spirit which obviously does not do things anyhow. It is my prayer however that in whatever type of praise that we indulge in, we pay heed to

***1Corinthians 14:40** which says that:*

*'**40** But all things should be done with regard to decency and propriety and in an orderly fashion.'*

10.1 *PRAISE—ACCOMPANIED BY MOVEMENTS*

Biblically, physical movements can express praise to God. Such movements may include the following:

▶ Raising of hands

The raising of hands in praise and worship could mean a couple of things depending on how it is done. Some primary well known expressions of praise made with human hands are *Yadah* and *Todah* or *Towday* as expressed in Hebrew.

Yadah is to give public gratitude to, and expresses the core meaning of praise. It implies worshipping with raised hands by, extending the hands in reverence or worship and is often associated with thanks giving. This expression usually depicts being in need and the dependence on God and may also portray the confession of sins.

TODAH OR TOWDAY

Here, the extending of the hands is an act of confession or thanks and is completely an act of the will. It is commonly used in songs and is interpreted as praise and thanksgiving.

Though I mentioned earlier that the raising of hands in praise and worship could mean a number of things depending on how it is done, it is not a hard and fast rule. The following interpretations of certain gestures are as well generalized and may mean different things to different individuals but basically, the lifting of hands straight up high, with palms facing outwards could indicate a sign of surrender or submission. I remember during my childhood days we used to play a game we at the time called 'police and thieves'. Others may call it 'hide and seek'—yet I prefer to use the 'police and thieves' because it paints a better picture of what I intend to emphasize. You can also imagine the scenario from films or even some arrests we occasionally see being made on the evening news. Just about the first thing the thieves do when they have been captured is to stick their hands up high in the air as a sign of surrender. Note that, even when they don't do it willingly the police most certainly upon arresting them will demand that they raise their hands or at least place them where they can be seen. This is to ensure maybe amongst other things that the thief does not pull a fast one on the officer and in so doing the thief implicitly says, I have nothing more to hide. Now, this expression during praise could be an indication of total surrender to God and a sign that we have nothing to hide—that we have been stripped 'naked' under the limelight of His Holiness.

Our hands speak volumes in our praise and worship to God. For instance, the outstretched hands, slightly tilted forward with the palms still outwards in praise may also show an extension of our love in praise to God.

Hands raised straight up with palms turned inwards could however indicate our plea for more of the filling of the Spirit of God.

Generally therefore the raising of hands may also be a sign of our willingness to grow heavenwards, a sign of surrender and an expression of ascending worship and of spiritual thirst.

> *'2 Let my prayer be set forth as incense before You, the lifting up of my hands as the evening sacrifice.'*
> **Palms 141:2**

> *'6 I spread forth my hands to You; my soul thirsts after You like a thirsty land [for water]. Selah [pause, and calmly think of that]!*
> **Psalms 143:6**

The following Scriptures are just a few of the many I would want to share with you to clear any doubts in your mind as regards the Biblical basis for lifting hands in praise and for that matter worship too.

> **Psalms 63:3, 4:**
> *'3 Because Your loving-kindness is better than life, my lips shall praise You. 4 So will I bless You while I live; I will lift up my hands in Your name.'*

'2 Lift up your hands in holiness and to the sanctuary and bless the Lord [affectionately and gratefully praise Him]!'
Psalms 134:2

'8 I desire therefore that in every place men should pray, without anger or quarrelling or resentment or doubt [in their minds], lifting up holy hands.'
1 Timothy 2:8

It is with such an understanding that we can now sing the following songs with meaning:

*'**WHO IS THERE LIKE YOU**' Who is there like you oh God; You created us in your likeness,*
Who is there like you oh God, It's an honor Lord to stand and worship you
***We lift our hands to the great I Am**; Who was and who is and is to come—**We lift our hands to the great I Am**; Who can compare with You*

*'**FATHER WE DECLARE**'*
And we will say that you are good; and all the miracles You've done have brought us joy
*For we are changed; **and all the hope we have***
We place in you right now
Father we declare that we love you
We declare our everlasting love for you

*'**LIFT UP YOUR HANDS**'*
Lift up your Hands; to the coming King

Bow before Him and adore Him sing
To His majesty; let your praises be
Pure and Holy, Lift your praises, to the King of King

► Bowing (characteristic of worship)

Worthy of mention is **Barak**, (Hebrew), meaning to bless the Lord by kneeling before Him in an act of adoration and reverence. **Psalms 103:2** says:

'*2 Bless (affectionately, gratefully praise) the Lord, O my soul, and forget not [one of] all His benefits . . . '*

And thereafter mentions these benefits.

Barak is that time of quiet expectancy as we wait on God and His response to our worship. It is important to bless God and this we do by not forgetting His benefits. This act of **Barak** bears a sense of kneeling and blessing God by adoring Him.

Bowing further depicts making obeisance, to bless or honor and to show deep respect or reverence to God. Bowing from the waist says I honor you. It is imperative that we learn from what David and the congregation did in *1 Chronicles 29:20*:

'*20 And David said to all the assembly, Now adore (praise and thank) the Lord your God! And all the assembly blessed the Lord, the God of their fathers, and bowed down and did obeisance to the Lord and to the king [as His earthly representative].'*

Now therefore knowing that it is Biblical to bow before God in worship and understanding the significance of such an act I bet we can better minister with understanding songs like:

'HERE I AM TO WORSHIP'

Light of the world You stepped down Into darkness
Open my eyes let me see
Beauty that made this heart adore You
Hope of a life Spent with You
Here I am to worship Here I am to bow down
Here I am to say that You're my God You're altogether lovely
Altogether worthy Altogether wonderful to me

King of all days Oh, so highly exalted
Glorious in Heaven above
Humbly You came to the earth You created; All for love's sake
became poor

Chorus

I'll never know how much it cost; To see my sin upon that cross

'I WILL COME AND BOW DOWN'

I will come and bow down at your feet Lord Jesus, In Your presence is fullness of joy; there is nothing there is no one; who compares with you
I take pleasure in worshipping (3X) You Lord

▶ Kneeling

Kneeling goes beyond honor into submission. This says you have power over me and will probably not be new to those who love to watch Chinese films. In some of these films where martial arts are performed, when, in a fight, one is overpowered, the overpowered one kneels before the one who has overpowered them and bows his head for it to be chopped off. Not a pleasant example I know, but it was just to illustrate that, that act symbolically says 'you have power over me, do with me as you please even of it means killing me'.

This is what it means when we come and kneel before God. We tell Him that He has power over us. It is total surrender and goes beyond honor.

Romans 14:11

'11 For it is written, As I live, says the Lord, every knee shall bow to Me, and every tongue shall confess to God [acknowledge Him to His honor and to His praise] . . .'

Isaiah 45:23

'23 I have sworn by Myself, the word is gone out of My mouth in righteousness and shall not return, that unto Me every knee shall bow, every tongue shall swear [allegiance].'

▶ *PROSTRATING*

'11 And all the angels were standing round the throne and round the elders [of the heavenly Sanhedrin] and the four living creatures, and they fell prostrate before the throne and worshipped God.'
Revelations 7:11

To fall on one's face signifies extreme reverence and respect. In some parts of Nigeria people still fall prostrate when addressing others of higher authority. I can quite remember years back when I was Anglican; I found it so awesome to see young priests fall prostrate during ordination services. Regardless of the fact that I was still a little boy I can vividly remember how much it touched me to see these young priests lying on their faces before God, and at the time, I just wished I could do it too. Now, thank God, I am at liberty to do just that before God and with the right understanding too.

ALL HAIL THE POW'R OF JESUS' NAME!

All hail the pow'r of Jesus' name! Let angels prostrate fall; Bring forth the royal diadem, And crown Him Lord of all;

Ye chosen seed of Israel's race, Ye ransomed from the fall, Hail Him who saves you by His grace, And crown Him Lord of all; Hail Him who saves you by His grace; And crown Him Lord of all!

Let ev'ry kindred, ev'ry tribe, on this terrestrial ball, To Him all majesty ascribe, And crown Him Lord of all; To Him all majesty ascribe, And crown Him Lord of all!

O that with yonder sacred throng; we at His feet may fall! We'll join the everlasting song; and crown Him Lord of all; we'll join the everlasting song; and crown Him Lord of all

2 Chronicles 20: 18-20

'18 And Jehoshaphat bowed his head with his face to the ground, and all Judah and the inhabitants of Jerusalem fell down before the Lord, worshiping Him. 19 And some Levites of the Kohathites and Korahites stood up to praise the Lord, the God of Israel, with a very loud voice. 20 And they rose early in the morning and went out into the Wilderness of Tekoa; and as they went out, Jehoshaphat stood and said, Hear me, O Judah, and you inhabitants of Jerusalem! Believe in the Lord your God and you shall be established; believe and remain steadfast to His prophets and you shall prosper.'

▶ *STANDING*

Standing up on one's feet can indicate honor, recognition, or a salute and shows an urgency and keenness for serious business. I remember hearing about this man who received a phone call from his boss. According to the story, although the person who had called was abroad (thousands of miles away) this man immediately upon hearing his boss's voice on the other end of the line jumped to his feet as a sign of respect.

Whatever the case, you just need to find the right posture that fits the condition of your heart whilst praising God. This is what makes praise authentic.

10.2 PRAISE—ACCOMPANIED BY SONG (A VOICE OF MELODY)

Usually singing accompanies our praises as indicated by another Hebrew idiom for praise—**Tehillah,** which translates into, 'the **praise that God inhabits'** and there are also the **Halals** (as used in *Psalms*

22:3). This refers to a special type of singing which can be best described as 'singing in the Spirit'. These are the songs and utterances that only God can understand. Tehillah is the manifestation of songs that are born from a heart and spirit of the believer. These songs are usually not prewritten or arranged.

Halal on the other hand translates into demonstrating excitement about God with boasting, raving, showing off, celebrating and making a spectacle. This is the root word for Hallelujah which is usually translated as *'Praise the Lord'*. This

expression of praise causes a person to throw off their dignity and release themselves to be clamorously foolish for the Lord. In all of this we should however understand that it is not the singing in itself that is what God requires. He desires a rightly conditioned heart.

'HEART OF WORSHIP

When the music fades, and all is stripped away; And I simply come

Longing just to bring something that's of worth; That will bless your heart

I'll bring You more than a song For a song in itself; Is not what You have required You search much deeper within through the way things appear—You're looking into my heart

I'm coming back to the heart of worship
And it's all about You It's all about You, Jesus
I'm sorry Lord For the thing I've made it; it's all about You
It's all about You, Jesus

King of endless worth No one could express
How much you deserve though I'm weak and poor
All I have is yours every single breath

Having said all this, it is extremely important it is to remember that God's grace in our hearts can also make melody.

'16 Let the word [spoken by] Christ (the Messiah) have its home [in your hearts and minds] and dwell in you in [all its] richness, as you teach and admonish and train one another in all insight and intelligence and wisdom [in spiritual things, and as you sing] Psalms and hymns and spiritual songs, making melody to God with [His] grace in your hearts.'
Colossians 3:16

'1 PRAISE THE Lord! Sing to the Lord a new song, praise Him in the assembly of His saints!'
5 Let the saints be joyful in the glory and beauty [which God confers upon them]; let them sing for joy upon their beds.'
Psalms 149:1&5

'1 MAKE A joyful noise unto God, all the earth; 2 Sing forth the honor and glory of His name; make His praise glorious!.'
Psalms 66:1&2

'16 But I will sing of Your mighty strength and power; yes, I will sing aloud of Your mercy and loving-kindness in the morning; for You have been to me a defence (a fortress and a high tower) and a refuge in the day of my distress . . .'

Psalms 59:16

'1 SING ALOUD to God our Strength! Shout for joy to the God of Jacob!.
Psalms 81:1

'14 Deliver me from blood-guiltiness and death, O God, the God of my salvation, and my tongue shall sing aloud of Your righteousness (Your rightness and Your justice).'
Psalms 51:14

'3 For the Lord will comfort Zion; He will comfort all her waste places. And He will make her wilderness like Eden, and her desert like the garden of the Lord. Joy and gladness will be found in her, thanksgiving and the voice of song or instrument of praise.'
Isaiah 51:3

Again we are explicitly commanded in **Ephesians 5:7** to speak to ourselves in Psalms, hymns SINGING and making melody in our hearts to God.

'17 Therefore do not be vague and thoughtless and foolish, but understanding and firmly grasping what the will of the Lord is. 18 And do not get drunk with wine, for that is debauchery; but ever be filled and stimulated with the [Holy] Spirit. 19 Speak out to one another in Psalms and hymns and spiritual songs, offering praise with voices [and instruments] and making melody with all your heart to the Lord,'
Ephesians 5:17-19

Hence another manner in which we can praise God constantly is to make melody unto God in our hearts. That should not be too hard to do. Or am I belittling the effort that goes into that?

10.3 *PRAISE—ACCOMPANIED BY MUSICAL INSTRUMENTS*

Biblically, praise can also be expressed and accompanied by instruments. This is the concept described in Hebrew as *Zamar*. The word itself means to touch the strings and carries the idea of instrumental praise and worship as indicated in ***Psalms 150***.

'1 PRAISE THE Lord! Praise God in His sanctuary; praise Him in the heavens of His power! 2 Praise Him for His mighty acts; praise Him according to the abundance of His greatness! 3 Praise Him with trumpet sound; praise Him with lute and harp! 4 Praise Him with tambourine and [single or group] dance; praise Him with stringed and wind instruments or flutes! 5 Praise Him with resounding cymbals; praise Him with loud clashing cymbals! 6 Let everything that has breath and every breath of life praise the Lord! Praise the Lord! (Hallelujah!)'

Psalms 149:3

'3 Let them praise His name in chorus and choir and with the [single or group] dance; let them sing praises to Him with the tambourine and lyre!'

Psalms 144:9

'9 I will sing a new song to You, O God; upon a harp, an instrument of ten strings, will I offer praises to You.'

10.4 *PRAISE—ACCOMPANIED BY TEARS FOR JOY*

The following passage narrates how this woman in the city, a sinner as the Bible describes her, understood how to express herself in the presence of the Lord which pleased Him.

'36 One of the Pharisees asked Jesus to dine with him, and He went into the Pharisee's house and reclined at table. 37 And behold, a woman of the town who was an especially wicked sinner, when she learned that He was reclining at table in the Pharisee's house, brought an alabaster flask of ointment (perfume). 38 And standing behind Him at His feet weeping, she began to wet His feet with [her] tears; and she wiped them with the hair of her head and kissed His feet [affectionately] and anointed them with the ointment (perfume). 39 Now when the Pharisee who had invited Him saw it, he said to himself, If this Man were a prophet, He would surely know who and what sort of woman this is who is touching Him-for she is a notorious sinner (a social outcast, devoted to sin). 40 And Jesus, replying, said to him, Simon, I have something to say to you. And he answered, Teacher, say it. 41 A certain lender of money [at interest] had two debtors: one owed him five hundred denarii, and the other fifty. 42 When they had no means of paying, he freely forgave them both. Now which of them will love him more? 43 Simon answered, The one, I take it, for whom he forgave and cancelled more. And Jesus said to him, You have decided correctly. 44 Then turning toward the woman, He said to Simon, Do you see this woman? When I came into your house, you gave Me no water for My feet, but she has wet My feet with her tears and wiped them with her hair. 45 You gave Me no kiss, but she from the moment I came

*in has not ceased [intermittently] to kiss My feet tenderly and caressingly. **46** You did not anoint My head with [cheap, ordinary] oil, but she has anointed My feet with [costly, rare] perfume. **47** Therefore I tell you, her sins, many [as they are], are forgiven her—because she has loved much. But he who is forgiven little loves little. **48** And He said to her, Your sins are forgiven! **49** Then those who were at table with Him began to say among themselves, Who is this Who even forgives sins? **50** But Jesus said to the woman, Your faith has saved you; go (enter) into peace [in freedom from all the distresses that are experienced as the result of sin] . . . .'*

Luke 7:36-50

We can learn from this woman and the acts she expressed. The lessons will however be dealt with later on in this book, but for now I just want to establish that just as we are able to relate to each other by means of our emotions, in like manner, our praise to God can be accompanied by expressions of our emotions as well.

10.4 *PRAISE—ACCOMPANIED BY LAUGHTER*

It may seem a bit weird but it's true. Praise can be accompanied by laughter. I can recall one of the few such experiences I had. It was at my sister's place and we had gathered with a brother from our local assembly. I can't really remember if it was a prayer meeting or it was just a visit but all I can remember is that, my brother in-law, an anointed pastor and instrumentalist started playing softly on the keyboard. I remember the song was 'You deserve the Glory and the Honor, as we lift our hands in worship . . . .' and we must have just started singing along, when all of a sudden there was this sudden change in the atmosphere. One I cannot explain in words but I surely know it was the presence of the Spirit of God that was brooding over us. Suddenly, Gloria, my only sister started to giggle, then burst out into laughter and then within moments we were all caught up in it. We all laughed uncontrollably. This was definitely more than the 'laughter is infectious' saying. This was something supernatural. It was so sweet, so refreshing and so inspiring. It was really an experience!!! And it continued for a good few minutes. At the end of it we all felt so refreshed and I am sure God enjoyed it Himself. Will it therefore surprise you what scripture says in *Psalms 126:2*?

> '2 *Then were our mouths filled with laughter, and our tongues with singing. Then they said among the nations, The Lord has done great things for them.*'

CHAPTER 11

THE KING'S MODEL PRAISE

1 Chronicles 15:16-28

'*16 David told the chief Levites to appoint their brethren the singers with instruments of music—harps, lyres, and cymbals—to play loudly and lift up their voices with joy. 17 So the Levites appointed Heman son of Joel; and of his brethren, Asaph son of Berechiah; and of the sons of Merari their brethren, Ethan son of Kushaiah; 18 And with them their brethren of the second class: Zechariah, Ben, Jaaziel, Shemiramoth, Jehiel, Unni, Eliab, Benaiah, Maaseiah, Mattithiah, Eliphelehu, and Mikneiah, and also the gatekeepers, Obed-edom and Jeiel. 19 So the singers Heman, Asaph, and Ethan, were appointed to sound bronze cymbals; 20 Zechariah, Aziel, Shemiramoth, Jehiel, Unni, Eliab, Maaseiah, and Benaiah were to play harps [resembling guitars] set to Alamoth [probably the treble voice]; 21 Mattithiah, Eliphelehu, Mikneiah, Obed-edom, Jeiel, and Azaziah were to lead with lyres set to Sheminith [the bass voice]. 22 Chenaniah, leader of the Levites in singing, was put in charge of carrying the ark and lifting up song. He instructed about these matters because he was skilled and able. 23 Berechiah and Elkanah were gatekeepers for the ark. 24 Shebaniah, Joshaphat, Nethanel, Amasai, Zechariah, Benaiah, and Eliezer the priests were to blow the trumpets before the ark of God. And Obed-edom and Jehiah (Jeiel) were also gatekeepers for the ark. 25 So David, the elders of Israel, and the captains over thousands went to bring up the ark of the covenant of the Lord out of the house of Obed-edom with joy. 26 And when God helped the Levites who carried the ark of the covenant of the Lord [with a safe start], they offered seven bulls and seven rams. 27 David was clothed with a robe of fine linen, as were the Levites who bore the ark, and the singers, and Chenaniah, director of the music of the singers. David also wore an ephod [a priestly upper garment] of linen. 28 Thus all Israel brought up the ark of the covenant of the Lord with shouting, sound of the cornet, trumpets, and cymbals, sounding aloud with harps and lyres'*

Let's see in *2 Samuel 6:14* the person who was dancing the most.

'14 And David danced before the Lord with all his might, clad in a linen ephod [a priest's upper garment].'
2 Samuel 6:14

David must have known what it really meant to praise God. Actually, the Hebrew word which translates into praise here is **Hallal**, which means *to go clamorously crazy, foolish or mad before the Lord, from which as mentioned, we derive* the word **Halleluiah**. It is to be boastful, to be excited and to be enjoyed. I pray that we all, like David, will come to the point of understanding and doing what is right before God. You see, he was the king yet he did not care about who was looking and who was not. As a matter of fact, the Bible records that he danced openly before all Israel.

There are times when, because of our position or stature in society, we are wary of those around us, when we have to offer a dance to the Lord. At times we are intimidated by others or circumstances around us. I believe that there is so much we can learn from David. He, who was king, put aside all the protocol that accompanied kingship and honored God with a dance. He would not be intimidated or shy. He would not allow himself to be bothered about those around and what they would think of or say about him. All he knew was that he had to honor the one who was greater than him and greater than anyone and any circumstance around him. The one from whom he got His position, for the Bible says promotion comes from God.

For him, God's presence was coming to Jerusalem and that was what was important.

> *'15 So David and all the house of Israel brought up the ark of the Lord with shouting and with the sound of the trumpet.'*
> **2 Samuel 6:15**

Unfortunately, nowadays many Christians are intimidated in corporate praise. The question is, why can't we praise God openly? Is it because we think, whatever restrains us is bigger than the Lord we serve? And what could that be? Friends? Sickness? Emotions? Stature?

I believe that if something really 'good' happened to us during the day at work, we would hasten home just to break the news to our loved ones. How many times have we not said, 'I just can't wait to get home to tell someone about some good news'? We are happy and willing to talk about or share the good that happens to us with others. Sometimes regardless of the time, venue or circumstance, we are still eager to share the good news. We just want to declare it. Usually, depending on how great we perceive the news to be and in our excitement, it is even when we get into the midst of people that we want to talk about it most, and at times, we tend to intentionally drop hints about it for people to ask questions that will eventually give us the opportunity to share the news. So if we are not praising God does it mean we do not see Him as good news enough? God forbid!!!

There are quite a number of reasons that account for our not praising God the right way or not praising Him at all but before treating a couple of them permit me to mention some giants of praise as recorded in the Bible.

- ► As mentioned earlier, David was a praise 'monster' and we realize the manner in which he brought the Ark of God to Jerusalem. The Bible says he did it with shouts of praise and with dancing.
- ► At the dedication of the temple, the Bible says that Solomon led his people in praise.
- ► Again God allowed the shepherds in Bethlehem to hear the chorus of praise of the Angels.
- ► In accordance with Scripture, Mary the mother of Jesus together with the twelve disciples gave praise to God continually and
- ► The Children of Israel led by Moses in songs of praise and Miriam gave praise to God after crossing the Red Sea.

It is therefore a good thing, to give praise to God and when we do, we are assured of being in good company or at least carrying on the good work that these children of God executed, and I can say with all certainty that, provided we are doing it well, with a right heart and attitude, God credits our accounts with pleasure and blessings.

Isn't it a wonder then that, we sometimes find it so hard to come before God with the right attitude to praise Him in spite of us knowing well that praising God is of so much importance and benefit to others and most importantly to ourselves? Having been taught some truths, I have been on my guard and it is my hope that reading further will also put you on the alert as well. Immediately you identify with anyone of the following which may have hindered you from praising God, may I advice that you work on yourself in order to break away from them before they eventually destroy you.

CHAPTER 12

HINDRANCES TO OUR PRAISING GOD

HAVE you ever considered why it becomes so difficult to praise God even though the benefits of praising Him are so enormous? I am sure that if we are able to identify those hindrances to our praise then we will be able to remove them in order to praise God freely.

A. QUEST FOR FORMULAE

It is essential to emphasize that praise is not mimicking what other people say or do. No two people experience God in exactly the same way, because we don't have the same encounters in life and even if we do, by the way we were created, we are all different, which makes every person's experiences unique to every person. It is unfortunate that in our contemporary world, we have what I call 'Lotto Working Christians'. Many people use formulae to achieve goals but praise is not a program and as such has no simple formulae. This explains why no two people will praise God in exactly the same way. Yes, in corporate praise, we may sing the same songs of praise but the truth is our hearts which back our praise and our expressions which accompany our praise surely differ.

Now those who seek out a formula for praising God, sometimes tend to emulate other people's way of praising God. So when they have the opportunity, they would want to use the same sequence or 'formula'. They may have heard a certain 'flow' or medley of songs on a certain recording and thus try to adopt it to the letter, thinking that, that is what will bring down God's glory; yet many a time it turns out to be disastrous basically because of the lack of an understanding of what they are doing. All they try therefore to do is to 'work out' a formula to praise God which should not be the case. And then when the expected does not happen, they get frustrated and give up. This is due to the fact that, they missed the point right from the start themselves when they had set off, seeking for their own 'selfish end results'—to receive human praise rather than to give God praise.

The fact has always remained—there has never been and will never be any such 'hot-keys' that we can strike to manipulate God. Of course, by the Bible, we can be guided to know fundamentally what is allowed and what is not in genuine praise to God. There is Biblical indication of what God expects from us and what we can do to please him, but that is quite different from having a laid down formula. Searching for, and relying on formulae, will only lead to frustration and destruction.

B. REVULSION FOR TRANSFORMATION

Praising God, places a demand on us to amend various aspects of our lives but before I venture into talking about these inevitable required changes, it's important to note that human beings by nature do not welcome CHANGE.

Regardless of whether change may or may not bring improvement, human beings by nature, would usually shun 'change' due to the fear of or discomfort associated with uncertainty and unfamiliarity.

The good news however is that those transformations that are brought about by the true attitude of praise results in us becoming better people, in that it causes us to become like the One we worship. Why do I say this? In speaking of those who worship idols *Psalms 115:8* says:

> '*8 They who make idols are like them; so are all who trust in and lean on them.*'

From inference therefore one is bound to be like that which or whom he trusts. If so, then it should hold true for Christians as well. Through the wonderful experience of praising God and worshipping Him we tend to be transformed to be like the One we worship—who is God Himself. Hence when we worship God in the beauty of His holiness we will be like Him.

> '*2 Give to the Lord the glory due to His name; worship the Lord in the beauty of holiness or in holy array.*'
> *Psalms 29:2*

Therefore from the two aforementioned Scriptures, when we praise and worship God, we become beautiful. I have encountered some young Christian ladies who honestly would not pass to be good examples of pretty ladies. Yet, there appeared to be something about them that made everyone yearn to be around them for ages—something which I cannot describe, other than to call beauty. I can say with all certainty therefore that the more we trust in God, the more we become like Him—Beautiful!!!

For those who are serious about really praising God, be prepared to yield to changes in at least five different facets of your life because in authentic praise, transformation in these areas of our lives are inevitable.

► In the state of our souls

It is important that we examine ourselves and our lives each time we go before God in praise. Our mind-set, feeling and will—(the soul's state) with which we approach God in praise is pivotal to the effectiveness of our praise. If our feelings are negative, there is no way we can express true praise to God. It is impossible to harbor hatred, anger, bitterness and other negative feelings and genuinely praise God. The crux is that, we cannot have a negative spirit and render positive praise to God. It is not practicable. In view of that, I trust that, our souls will be tasked in demand of an amendment to all the negative attitudes that we sometimes harbor in order for us to praise God with a positive attitude. That is why David's spirit called out to his soul in saying, 'Bless *the Lord, oh my soul'*. Obviously his soul or part of his soul must have been in a state, not willing to yield to praising God. It could have been his mind frame (intellect), his feelings or his will, but the right thing as we learn here is to ensure that all our soul is set right.

► In our power and strength

There are times when because of the demands on our physical bodies, souls and at times our spirits, we grow faint and exhausted. If you are a little like who I used to be, then you would have realized that there are times when you could get so dead beat or worried that, you cannot even sleep. When we come before God's presence in praise, our strength is renewed as we exchange our weakness for His strength. Hence our energy levels also change.

> *'28 Have you not known? Have you not heard? The everlasting God, the Lord, the Creator of the ends of the earth, does not faint or grow weary; there is no searching of His understanding. 29 He gives power to the faint and weary, and to him who has no might He increases strength [causing it to multiply and making it to abound]. 30 Even youths shall faint and be weary, and [selected] young men shall feebly stumble and fall exhausted; 31 But those who wait for the Lord [who expect, look for, and hope in Him] shall change and renew their strength and power; they shall lift their wings and mount up [close to God] as eagles [mount up to the sun]; they shall run and not be weary, they shall walk and not faint or become tired.' Isaiah 40:28-31*

▶ In our relationships

We have come to understand the fact that praise is a sacrifice. Now the Bible admonishes us to lay our sacrifices or offerings before the altar and go and make peace with those who have offended us before coming to God. Doesn't that tell us something? I believe then that it is impossible to come before God with a sacrifice—and in this case praise, whilst we are still at odds with other people or for that matter whilst others are at odds with us. I believe that before we come before God in praise we need to ensure that to the best of our knowledge, our relationship with God and with fellow men is right. In the account of the sacrifices offered by Cain and Abel, the Bible mentions that God had respect for Abel (first) and then for his sacrifice. If you are going to earn God's respect, then you will have to be a person worthy of that respect, not that person who has problems with everybody.

The truth of the matter is that it is impossible to remain at odds with others over temporary human differences and yet be in agreement with the greatness and goodness of God. How do you win God's respect when you are struggling to win even your fellow man's respect? In order to praise God sincerely, there is a demand on us to have a healthy relationship with fellow men. This is yet another aspect of our lives, in which praising God will demand a transformation. Remember that, while we were yet sinners, God sent His Son to die for us all.

True praise should transform our relationships with our fellow men. I can't envisage how people are able to strive amongst themselves (worst of all, within the same congregation) and yet praise God effectively and more so enjoy the corporate benefits of praising God. Really Strange!

▶ In our spiritual judgment and sensitivity

If we praise God with the right attitude, we give God all our attention. That way, (having taken over all our attention) we can be sure that when He speaks to us we will be in the position to hear Him even more clearly. Even in our normal academic setting, you will realize that it is when you give your lecturer your full attention that you hear more clearly and understand better what he says. The fidgety and easily distracted student is usually the one who is at a loss. Ideally, when we praise God, we must give Him our attention which means our focus has to move from earthly, worldly and carnal things to the things of God, which consequently cause modifications to our spiritual discernment, receptiveness and sensitivity to the things of God.

*In **Matthew 11:15**; Jesus declared:*

'15 He who has ears to hear, let him be listening and let him consider and perceive and comprehend by hearing.'

Matthew 13:19

'19 While anyone is hearing the Word of the kingdom and does not grasp and comprehend it, the evil one comes and snatches away what was sown in his heart. This is what was sown along the roadside.'

▶ In our pitiful conditions

There is a gap between our desires and satisfaction that is bridged by PRAISE. There are some who will want to continue in their state and not change their status for fear of the fact that if they should move from that state, they may lose the small benefits that they get from those who pity them. Such people abhor even change that will bring them a better circumstance. In any case, it does not erase the fact that there is a gap between desire and satisfaction, and until we yield to the change that praise will bring to our lives this gap will never be bridged. Remember that we previously discussed the atmosphere of praise in which praise and faith build on each other and where as a consequence, needs or desires are met.

C. SATAN'S DECEIT

▶ Arrogance

Another reason why it becomes difficult for us to praise God right sometimes is as a result of the material and social authority we are blessed with. Having received these blessings from God by grace, satan then tries to make us feel as though we are more favored, more important and of a higher value than others but we need to always remember where our blessings come from and acknowledge the source and consequently let our attitude portray it thoroughly.

> *'17 Every good gift and every perfect (free, large, full) gift is from above; it comes down from the Father of all [that gives] light, in [the shining of] Whom there can be no variation [rising or setting] or shadow cast by His turning [as in an eclipse].'*
> **James 1:17**

When this pride is not dealt with, we consequently drop our guard and allow ourselves to be deceived into thinking that we earned it by some work of ours and then find it unnecessary to give God praise.

▶ 'I Am In Control' Syndrome

Satan tries to cause us to dissociate our emotions from our expressions in praise. Most of us have grown up (especially as African men) equating maturity to lack of outward expressions of our emotions, such that it is alright for a child to cry but it's uncomely for an adult to cry (more so in public). Yet we need to realize that God created our emotions (which may serve as channels via which we may empty ourselves before Him). I have mentioned earlier that praise and worship has an emotional dimension yet we must be careful not to allow our emotions to dictate our praise and worship especially when they are negative. I once entered a relationship with a lady who had a problem accepting the manner in which I unashamedly expressed some of my emotions. I had come to realize with time that there were times that I might have mismanaged my emotions and had made them get the better part of me which was wrong, but I have never seized to stand by the fact that the expression of one's emotions in itself is not a bad thing. After all, God created our emotions and He Himself as the Bible teaches, expresses His emotions. God laughs, Jesus wept and He was angry on at least one occasion. All these I believe are emotions and expressing them in itself may not be wrong. We must however be mindful of how we manage them.

May I therefore suggest that the praise and worship we offer to God can be expressed with the help of a wide range of human emotions? After all, the Bible admonishes us to bless the Lord with all that is within us which includes our emotions. But as mentioned earlier about being mindful of how we manage our emotions, when for instance we pour our tears and hearts out to God we need to be cautious that it doesn't come across as a criticism of God's being. It is alright to lament in our praise to God. After all, it is said that almost 70 per cent of the Psalms are laments. Yet it is worth emphasizing that a true lament never criticizes or challenges God's worth. True laments rather show forth the goodness and greatness of God and shows that He is our only hope. There is a thin line between lamenting and complaining though and as we walk this thin line, we need to be cautious and hasten slowly so that we do not slip unto the side of complaining. The key is that lamenting always has an element of recognition of God's greatness and goodness in spite of the conditions or circumstances we find ourselves in.

> '1 MY GOD, my God, why have You forsaken me? Why are You
> so far from helping me, and from the words of my groaning?'
> **Palms 22:1**

Again, the Psalmist says in **Psalms 31:5** that:
> '5 Into Your hands I commit my spirit; You have redeemed me,
> O Lord, the God of truth and faithfulness.'

This is almost like Jesus' words on the cross but do you also realize that He was not complaining?—The part 'You have redeemed me, O Lord, the God of truth and faithfulness' turns the statement around from being a complaint to a lament.

▶ Sinful Adam-Inherited Pride

The devil causes us to find solace in thinking that religion in modesty is alright and that boldness is over the top. In so doing, we just tend to value our self image above what we are supposed to do right.

> '29 As the ark of the covenant of the Lord came to the City of David, Michal [David's wife] daughter of Saul, looking from a window, saw King David leaping as in sport, and she despised him in her heart . . .'
> **1 Chronicles 15:29**

Evidently, David's wife displays pride as opposed to David's boldness in Praise.

I have asked myself how many times people have acted similarly towards others who have come out boldly to praise God (even in church). I must have fallen victim to reacting negatively towards some people who boldly expressed praise in the past when I didn't have the right understanding, yet, now being privileged to have attained an understanding as regards these spiritual things, I have repented, asked for forgiveness from God and can now be positive towards praise and worship (whether as expressed by others or myself).

I propose same for you, if you happen to be the type who criticizes bold expressions of praise.

Note that David's wife could have decided to join in the praise or at best shut up. Really she had nothing to lose, yet she was angry and when her anger got the better part of her, in sarcasm, all she could say was:

> *'20 . . . How glorious was the king of Israel today, who stripped himself of his kingly robes and uncovered himself in the eyes of his servants' maids as one of the worthless fellows shamelessly uncovers himself!'*
> **2 Samuel 6:20**

In certain situations if we allow someone's expression of praise to God to infuriate us, we can fall prey to being sarcastic and utter words that can cause our own doom.

I am convinced that her problem was not really about the fact that David had danced before God or changed his royal robes. I suppose her real problem must have been her own 'dignity' as a king's wife which she must have thought had been wounded and her concern about what people would say and think of her.

Sometimes we find ourselves in similar situations thinking alike and even assuming that people may hold our faith against us if we expressed our praise to God in certain ways. We feel that, when people see us or others close to us boldly expressing praises to God, they may form some impressions about us and even mock us. In extreme cases some may even feel that a bold expression of praising God could cost them their jobs, relationships or some other thing(s) they humanly value so much and it's the fear that their pride may ultimately be wounded which hinders them. The thing is we have often worried about our self image which is a dangerous mind-set to remain in.

▶ The Notion That Pride Is Not Detrimental

The devil causes us to sometimes think that pride is harmless. Remember that despite all the great accomplishments of Uzziah, his ruin was as a result of pride *(2 Chronicles 26:16; 19-21)*

*'16 But when [King Uzziah] was strong, **he became proud to his destruction;** and he trespassed against the Lord his God, for he went into the temple of the Lord to burn incense on the altar of incense . . .'*
2 Chronicles 26:16

'19 Then Uzziah was enraged, and he had a censer in his hand to burn incense. And while he was enraged with the priests, leprosy broke out on his forehead before the priests in the house of the Lord, beside the incense altar. 20 And as Azariah the chief priest and all the priests looked upon him, behold, he was leprous on his forehead! So they forced him out of there; and he also made haste to get out, because the Lord had smitten him. 21 And King Uzziah was a leper to the day of his death, and, being a leper, he dwelt in a separate house, for he was excluded from the Lord's house. And Jotham his son took charge of the king's household, ruling the people of the land.'
2 Chronicles 26:19-21

For a fact, pride is destructive and I pray that it does not hinder you from praising God like you should.

Remember Jesus said the Sunday before his crucifixion that if the people refused to render praise, stones would rise up and scream praises. I'm definitely not sitting down in pride for some stone to perform my duty of praising God—I will have no excuse whatsoever for that!!!

In David's case as aforementioned, neither protocol nor what people would say, was to stop him from praising God. In fact, check out his response to his wife in *2 Samuel 6:21, 22*. Literally he says,

'Woman, you ain't seen nothing yet'.

> *'21 David said to Michal, It was before the Lord, Who chose me above your father and all his house to appoint me as prince over Israel, the people of the Lord. Therefore will I make merry [in pure enjoyment] before the Lord. 22 I will be still more lightly esteemed than this, and will humble and lower myself in my own sight [and yours]. But by the maids you mentioned, I will be held in honor.'*
> *Samuel 6:21& 22*

You will realize that due to this attitude, David's wife became barren.

> *'23 And Michal the daughter of Saul had no child to the day of her death.'*
> *2 Samuel 6:23*

How many times, and in how many aspects of our lives, have we not pronounced barrenness upon ourselves as a result of our sinful pride, regard for our self image, what we say about others who express praise boldly and our total disregard for God?

The devil works to get us to hold on to pride and our 'valued' self image but praise exposes and wars against our pride and consequently helps us submit to God's rule.

Note that though Peter and Judas both denied Christ, one allowed pride to ultimately lead him to destruction whilst the other defied and defeated his pride thereby continuing his service to God.

▶ Distractions

Satan seeks to distract us so that we use our time to ultimately pump up our self-image and inflate our sense of pride. How many times have we not been late for or missed an opportunity to have joined in corporate praise. Our reasons may seem 'legitimate' but truly and sincerely ask yourself whether your excuse can exonerate you from God's wrath. How many times our phones have not rang during times when we should have been focusing on God? How many times have our babies not burst into one of those uncontrollable tantrums where nothing would calm them except for our abandoning the praise session? Immediately things of the sort occur, our focus on God goes right through the window. How many times have we not stepped out of church or even right in the congregation, not stopped praising God to greet others and even engage in a hearty chat with them—right in the midst of corporate praise and worship?

Satan is very cunning. He now uses more advanced strategies to distract Christians from praising God. Now, he may not stop you from going to church or from attending that Christian gathering but he may batter you with all sorts of distractions whilst you are still in the meeting. Note that, not participating is as bad as not being there in the first place, so if he is able to distract you from participating in the praise and worship and other aspects of the meeting—all well and good for him; his work is done!!! We have all fallen prey to some of these tricks of the devil for far too long but what is important is for us to know these tricks, realize our shortfalls, repent, get on with it and guard against falling prey to his foolish antics again.

I'm sure we comport ourselves better in some places. If for instance you were on an aircraft where you were asked to turn off your phone because it could interfere with the aviation or communication equipment onboard the aircraft, I am convinced that you would comply immediately without reservation, regardless of what important calls you might be expecting. You know what? If your phone is left on during a service, it also interferes with the spiritual atmosphere.

Have you ever considered that, just as your phone's interference with aviation equipment could cause a tragic accident which could consequently cost your life as well as those of many other innocent passengers, such distractive behaviors (such as using your phone in church) could equally cause a tragic spiritual crush which could cost you your soul and the souls of many other innocent members of the congregation?

Even when we visit libraries, hospitals or we find ourselves in the presence of some people we see as important, we behave properly so why can we not defy all other distractions satan tries to bring our way and give God our full attention when we are in His presence?

If you were sitting in a meeting with a king or a president, I am sure you wouldn't just walk off to have a hearty chat with a friend who just entered the conference room, just because you feel like it. I am convinced that you might even ignore the friend's presence whilst you are in that 'serious' meeting and give your full attention to the king or president and at best later apologize to the friend, expecting to be understood and forgiven. Why then can we not give God our full attention and ignore all other unnecessary chats, conversations, phone calls, greetings and exchange of pleasantries whilst we meet with the Lord God Almighty? Or do you think He is not worth that? If even our earthly kings get to enjoy our full attention, how much more God!!! And the unfortunate thing is that even pastors, church leaders and other ministers fall victim to such distractions with reckless abandonment and total disrespect for God. For them I refuse to assume that their attitude is as a result of ignorance. As ministers of God I believe that such reckless behavior shows that they just don't care. SHAMEFUL isn't it? Have you not seen pastors during praise and worship standing outside chatting with church members? Could whatever it was not have waited till afterwards? Was God not able to take care of it till afterwards? I only assume situations like that arise from either of two causes. Either someone neglected a duty that should have been attended to earlier which might have come back to compete for the attention that is due God or on the other hand they just don't have enough respect for God. Now I am speaking to the ministers. If you as the shepherd will behave in such a shameful manner, I have a fair picture of what you expect from your flock. Sorry but it's about time someone said it without fear or favor. If ministers will continue acting in such manner, then how can we correct other church members? Remember that in the church or in life generally, there is always someone who looks up to you as a Christian, and your actions or inactions teach them how to comport themselves. Are you proud of what you have just taught that person who looks up to you by the way you last comported yourself in the gathering of the saints?

It is understandable that there are some situations or circumstances under which nothing can be done and we may have to run off to attend to some pressing issues but remember that God knows the intent of every heart and He knows the thoughts behind our every action, so sincerely ask yourself whether the reason for your putting aside the praise and worship of your creator and redirecting the attention is really worth it.

Honestly, these distractions are either of our own making or are from satan and we often allow them to get the better part of us but truly, with determination we can overcome them. For me, nothing and for that matter no one is bigger and more important than God, so at least as a matter of principle, I switch my phone off to prevent it from distracting me when I am in the presence of my maker. I usually say that if you switch just the ringer to 'silent mode', it sometimes becomes an even greater distraction since you are then compelled to keep looking at it to see whether or not you have missed a call. Isn't it hypocritical then that when people notice that they have missed a call, right during service they would step out to call the person back or hold their phones in anticipation that the person would call back for them to pick it? Well in order to avoid all that, I think it is better to put it off completely. Whilst in the presence of God, everything else can wait.

If that is what it takes I challenge you to let others see you as being rude or weird, because regardless of the effort it draws, we must determine within our hearts to deal with and overcome anything that tries to distract us from praising and worshipping God. If there is anything we can do to minimize or ultimately eliminate these distractions, I believe it is ideal to do it.

Some orthodox churches for instance bar their doors at some particular times during services so as to minimize all distractions which would have otherwise been caused by people leaving and entering the church during service and I think we can all pick a cue from the practice.

▶ Feeling of Lack

Again, at times, satan tends to deceive us into thinking that we do not have what it takes to praise God. I have heard a couple of people brandishing the lack of a good voice as an excuse for not praising God. You see, one thing we need to establish is the fact that there is quite a big difference between ordinary singing and ministering unto God in song. I was guilty of the 'I don't have a good voice' excuse but when I came to understand the difference between singing and ministering to God in song, I realized that I really had no excuse.

Actually, I am sure if God wanted to hear what you may term 'beautiful voices', then even if your voice and the voices in heaven were not good enough for Him, He could have created another being, with a customized 'beautiful voice' and forgotten about you and I and all the angels in heaven. But thank God it is not like that. God is not so wicked as to ask of you what He knows very well you do not have. He knows you have such a voice yet asks you to offer praise unto Him with it.

Years back I awoke from my folly and said to myself, 'If this is what God gave me then He surely would love to hear it'. I may have been lazy in training my voice at the time yet in spite of that challenge I still ministered unto God in song and it worked. If it has worked for me, my dear, and it will work for you as well. There is beauty in variety you know, so even if you cannot carry a tune, just use what you have any way to praise Him.

Praise can be expressed in many forms so even if you still claim you cannot 'Tehillah' (sing in the Spirit), I am sure you can 'Nagad' (declare), 'Rum' (extol), 'Ruah' (shout in joy), 'Towdah' (stretch out hands), 'Shabach' (address in a loud tone, command triumph, glory, shout), 'Zamar' (touch the strings or use instruments), or even 'Barak' (simply bless), 'Halal' (boast and be excited and explode with enthusiasm) or 'Yadah' (publicly acknowledge) God.

After all, you will soon get to know that the most important instrument in praise and worship is not your voice. The most important instrument is your heart.

Please go on and make melody with and in your heart to the Lord and let the abundance spill through your mouth, regardless of what you think of your voice.

> '19 Speak out to one another in Psalms and hymns and spiritual songs, offering praise with voices [and instruments] and making melody with all your heart to the Lord,' Ephesians 5:19

THE CHALLENGE OF APPROACHING GOD WITH A TRUE HEART

It is possible to sing to God with our lips and still harbor bitterness in our hearts. That way, all we succeed in doing is to sing empty choruses rather than sacrifice and minister to God. How many times have we not carried our hurts and bitterness and all the other negative feelings into the house of the Lord and attempted to enter His courts with praise with all that baggage. In doing that, we end up distancing ourselves and others from God and we become ordinary hypocritical actors. Search your heart and find out how many times you have been guilty of this. It is clear now, how subtle the devil is when it comes to designing schemes to get us to lose out on the privilege of enjoying God's presence.

> '22 Let us all come forward and draw near with true (honest and sincere) hearts in unqualified assurance and absolute conviction engendered by faith (by that leaning of the entire human personality on God in absolute trust and confidence in His power, wisdom, and goodness), having our hearts sprinkled and purified from a guilty (evil) conscience and our bodies cleansed with pure water.'
> **Hebrews 10:22**

It is paramount therefore that we ensure that our hearts are right as we draw near to God. We should be wary of the possibility of making a confession without a commitment. I heard this story about a young student who was being punished by his senior in school to kneel down. He obviously didn't see himself in the wrong and so refused to kneel down. After being beaten for a while, the poor young boy had no other option but to submit to the physical abuse. He goes down on his knees and the first thing he utters is—'You have forced me to kneel down but I know that in my heart I am standing'; and I believe that he was really standing in a sense. I mean if Abraham in his heart had sacrificed Isaac and the Bible says it was accounted unto him as righteousness then it is possible for us in some instances to act visibly in one way but contrary still to what is in our hearts. Note that Abraham had not physically sacrificed Isaac but due to the state of his heart, God recognized him as having already sacrificed Isaac.

> '7 You pretenders (hypocrites)! Admirably and truly did Isaiah prophesy of you when he said: 8 These people draw near Me

144

with their mouths and honor Me with their lips, but their hearts
hold off and are far away from Me. 9 Uselessly do they worship
*Me, for they teach as doctrines the commands of men.' **Matthew***
15:7-9

IDOLATRY IN THE CHURCH

By now, it should not come as a surprise that people practice idolatry
in church. An idol is anything that draws one away from God. It could
be food, entertainment, family, relationships, work or even a thought.
If whilst in church (a time when one should be focusing on God) one
decides to pick a phone call or lend attention to some other thing other
than God, be it a problem or any other person or thing, may I suggest to
you that, such an action is tantamount to idol worship in God's house.
You see how 'Christians' of today carry idols into the church without
shame or fear and with no reverence to God Almighty?

SATISFYING THE DEMANDS OF IDOLS

You must understand that every idol demands three things—stewardship,
service and work. As regards stewardship, they expect that you bow
before them. As regards service they expect that you serve them and as
regards work, they expect that you do after their works.

In being subdued by the pressures of the devil we may have sometimes
been brought to the point of bowing and succumbing to him in several
ways—one of which as mentioned is how we sometimes, sit in church
and yet bow to the devil by giving him our attention rather than focusing
on God.

When we harbor all the hurt and negative attitudes within us, we not
only render service to the devil but also, exhibit a rebellious attitude

which is the very nature of the devil himself. Sometimes, by our actions or inactions, we refuse to yield to the awesome power of God that has been made available to us all and that is practically the same as doing satan's works. After all, we know how lucifer was thrown out of heaven—rebellion wasn't it? Is it not scary therefore that 'Christians' (or so as we call ourselves) tend to be daring enough to carry idols into the house of God and practice idolatry right there? Beloved, we can choose to fool everyone around us but God knows the hidden thought behind our actions. The Bible says of His word which is Himself, that He is the discerner of the intent and thought of every heart. He knows whether or not your heart is right. The good thing to know however is that, if you have some wrong in the past, you can do something about it now. Let us guard against being battered by the presence, perceptions, or otherwise of our pastor or any other person into submitting to insincere, empty expressions such as kneeling or the raising of hands before God. How many times have we not offered praise to God insincerely? Let us lend our hearts, attention and our all to God and not offer praises and worship 'mechanically' for as we draw closer to Him with the right heart He will in turn draw closer to us.

THE CHALLENGE OF SACRIFICING & SUBMITTING

'15 Through Him, therefore, let us constantly and at all times offer up to God a sacrifice of praise, which is the fruit of lips that thankfully acknowledge and confess and glorify His name . . .'
Hebrews 13:15

Every sacrifice costs something and requires total submission, devotion and self denial. David said he would not offer a sacrifice that cost him nothing. He could have gotten that threshing ground for free but he still did not take it for free since he understood the fundamental truth about sacrificing—that a sacrifice must cost something. I remember when I was young both spiritually and otherwise; it was the monies that my parents gave me for offering that I would put into the offering bowl. That was fine but you see though that might have tasked my parents hard enough to be counted as sacrifice, it did not affect me, and hence, I had not made the sacrifice. After all I did not strive for it. All I had to do was just to walk to the front and drop it into the offering bowl-(even with that, sometimes people used to steal from it). Actually, I suppose our parents must have been instilling in us the practice of having to always come before God with 'something' and that is fine—in fact that is the right thing to do. We must always come before God with a gift. Yet one thing parents always lose sight of is the fact that it is not just the 'something' that counts but rather how much it costs the one making the sacrifice that matters. Most of the time, children grow up with an attitude of depending on others for their offerings to God and so when they turn into adults and no one blesses them with anything, they in turn refuse to give anything to God.

I have always said that we can teach our children to start sacrificing at tender ages and when they understand the concept they will grow with it and sacrifice genuinely with a pure heart to God. At the child's infancy you may encourage them to give a bit of what they so much cling unto as their own—be it money from their piggy banks or in kind (such as a ball or a doll they love so much). Let them understand the need to sacrifice to God. I suppose that it is at the 'possessive stage' of the child that we should as parents, even more than ever, teach them the concept of sacrificing to God and sowing seeds in His vineyard. T rust me—teaching them this will become one of the biggest assets you would have ever given your children. Remember what the Bible says about training up a child in a way that they will never depart from? As a parent, don't underestimate your children and deceive yourself into thinking that they are too young to learn about sacrificing to God.

Still to do with sacrifices, for many, you would have noticed that in times when they get some bonuses or financial windfalls, they are happy to give fat offerings but when nothing has come in they are reluctant to give of the little they have. Really, it is not so much the amount we give; rather it is the extent to which it costs us. If I had one million Cedis and I gave hundred thousand as offering, I would have given 10% of what I had (which might not have cost me much). However, if I had a thousand Cedis and gave an offering of five hundred Cedis, that would have been 50% (which might have cost a greater sacrifice), even though nominally the hundred thousand Cedis is more than the five hundred Cedis. This I believe was the understanding David had about sacrificing to God. I suppose it is not only about the nominal value but even more importantly, it is about the percentage of the total that is being sacrificed that shows how much the sacrifice really costs. Many of us are happy to sacrifice gifts that don't cost us anything to God rather than things which task us. At times it is even the small change from our taxi fares, and our dirty currency which we deem fit to give to God. Do we praise God because we have some extra strength or exuberance? Will we praise God with all we have even through situations which task our health, logic, strength and emotions? In times when we don't have 'extra' health, wealth and strength, will we still praise God wholeheartedly?

In *Genesis 22* Abraham's obedience was equal to submission of his intellect. It did not make sense humanly, considering that God had given His word and promise concerning Isaac. Then He tells him to sacrifice the lad. There are times when God expects us to make some humanly 'crazy' sacrifices which logically may not make sense to our human understanding. I think that, had Abraham made mention of this particular sacrifice of Isaac to any one, they probably would have thought of it as a big joke. There are times when people may make fun of you and blame your actions on certain things they may logically feel are causes of your 'crazy' actions but all I have to say is that, if it is God who has demanded the sacrifice, defy logic and human understanding and go right ahead and give God the praise (sacrifice) due Him.

Again, Abraham had to sacrifice his feeling or emotions. Can you imagine having to kill your own child. I can almost feel the emotions every time I read that Scripture when Isaac asked his father where the animal for the sacrifice was. The mental agony of having to find an answer for the 'sacrifice' about the whereabouts of the 'sacrifice', when the 'sacrifice' asks you where the 'sacrifice' is. And so it is, when many times our pride and all the other negative emotions that need to be sacrificed tend to question us about the where abouts of the 'sacrifice' and we need to go through the torture of standing up to demonstrate that they are actually the real sacrifices.

Beloved, though it might be as agonizing, as it was for Abraham, we should demonstrate faith by being prepared to sacrifice what God demands of us with a true heart of surrender. If God doesn't need a particular thing or person to be sacrificed, He will not require it of you, and if that is not what He expects to be sacrificed, He will provide.

In sacrificing we surrender our will to God as seen in *Matthew 26:39* where Jesus teaches us a big lesson by saying:

'39 My Father, if it is possible, let this cup pass away from Me; nevertheless, not what I will [not what I desire], but as You will and desire.'

CHAPTER 13

THE VANITY OF MERE TRADITIONS

P RINCIPLES and orderliness in praise and worship are of great importance and without them our services could be chaotic. However, following such customs without the right God-enabled understanding, results in our participating in mere repetitive and vain traditions which are of no benefit to us nor of any use to God. Such useless traditions make us 'mechanical' worshippers rather than True Worshippers.

WITH A WRONG HEART ALL THAT WE DO IS FUTILE

'21 I hate, I despise your feasts, and I will not smell a savor or take delight in your solemn assemblies. 22 Though you offer Me your burnt offerings and your cereal offerings, I will not accept them, neither will I look upon the peace or thank offerings of your fatted beasts. 23 Take away from Me the noise of your songs, for I will not listen to the melody of your harps.' ***Amos 5:21-23***

Note that even God still referred to their assemblies as solemn. There might be no doubt about the fact that our assemblies may be solemn. Again, God recognizes that the people were (at the time) offering fat burnt offerings and meat sacrifices. Imagine God himself acknowledging that their offerings were of fat beasts. That says to me that the sacrifices were really big. So then, like them, our 'rituals' may no doubt be seen, and acknowledged as fat and solemn by both God and man but it is not solely about how big or solemn the sacrifices are. One may offer a beautiful dance or beautiful voice for instance, and offer the most solemn gestures and services but notice what God says in the next verse to His people.

He says *take away the noise of thy songs*, which tells me that even though God acknowledged that they were singing and even making melody, He still referred to it as noise. That scares me at times. How many times have we not supposedly come before God with songs whilst lending our attention to the petty details of creating the right melody, whilst in truth our hearts were far from Him. Brethren, in such times God might have only heard our melody as noise and it might have not even registered on His radar as reasonable service. I pray that it will be far from us that our songs and melody register as noise in God's ears. Public worship is worse than useless if it's done without sincerity and righteous living.

WORSHIP ENTAILS GIVING GOD THE BEST WE HAVE

The wise men brought gifts and worshipped Jesus for who He was and still is.

The essence of true worship is to honor God for who He is and to be willing to give Him what you value most. We worship God because He is perfect, just, and the Almighty Creator of the universe, worthy of our very best.

A TRUE WORSHIP EXPERIENCE IS OFTEN A DIRECT RESULT OF PREPARATION FOR WORSHIP

The time taken in preparation for worship in the olden days gave God's people the opportunity to prepare their heart for worship. Unless our hearts are ready, our worship is meaningless.

CHAPTER 14

WORSHIP

THE worship of God is quite a difficult experience to explain in words since worship has not been defined anywhere in the Bible. Some peoples' experiences in or revelations of worship have been described in the Bible but I am still convinced that these experiences and revelations do not amount to a definition of worship.

To worship is to ascribe ultimate value to an object, person, or God, and to revere, adore, pay homage to, and obey by ordering the priorities of our lives around that which we worship. The Bible teaches that God alone is worthy of our worship.

Really, worship relates to the holiness of God which in itself cannot be explained but can only be revealed and experienced. So if your expectation is for this book to define worship, then I am sorry to disappoint you. Even so, if your anticipation is for this book to offer some hot-keys to just punch in order to reach into God's presence, then again you must be reading the wrong book. You see, holiness is not a set of rules to be followed. It is far more than that, and that explains why it is impossible (at least for me) to define the worship of God.

It is impossible to worship God if you don't know Him and if you don't have a relationship with Him because in worship there is communication between the Spirit of God and the human spirit. Communing with God will thus be impossible if you are not born of His Spirit.

Remember what happened on the Island of Patmos when Jesus had to reveal Himself prior to true worship? Furthermore it's worth mentioning that our worship is based on faith and not particularly confined to praise though praising God can lead us into worship.

Worship is to an extent, a response to the holiness of God and therefore should be respectful. In **Revelations 2**, Jesus intimates that He longs for the church of Ephesus to do the things that she first did.

> '5 Remember then from what heights you have fallen. Repent (change the inner man to meet God's will) and do the works you did previously [when first you knew the Lord], or else I will visit you and remove your lamp stand from its place, unless you change your mind and repent.'
> **Revelations 2:5**

Having read the entire account (which I entreat you to do as well), I get the impression that, out of love, the church was *enduring* hard times and yet not really enjoying Jesus. What kind of relationship does the church and its members have with Jesus Christ today? Time and again we come across people who are enduring Christianity and all sorts of Christian *'rituals'* and ceremonies *yet not enjoying God*. People run around church programs, working their fingers to the bone endlessly (supposedly for God) and yet never get to enjoy God like they should or seek to for that matter. Is that the kind of situation you have been saddled with? Could it be that *the lamp stand has been removed from its place? God admonishes us to Repent (change the inner man to meet God's will) and to do the works we previously [when first you knew the Lord] did.*

Quite a number of believers quote *Revelations 3:20* when we go out to win souls for Christ, thinking that it is a piece of Scripture reserved for only the unsaved yet we lose sight of the fact that it was the church of Laodicea that was being reminded of this invitation. This was a church that was already in God's business, yet not up to speed with His standards. I suppose it was an invitation to a much more powerful and intimate relationship and not just a call to be followers of Christ. Many churches and individuals today are like the church of Laodicea—lukewarm and not 'up to speed', and to such churches and individuals, God is reaching out with an invitation to have a more meaningful companionship today. He says:

> *'20 Behold, I stand at the door and knock; if anyone hears and listens to and heeds My voice and opens the door, I will come in to him and will **eat** with him, and he [will eat] with Me . . .'*
> *Revelations 3:20*

Sup or eat used here is derived from the Greek noun *'Deipnon'* which is descriptive of the main meal of the day—usually the evening meal—supper or dinner for that matter. At this table, as was the practice in those days, it was not only about the food, (though that was important) but it was more about the quality time spent together as a family unit and it was at that meal time that all the quality time was spent after a hard day's work.

You see, that was where intimacy was shared and built. The main reason for this gathering for sure, had more to do with the fellowship and quality time spent, than anything else. It is important to note that, the meal as mentioned, was not to be a hurried meal but one that entailed eating and spending time (fellowshipping) with others, in order to build closeness.

Hence, I see Jesus' invitation as one which transcends just an ordinary invitation to eat with Him to one which beckons a more intimate letting-in. Note that this is not a call for us to act as waiters around His table either. This is an invitation to sit and dine with him and grab the opportunity to build a stronger bond with Him by getting to know him more intimately and to have Him fellowship with us and get even closer to us. Isn't that an honor? Yet, we have often turned Him away, and even when we have let Him in, we have behaved as though we were just waiters at His table, with an inferiority complex. At times we even abandon Him at the table, but God wants to sit with us and enjoy more than just a meal.

I can say without any doubt that had a president of the land you reside in (whom you respect) come knocking at your door, ready to sit, dine and share intimate fellowship with you, you would cancel all outstanding appointments just to make the best out of the time you would set to spend with Him. I am sure that you would make it the most quality time of your life. Yet when God knocks at our doors and we even let

Him in, our attitude almost says to Him, *"Can you please hurry up and leave because I have another appointment."* You see, you may even politely be saying to Him (through your actions or otherwise) *"I am sorry I have to make a quick dash to town, but you relax, enjoy the meal and feel at home. When you are through with it and I am not back, you may take your leave. Never mind we shall meet some other time."* This may sound really strange to you but in reality, that is a picture of what we do. Many times when we have the opportunity to sup with Him, we are in such a hurry to leave. Worship is to be an act of respect and reverence and we need to learn to spend quality time with God and not just wait at His table and, or hurry off.

I picked up a lot about children from my four beautiful nieces, Nana Araba, Adwoa, Adom and Esi who I have been privileged to see grow up through different stages of childhood. In like manner if we grow up (spiritually) around God, having spent time in His presence, we are bound to learn a lot through the quality intimacy we build as a result of fellowshipping with Him.

Truly these experiences with my nieces, have built up a dense resource of my understanding of God. No wonder He says we need to become like children to be able to inherit the kingdom—it is true. You can imagine how frustrating it could get when my nieces (whilst they were still toddlers) would run to Uncle with an issue but run off almost immediately even before I could respond. Then again and again, running back and forth doing the same thing, and yet, never having time for me to respond. Well, do we not often do same when we go before God? Instead of spending quality time in His presence, relishing and taking advantage of the opportunity to hear His voice, we constantly seem to be in a hurry to leave, short of the intimacy and quality time we could have spent with Him and benefitted from.

Obviously, those few minutes we get to spend in church are not enough and really are an apology of a true life of worship. As a matter of fact, our whole lives need to be worship unto God. So we should not wait till it's a church meeting before we struggle to enjoy God's presence. Like I said at the very beginning, God's presence is the ideal environment in which we as living souls are able to live to our fullest potential, outside of which we malfunction.

I have been privileged to learn quite a bit of law and have been blessed with some lawyer friends as well so I know that when dealing with criminal cases, a person charged with a crime is judged to be guilty when it has been proven *'beyond all reasonable doubt'* that that person actually committed the crime for which he or she stands trial. There are also other cases which are judged based on *'the balance of probabilities'* whereby a person's actions or inactions are assessed by a jury, as to whether or not he or she had acted as a **reasonable person** under the same given circumstances. Such cases are therefore assessed on the basis of whether or not a person's actions fall short of that of a reasonable person.

As Christians there is a reasonable standard we need to live up to or better still a reasonable service we need to render and anything short of that pronounces guilt upon us.

'1 I APPEAL to you therefore, brethren, and beg of you in view of [all] the mercies of God, to make a decisive dedication of your bodies [presenting all your members and faculties] as a living

160

sacrifice, holy (devoted, consecrated) and well pleasing to God, which is YOUR REASONABLE (RATIONAL, INTELLIGENT) SERVICE AND SPIRITUAL WORSHIP.' **Romans 12:1**

It is our REASONABLE SERVICE to present ourselves as a living sacrifice, holy and acceptable to God. This to me is a life of worship.

The overwhelming explosion of excitement which congregations of possessed football fans experience when their teams win a match (in say extra time) is what could pass as an expression of the Hebrew word *Hallal* which translates into praise. Again the manner in which many youth scream and throw themselves at the stage when their hip-hop or hip life star idols are performing are all expressions we could as well render to the Lord God Almighty, yet in the house of God those who express praise and worship to these limits are usually accused of going overboard.

Human beings were naturally created to worship but it's who or what we worship that is of importance. The Bible teaches that God alone is worthy of our worship.

To worship as per the dictionary's definition, is "to ascribe ultimate value to an object, person, or God-and then again to revere, adore, pay homage to, and obey by ordering the priorities of our lives around that which we worship".

Sometimes, it's unfortunate that it is rather when we come to God in worship that we are most casual (without any sense of having been invited by a King). We need to fine-tune our attitude to befit our approach to a Holy God. Undoubtedly, if we had to catch a flight abroad we would strive to get to the airport on time and even if we arrived late, I'm sure we would have exploited all opportunities to have gotten there on time and the frustration would be evident. Yet what do we see in our churches today? Late comers strolling into services so leisurely and with no regrets nor regard for God. I think that is totally unacceptable. How can we for instance, right in the middle of sweet worship, pick up a phone call and chat heartily with others. For me, this is appalling, considering that in the presence of our earthly presidents, kings, prime ministers and even some ordinary persons, we are careful not to dare behave in such a manner.

If truly God means so much to us we can ask whoever is competing for God's due attention to wait and be attended to later. Worship relates to God's holiness and is derived from the old English word "Worth ship"—indicative for the homage that directly reflects our sense of value for our object of worship who in our case as Christians is God. Hence our worship as Christians reflects how much we value and rely on God.

Let me quickly mention something really profound which I once heard Elder Bethel Odonkor (an Elder of my church) teach. He mentioned that in our praise and worship we need to recognize God as our **SOS**—Our Source, our Object and our Subject.

Worship is thus honor, reverence or homage paid to any superior being or power—we could make superior beings or powers out of men or angels but as mentioned before, in our case as Christians, the only person worthy of our worship is God, and our worship expresses to Him what worth we place on Him.

SOME ROOT WORDS WHICH TRANSLATE INTO WORSHIP

Two frequently used Hebrew and Greek expressions of Worship are **Shachah** and **Proskuneo** respectively, which suggest utter submission, lying prostrate or doing obeisance. Thus, for us as Christians, worship must be perceived as a total surrender in love and loyalty to God as well as an absolute dedication to Him.

Remarkably, none of the root words aforementioned make direct reference to music, though many people assume worship is simply about singing slow tempo songs and about the music.

As a matter of fact, worship transcends that which is visible. Singing and music are just tools used to discharge into God a heart of submission, love, obedience and devotion. Music helps lift a person's thoughts and emotions to God and through music we can reflect upon our needs and shortcomings as well as celebrate God's greatness.

Prior to taking a look at some models of worship, let's quickly run through some derivatives from which the word Worship came.

a. **Proskuneo:** As mentioned before means "to do obeisance to". It is used to describe an act of paying homage or reverence.

b. **Sebomai:** Is indicative of the act of revering, whilst stressing the feeling of awe or devotion.

c. **Sebazomia:** Is similar to Sebomai and refers to the act of honoring religiously as mentioned in ***Romans 1:25:***
   '25 Because they exchanged the truth of God for a lie and worshipped and served the creature rather than the Creator, Who is blessed forever! Amen (so be it).'

d. **Latreuo:** Is descriptive of serving or rendering religious service or homage as contained in the following scriptures:

'3 For we [Christians] are the true circumcision, who worship God in spirit and by the Spirit of God and exult and glory and pride ourselves in Jesus Christ, and put no confidence or dependence [on what we are] in the flesh and on outward privileges and physical advantages and external appearances.'
Philippians 3:3

'42 But God turned [away from them] and delivered them up to worship and serve the host (stars) of heaven, as it is written in the book of the prophets: Did you [really] offer to Me slain beasts and sacrifices for forty years in the wilderness (desert), O house of Israel?'
Acts 7:42

'14 But this I confess to you, however, that in accordance with the Way [of the Lord], which they call a [heretical, division—producing] sect, I worship (serve) the God of our fathers, still persuaded of the truth of and believing in and placing full confidence in everything laid down in the Law [of Moses] or written in the prophets;.'
Acts 24:14

'2 For if it were otherwise, would [these sacrifices] not have stopped being offered? Since the worshipers had once for all been cleansed, they would no longer have any guilt or consciousness of sin . . .
Hebrews 10:2

e.   **Eusebeo:** Is to act piously towards an object as illustrated in *Acts 17:23:*

> *'23 For as I passed along and carefully observed your objects of worship, I came also upon an altar with this inscription, To the unknown god. Now what you are already worshipping as unknown, this I set forth to you.' Acts 17:23*

WHO DETERMINES OUR WORSHIP?

Basically as taught by the Bible, worship is not and should not be determined on our terms or conditions. It is all about God. In other words, we cannot claim to worship God our own way or anyway for that matter. As a matter of fact, we can only worship God by His Spirit. I have on occasions heard people say things like 'you go on and worship God your own way' whilst trying to encourage congregations during worship and I have always wanted to believe that it is for want of a better expression that they utter such blunder because I beg to differ. We can only worship God His way.

> *'3 For we [Christians] are the true circumcision, who worship God in spirit and by the Spirit of God and exult and glory and pride ourselves in Jesus Christ, and put no confidence or dependence [on what we are] in the flesh and on outward privileges and physical advantages and external appearances-.'*
> ***Philippians 3:3***

From the above, note that we worship God in spirit and by the Spirit of God.

'6 O come, let us worship and bow down, let us kneel before
the Lord our Maker [in reverent praise and supplication] . . . .
' Psalms 95:6

The Psalmist here of course is not only calling on us to perform
some meaningless gestures and movements but now with a better
understanding of some of these gestures and expressions earlier
discussed under praising God, we can express our total surrender to God
thereby subjecting our ways and rights to God's own sweet Spirit.

You might be asking by now what God's way of worship is, since I
mentioned that we can't just worship God our own way.

In *Genesis 22* with reference to the account of Abraham and his sacrifice
of Isaac, though the Bible says Abraham had already sacrificed Isaac in
his heart, God still provided a ram.

'17 By faith Abraham, when he was put to the test [while the
testing of his faith was still in progress], had already brought
Isaac for an offering; he who had gladly received and welcomed
[God's] promises was ready to sacrifice his only son, 18 Of
whom it was said, Through Isaac shall your descendants be
reckoned. 19 For he reasoned that God was able to raise [him]
up even from among the dead. Indeed in the sense that Isaac
was figuratively dead [potentially sacrificed], he did [actually]
receive him back from the dead.'
Hebrews 11:17-19

Now note that God revealed to Abraham his own mode of worship after which Abraham said in *Genesis 22:5:*

> *'5 And Abraham said to his servants, Settle down and stay here with the donkey, and I and the young man will go yonder and worship and come again to you.' (According to God's own dictates).*

Are you able to say that you and your crown, your job, the authority you have, your stature or your every valued asset will go yonder (the extra mile) and worship according to God's own ordinance as Abraham did, knowing that, that which you are going before the Lord with is the same thing or person you are going 'the extra mile' to sacrifice and that there is the possibility that it may never return?

God's way in worship is for us to surrender our 'all in all' including our human will, intellect and feelings (our entire soul), in faith. This is the proper way to worship God and not to worship God our 'own way' as some say. It is my prayer that we yield our all to God so as to be sensitive enough to hear Him and know which way He wants us to go in worship.

Matthew 15:8-9 suggests that without submission, obedience and love we indulge in vain hypocritical worship which is just ritualistic, merely traditional, empty and void of God's presence.

> *'8 These people draw near Me with their mouths and honor Me with their lips, but their hearts hold off and are far away from Me. 9 Uselessly do they worship Me, for they teach as doctrines the commands of men. 'Matthew 15:8&9*

The Holy Spirit is the means to every meaningful thing that happens in our worship. As mentioned earlier in *Philippians 3:3,* we worship **by the Spirit of God**. Hence the human being follows or should follow the Holy Spirit. It is the Spirit of God who leads and takes us into God's presence and all that is required of us is to follow in obedience and reverence. So if we agree that it is the Holy Spirit who leads us in worship, then the only true **worship leader is the Holy Spirit**. You would have noticed if you were observant that when referring to praise I say praise leaders, yet I cautiously refer to ministers in the office of helping congregations in worship as lead worshippers. I may be the only one with this conviction but I believe that there can be only one worship leader—the Holy Spirit. For me, He is the worship leader and I am a lead worshipper.

I suppose you would say a 'lead microphone' rather than a 'microphone leader'. Why? The reason being that, the microphone does not lead the singer or the other microphones. Someone else uses the microphone in that role. Therefore in the same way, the Holy Spirit uses us, by leading us as to how to help others reach into God's presence. If that is true, then I think we are rather lead worshippers and not worship leaders. *What do you think?*

With this at the back of my mind I am compelled, and I will encourage you also, to yield to the real Worship Leader who is the Spirit of God whenever you are privileged to render your reasonable service in any congregation. Again it brings to the fore the fact that, we worship on God's conditions or stipulations. He directs us whenever we yield to His Holy Spirit who leads us into all truths. We need to be totally dependent on God. Actually, if it is not the Holy Spirit that is leading, no amount of musical arrangements can get us into God's presence.

Don't get me wrong. I am not saying that music is not important in worship. What I am saying is that, worship is foremost spiritual and the music enhances it. All in all, the bottom line is that, the Holy Spirit is the key to authentic worship.

CHAPTER 15

THE EXPRESSION OF WORSHIP:

AS PORTRAYED BY THE WOMAN WITH

THE FLASK OF FRAGRANT OIL

Luke 7:37, 38:

'37 And behold, a woman of the town who was an especially wicked sinner, when she learned that He was reclining at table in the Pharisee's house, brought an alabaster flask of ointment (perfume). 38 And standing behind Him at His feet weeping, she began to wet His feet with [her] tears; and she wiped them with the hair of her head and kissed His feet [affectionately] and anointed them with the ointment (perfume) . . . '

Luke 45-47:

45 You gave Me no kiss, but she from the moment I came in has not ceased [intermittently] to kiss My feet tenderly and caressingly. 46 You did not anoint My head with [cheap,

ordinary] oil, but she has anointed My feet with [costly, rare]
perfume. 47 Therefore I tell you, her sins, many [as they are],
are forgiven her-because she has loved much. But he who is
forgiven little loves little.'

From the aforementioned references there is a lot we can learn from
this Pharisee woman as regards worship.

UNPREDICTABILITY

Praise leaders and lead worshippers especially must ideally allow room
for the unpredictable because in His own wisdom God may decide
to lead you through certain ways that may seem 'foolish' to you yet
via these paths of righteousness, He will eventually lead you into an
entirely wonderful and powerful depth of His throne room. You see,
God sometimes takes us on routes we have never journeyed before.

Mark 14 tells of Jesus in the house of Simon in the week leading to
His crucifixion. Through all the mental agony of facing what was yet
to befall Him, suddenly a woman with a jar of perfume enters and
without observing protocol, breaks off the top of the jar and unsparingly
empties the whole jar of perfume on Jesus' feet with abandon. For sure
those looking on must have deemed her as having lost her marbles and
must have seen her act as an exaggerated waste of resources. This was
perfume that was supposed to be measured out drop by drop. Nowadays
when we buy our relatively cheap Boss, D&G etc fragrances, just see
how mindful we are of the amount we spray on ourselves. Yet, though
others must have thought this woman was crazy, Jesus said she had
done a beautiful thing.

What the woman did was a well timed, unexpected, unusual and yet such a meaningful act of deep devotion regardless of religious attitudes, protocol and traditions. Undoubtedly all these intimidating elements were still present but she would not let them weigh her down.

This was a woman who would not allow her act of worship to be trapped by traditions and who yielded to the unpredictability we should be willing to yield to regardless of the situations, circumstances, attitudes and protocol that surround us. Someone said 'worship is meant to be an encounter; an exciting meeting where love is given and received in an unprescribed manner.'

Planning is important yet to be open to the Holy Spirit and to yield to His directions into fresh areas is even more pertinent.

Garry Furr and Mc Iburn Price put it:

> *'Because worship is a conversation and not a mere review of the past, it is dynamic, unpredictable and open ended'*

Of course it is not bad to follow a certain order or format, after all every church has its own traditions and principles and such familiarities can as a matter of fact be comfortable and reassuring for the worshipper, but these traditions have the tendency to evolve into dead monotony—so rigid as to hinder spontaneous expressions of love in the presence of God. That is what we need to avoid. Yes, when we come before God in worship, structures and order are important but they must never be allowed to strangle or imprison our spirits let alone God's sweet Holy Spirit.

We must guard against losing the true spirit of worship to our getting accustomed to and familiar with vague traditions and repetitions. As in *Genesis 22:2 ff* let us yield to the commands of God in order to discover new places of worship—Probably not just physically but spiritually too.

As a matter of fact worship can be likened to a romantic relationship and hence is best experienced when expressions of love are passionate and unpredictable. A passionate heart (more often than not) seeks to find out fresh and inventive ways to reach out to the one it beats for and is unable to hold back or contain the response to the one it adores. People in love usually do a lot of crazy things which sometimes seem embarrassing to everyone else except those enjoying it and the feeling is often mutual. I have done more than my fair share of crazy things for love and I believe you have too. Just own up and let's get on with it!

You can then understand why just the other day, probably, except for Jesus and the woman herself, there might have been a couple of people in that room who felt embarrassed when the woman entered, broke the top of the jar of perfume and poured it over Jesus.

We must come to a point where we can break the top of our 'jar of perfume', refuse to be intimidated by on lookers and pour it all over our King Of kings without yielding to intimidating environments and traditions which are capable of hindering our worship.

I am quick however to point out that, I am not by this element of unpredictability imputing that lead worshippers and praise leaders must act so erratically and out of sync with the congregation and the team they are supposed to be working together with. That would be prescribing havoc and extreme folly which would rather hinder people from concentrating and focusing on God.

Note that the instruction to Peter was 'feed my sheep' not 'try experiments with my sheep' or 'teach my sheep new tricks in performing arts'.

THE FLASK OF FRAGRANT OIL

First of all, is the flask of fragrant oil. Bible scholars have it that the fragrance was very expensive and in those days such fragrance (as in our present day) was usually used sparingly. Here we learn our first lesson regarding expressions in worship—which is to give liberally of our material treasure we have earned through sweat and toil. I can't imagine how hard this woman must have worked to have earned enough to afford that amount and type of fragrance. Yet she counted it as nothing and sacrificed it all. How much of the material treasure you have toiled and worked for are you prepared and willing to worship God with?—And note that the Bible says

that she broke the jar and poured it ALL. Do you hold back some of your treasure when you approach God's presence in worship or do you give it all?

THE ACT OF WEEPING AT JESUS' FEET

This act of the woman was indicative of her true spirit of brokenness, submission and gratitude for what Jesus meant to her. One of the questions I often ask when I consider this expression of worship is whether we are truly broken before God when we come before Him in worship. Because if we truly are, then we can be sure that He will not cast us away since He says a broken and contrite spirit He will not cast away.

THE WASHING OF HIS FEET WITH HER TEARS

This to me was an ultimate expression of gratitude. I have witnessed people receive huge gifts on TV shows which were so much for them that, their immediate response was to break down in tears. I have also encountered people who have received some sort of miracle from God (whether healing or otherwise) and just could not contain their gratitude, and as a result have broken down in tears. For this woman to wash Jesus' feet with her tears, indicates to me extreme gratitude, and if only we would express such genuine gratitude (not by forcing fake tears but rather by expressing genuine gratitude from our hearts) before God, I am convinced that He will respond to us just as He did in the case of the woman we have just read about.

THE WIPING OF HIS FEET WITH HER HAIR

1 Corinthians 11:15 depicts the value of a woman's hair as her pride, glory and her covering:

> *'15 But if a woman has long hair, it is her ornament and glory? For her hair is given to her for a covering.'*

The act of wiping Jesus' feet with her hair could be symbolic of her investing her glory, power and substance into her worship. She was by that act actually giving the very basis of her dignity. Can we say that when we also come before God in worship we are able to give off the very basis of our dignity to the Lord?

KISSING HIS FEET

Kissing Jesus' feet for me was symbolic of true worship. The climax of her worship was to generously pour love on the master and Jesus in reference to this act mentioned that she had loved so much. How much do we lavish God with love when we go before Him in worship? Can

God also say of us that we have loved Him that much? Remember that the frequency, intensity and duration of our worship are a reflection of the value we place on Him and how much we rely on Him.

Also remember that **Romans 12:1** says:

> *'1 I APPEAL to you therefore, brethren, and beg of you in view of [all] the mercies of God, to make a decisive dedication of your bodies [presenting all your members and faculties] as a living sacrifice, holy (devoted, consecrated) and well pleasing to God, which is your reasonable (rational, intelligent) service and spiritual worship.'*

Worship therefore entails death to one's self. It is a sacrifice which must remain on the altar until it has been totally consumed, releasing a perpetual sweet savor into heaven. Now so long as we are still living it means we are not totally consumed and ideally should remain on the altar. This means that we are supposed to give off a constant sweet savor unto God in heaven (as we lead a life of worship as living sacrifices). Yet nowadays the living sacrifices (you and I) who are supposed to remain on the altar tend to jump off and go our ways, at our own convenience which is totally unacceptable.

CHAPTER 16

SOME CHARACTERISTICS OF
TRUE WORSHIP

IT is important that we consider some characteristics of true worship. Hence, this chapter highlights some of these characteristics.

WORSHIP ENTAILS BRINGING OUR BEST TO GOD

How many times have we not consciously or unconsciously chosen to give God our 'dirty' currency? At times it is even the notes we know very well no one else would accept as legal tender that we send to the church and dump in the offering bowl as our offering (part of our worship to God). And then as though without any shame, we keep the fresh notes to ourselves and try to defend our disgraceful and disrespectful acts with the excuse that the money will eventually be sent to the bank and so it does not matter. I can remember times when I would find my mum selecting the best notes from her purse, and when I asked what they were for, she would say to me that she was selecting the best notes for her tithe. At the time I was young and may not have seen the point but a couple of years down the line, I can now fully understand. Did you not know that God stands by the offering bowl and sees whatever you put into it? If not, how would He have known the other day that a certain woman had given more than anyone else?

Unfortunately, it is the same attitude we sometimes adopt when we offer all other forms of sacrifices during our worship. We just don't give God our best. It is in our spare time (when there is nothing else to do, no one else to visit or no business to transact) that we choose to consider attending church services. Your best sacrifice will demand that you sacrifice and surrender your self-made plans, your pride and even your intellect (which entails your understanding or reasoning) and to give off your all in all. It is such a sacrifice that will place a demand on God in heaven to come through for you.

BROKENNESS

> *'17 My sacrifice [the sacrifice acceptable] to God is a broken spirit; a broken and a contrite heart [broken down with sorrow for sin and humbly and thoroughly penitent], such, O God, You will not despise.'*
> **Psalms 51:17**

Brokenness in Hebrew **Dakah** means to crumble, to beat into pieces, to bruise or to crush. Brokenness is very fundamental in worship. In the Old Testament, animals to be sacrificed were required to be slain and for that matter broken. The gift of 'life' was therefore an indication of giving up one's own interest in honor of God. That is why the animal could not be blemished or crippled. However, since such animals were hard to come by, they commanded a relatively higher price which as a result must have created the wrong impression that more expensive gifts were better sacrifices consequently causing some to carry the wrong notion that more expensive gifts were more pleasing to God and for that matter commanded better or higher blessings. Brethren, I believe that what God was and still is interested in is not the nominal or financial value of our sacrifices, and for that reason the one who provides the most expensive sacrifice (financially) but rather the worshipper's heartfelt obedience as captured by David in *Psalms 51.*

> '16 For You delight not in sacrifice, or else would I give it; You find no pleasure in burnt offering. 17 My sacrifice [the sacrifice acceptable] to God is a broken spirit; a broken and a contrite heart [broken down with sorrow for sin and humbly and thoroughly penitent], such, O God, You will not despise.'
> **Psalms 51:16-17**

The background of this Scripture reveals what David said at the point in his life when he had committed adultery with Bathsheba and had murdered Uriah. As a wealthy man you can imagine that he could have offered extremely expensive sacrifices and in their thousands as well.

Just to remind you of David's sacrificing abilities, let's read
2 Samuel 6:12-13:

> '12 And it was told King David, The Lord has blessed the house of Obed-edom and all that belongs to him, because of the ark of God. So David went and brought up the ark of God from the house of Obed-edom into the City of David with rejoicing; 13 And when those who bore the ark of the Lord had gone six paces, he sacrificed an ox and a fatling.'

So then, what expensive sacrifice would you have put beyond David? Yet, caught in the circumstance he grabbed the revelation that it was not about offering expensive sacrifices but rather it was about offering a broken heart that was pivotal to his sacrifice. After all, we can never pay, bribe or buy God, can we? It is in such broken-heartedness that man loses his essence before God and depends totally on Him.

It is however imperative to note that it is God who does the crushing and it could turn out to be dangerous and displeasing to God if we allow ourselves to be broken before ordinary men.

HUMILITY

In the scripture that mentioned the woman who stood at the feet of Jesus and washed His feet with her tears, we notice how she made herself of no repute by using her hair to wipe Jesus' feet, and how she bowed before Him which in itself is an indication of humility. I can confidently say—you show me a true worshipper and I will show you humility personified. Humility is very essential to worship hence in our bid to become the worshippers that we should be, it is important that we strive to be humble. Pride will draw us away from God.

LOVE

In the same account of this woman as previously mentioned and seen in *Luke 7:47*, we notice that Jesus responded to her act of worship and said that she loved much. It goes without emphasizing then that another ingredient that is important to our worshipping God is an expression of love. Here, I am talking about an unashamed, non-sexual love as expressed by this woman.

GIVING

The true heart of worship gives freely and more so to God. In the same account in *Luke 7* we notice that the woman came to God in worship with an alabaster jar of perfume which could pass for a family costly treasure. What do you come to God with in worship? I am not by this imputing that the more expensive the gift, the better the sacrifice—I believe I debunked that notion earlier on. In any case regardless of the expense, a sacrifice would have to cost you something. Your gift might not be nominally expensive yet it could still have cost you more than some others which might have higher financial tags.

CORPORATE WORSHIP MUST BE BENEFICIAL

There seems to be excessive spiritual gymnastics in our churches today where *'ministers'* are indulging in choreographed performances and practicing 'psychology' to earn self recognition rather than pointing the flock to God. It is important to note that in corporate worship a lot of positive spiritual release can be experienced which should generally speaking be of benefit to the worshippers.

CHAPTER 17

WORSHIP AS A FRUIT

WE have already learned that worship is a sacrifice and is a fruit as well. In that regard I trust that if we all considered a couple of things vis-à-vis ordinary fruits, we could better understand how to produce good fruit in order to sacrifice our best to God.

GOOD FRUITS DON'T JUST APPEAR

It is of great importance to note that fruits don't just drop from outer space. Naturally, there is a process by which they grow.

A fruit may as well be seen as an end product and therefore it is essential to ensure that the entire processes of producing good fruit is sustained if not, we are bound to lose out on the fruit. It is important to know therefore that fruits grow off plants or trees and in view of that, if any part of the plant or tree stalls in its growth or functioning, ultimately our fruit will be affected, in which case, we may have an unhealthy fruit or no fruit at all. I believe just like me, you would want to sacrifice a healthy fruit to God. Remember what we discovered as regards Abel doing the right thing? Amongst other things therefore, in order to obtain a healthy fruit there is the need for:

► Strong roots
► Rich soil
► A good stem
► The sun

THE FRUIT

Now let's take the:

► **Strong Roots** to be symbolic of a truly surrendered heart to God
► **Rich Soil** to stand for the goodness and word of God
► **Good Stem** to signify a vital connection which is our relationship with God
► **The Sun** as a symbol of constancy and of beauty.

If we truly have surrendered hearts that are hungry for God, (symbolized by strong roots) drawing vital nutrients from (the rich soil which stands for) the goodness and the word of God by means of a good standing with God via a spiritually healthy relationship with Him, (symbolized by a good stem), and we also have (the sun shining over our plant, depicting) consistency, we can be assured of bearing healthy fruits—good enough and worthy of sacrifice to our God Almighty in worship.

It's worth emphasizing that the stem which in this case is taken to be symbolic of our relationship with God is very important to our worship. Now if any of these aforementioned is defective you can expect that the fruit will be defective or even nonexistent. As a matter of fact, one of the basis of worship is the covenant relationship whereby God has bound himself to those whom He has saved and claimed. If the fruit of a natural physical plant is its produce then worship should be seen to be the spiritual produce of a believer.

Psalms 24:3-5 says:

'3 Who shall go up into the mountain of the Lord? Or who shall stand in His Holy Place? 4 He who has clean hands and a pure heart, who has not lifted himself up to falsehood or to what is false, nor sworn deceitfully. 5 He shall receive blessing from the Lord and righteousness from the God of his salvation.'

Therefore acceptable worship requires "clean hands and a pure heart" and the willingness to express one's devotion in works of service as well as in words of adoration.

Beloved, WORSHIP originates from God and actually, the Genesis encounter was not the first worship experience. Even before man was created worship existed.

'1 AFTER THIS I looked, and behold, a door standing open in heaven! And the first voice which I had heard addressing me like [the calling of] a war trumpet said, Come up here, and I will show you what must take place in the future. 2 At once I came under the [Holy] Spirit's power, and behold, a throne stood in heaven, with One seated on the throne!'

'10 The twenty-four elders (the members of the heavenly Sanhedrin) fall prostrate before Him Who is sitting on the throne, and they worship Him Who lives forever and ever; and they throw down their crowns before the throne, crying out, 11 Worthy are You, our Lord and God, to receive the glory and the

honor and dominion, for You created all things; by Your will they were [brought into being] and were created.'
Revelations 4:1, 2; 10, 11

DOES GOD ENJOY OUR WORSHIP?

Revelations 4:11 tells us

'11 Worthy are You, our Lord and God, to receive the glory and the honor and dominion, for You created all things; by Your will they were [brought into being] and were created.'

The issue as to whether or not God is pleased with our genuine worship is now established but the question is why does He delight in our worship? Why as the song writer inquires, is He so mindful of us?

'3 When I view and consider Your heavens, the work of Your fingers, the moon and the stars, which You have ordained and established, 4 What is man that You are mindful of him, and the son of [earthborn] man that You care for him?'
Psalms 8:3-4

A songwriter says:

'Who am I that you are mindful of me? That you hear me When I pray?
Is it true that you are thinking of me? That you love me? It's amazing, so amazing
I am a friend of God—I am a friend of God
I am a friend of God, He calls me friend

In *Genesis 2:23* Adam finds completion with Eve since she was a part of him—in fact she had actually been formed out of, the man.

> *'21 And the Lord God caused a deep sleep to fall upon Adam; and while he slept, He took one of his ribs or a part of his side and closed up the [place with] flesh. 22 And the rib or part of his side which the Lord God had taken from the man He built up and made into a woman, and He brought her to the man. 23 Then Adam said, This [creature] is now bone of my bones and flesh of my flesh; she shall be called Woman, because she was taken out of a man . . . .'*

Now if we were also created in God's own image then I trust that He must obviously find satisfaction in us as well just as Adam found satisfaction in the woman.

Again, have you noticed that a mother even before conception expects that when her child is born the child will amongst other things look up to her for things like protection, daily earthly

guidance and provision, and refuge? These are a few of the things that may motivate a mother as she travels the road towards childbirth. I believe that God must have also been motivated by quality worship (the type that must have been better than that of angels) to have created us in His own image.

WORSHIPPING IN SPIRIT

> *'24 God is a Spirit (a spiritual Being) and those who worship Him must worship Him in spirit and in truth (reality) . . . .'*
> *John 4:24*

This Scripture admonishes us to worship in spirit and in truth which indicates that there exists a spirit of worship that is born out of a positive relationship with God. Take note of the word relationship and not Knowledge. It is possible for you to have knowledge about someone but not have a relationship with that person.

I might have knowledge of Mr. Kofi Annan, and about stuff he has done and even what he may be doing now, but that does not mean I have a personal relationship with him. Having knowledge of or about someone and having a personal relationship with the person are two different things. In the same way we may possess a generous amount of knowledge of or about God but the most important thing is for us to have a personal relationship with Him. Actually even if we do not have so much knowledge about Him but have a healthy personal relationship with Him we are bound to attain the knowledge as the relationship grows. I remember going for a job interview once. Honestly, I knew almost nothing about the outfit I was seeking employment with. Yet after being taken on and as a result of a healthy relationship with my colleagues and managers, I got to learn so much about the job within such a short time. Again, let me caution that the fact that someone might have amassed a wealth of knowledge deposited in a book does not necessarily mean that the person knows the author of the book. Even if I could regurgitate the contents of a History book written by F. K. Buah it does not mean I know the man. In much the same way, some may quote extensively from Scripture and yet may not I have necessarily had a personal relationship with the one who inspired it—the Holy Ghost or ultimately God.

In the olden days they knew God as the God of their fathers but we are privileged to know God in our day as our father. We have a Father—son relationship.

> *'16 What agreement [can there be between] a temple of God and idols? For we are the temple of the living God; even as God said, I will dwell in and with and among them and will walk in and with and among them, and I will be their God, and they shall be My people. 17 So, come out from among [unbelievers], and separate (sever) yourselves from them, says the Lord, and touch not [any] unclean thing; then I will receive you kindly and treat you with favor, 18 And I will be a Father to you, and you shall be My sons and daughters, says the Lord Almighty . . .'*

> **2 Corinthians 6:16-18**
> *'15 For [the Spirit which] you have now received [is] not a spirit of slavery to put you once more in bondage to fear, but you have received the Spirit of adoption [the Spirit producing son ship] in [the bliss of] which we cry, Abba (Father)! Father!'*
> **Romans 8:15**

> *'6 And because you [really] are [His] sons, God has sent the [Holy] Spirit of His Son into our hearts, crying, Abba (Father)! Father!'* **Galatians 4:6**

Hence God is always present and to worship in spirit is to be conscious of His presence. This spirit of worship is not to be imported from some other place. As true believers, this spirit of worship should be resident in us, ready to be naturally released.

Now the relationship between mother and child is paralleled to the spirit of worship in that, something in the child yields towards the mother and recognizes her person and presence. You would have noticed this if you have had the opportunity to hang around a family that has been blessed with a baby. Even at their tender ages, babies who may normally not be able to see or reason properly at times will cry and not stop at anything except for 'mummy' picking them up and one can only but wonder how they are able to recognize the presence of 'mummy'. Similarly, there is a spirit of worship that longs for the Creator within every believer and until the two are brought together, there is bound to be an unrest within the believer.

Hebrews 8:10-11 further teaches us that the New Testament worshipper has the law of God on his mind and heart which I believe should by default cause us on the inside to be naturally released to express worship.

> '*10 For this is the covenant that I will make with the house of Israel after those days, says the Lord: I will imprint My laws upon their minds, even upon their innermost thoughts and understanding, and engrave them upon their hearts; and I will be their God, and they shall be My people. 11 And it will nevermore be necessary for each one to teach his neighbor and his fellow citizen or each one his brother, saying, Know (perceive, have knowledge of, and get acquainted by experience with) the Lord, for all will know Me, from the smallest to the greatest of them.' **Hebrews 8:10-11***

In *John 4:24* Jesus admonishes us to worship God in truth because there is no way liars will be able to worship Him. The Bible says of liars in **Revelation 21:8** that their part will be in the lake of fire which indicates that they cannot have access into the presence of God.

Notice how Ananias and Sapphira perished in **Acts 5** as a result of their lies, and what the Apostle John says in **1 John 1:5-6:**

> '*5 And this is the message [the message of promise] which we have heard from Him and now are reporting to you: God is Light, and there is no darkness in Him at all [no, not in any way]. 6 [So] if we say we are partakers together and enjoy fellowship with Him when we live and move and are walking about in darkness, we are [both] speaking falsely and do not live and practice the Truth [which the Gospel presents].'* **1 John 1:5-6**

Again, Jesus mentions that He is 'the truth, the way and the light' and mentions that no one can enter the Kingdom of God except through Him. Now, if Jesus is the truth and again, the Bible teaches us that Jesus Himself is the Word of God, then it means that when He admonishes us to worship the Father in Truth, He is in other words saying we should worship the Father in Jesus Himself, who is the Word. From inference Jesus is reminding us that as true worshippers, we have to worship God in and according to His Word.

Once again, he admonishes us to worship in Spirit. As mentioned earlier, we are a composition of spirits, soul and body as indicated in **1 Thessalonians 5:23** and it is our spirit that has the supreme function of relating to God. Actually, it is with our spirits that we worship God.

'23 And may the God of peace Himself sanctify you through and through [separate you from profane things, make you pure and wholly consecrated to God]; and may your spirit and soul and body be preserved sound and complete [and found] blameless at the coming of our Lord Jesus Christ (the Messiah).' 1 **Thessalonians 5:23**

When man sinned in the Garden of Eden, our spirits were cut off from fellowshipping with God, and God drove Adam and Eve away from the Garden, which was where God's presence touched the earth and where He had fellowship with man. Having been driven away from the Garden therefore means that man was driven away from God's presence and fellowship. Now via the work that was accomplished on the cross by Jesus, our spirits have now been granted direct access into the presence of God to fellowship with Him again.

Yet, the fact that we have access into His presence does not necessarily mean that our spirits are there having fellowship with Him. You see, I could have a visa and a fully paid up invitation to share fellowship with the president of the United States of America, but until I have not made a personal decision to accept the invitation I may still be in the same place until the visa expires.

Can you imagine that Christ has secured for us, our 'visas' to access His presence, and we have the invitation and our 'paid tickets' all ready, through the redemptive work that was accomplished on the cross, yet instead of just accepting Him as our personal Lord and savior as our acceptance and acknowledgment of His invitation, some will stay put in one place until their 'visas' expire and they completely miss out on the opportunity to fellowship with God.

It is worth noting that, it is through the new born spirit of man, that we can relate directly to and have fellowship with God. It is a spirit-to Spirit relationship and without a re-born spirit, it is impossible to relate and have fellowship with God. That is why Jesus says we need to worship God in spirit.

And that is why I always emphasize that it is impossible for the unsaved to worship God. They may be able to praise God even though I suppose at times even their praises can end up being an abomination unto Him since the Bible says that even the prayers of the sinner is an abomination unto God. I am however convinced that the unsaved cannot truly worship Him—Why? Because without accepting Christ as your personal Lord and savior, there is no re-born spirit with which to relate let alone have fellowship with God's Spirit.

I wonder how you would perceive my mental state if you saw me trying to commune or share fellowship with say an orange or a tree. I am sure your perception about me might be that I have gone crazy and understandably so because regardless of how hard I may attempt to commune or communicate with the tree or the orange, you would realize that there is no existing basis of communion.

Now you can understand why I maintain that unbelievers are unable to truly worship God. One can only worship God by the Spirit of God which unbelievers do not have because they have not been born-again.

CHAPTER 18

MODEL WORSHIP

In teaching His disciples how to pray, Jesus says in **Matthew 6:10: '10** *Your kingdom come, Your will be done on earth as it is in heaven.'*

If this is how we pray according to how Christ taught us, then we must as well know that God has a specific will concerning everything and for that matter worship. Hence in order for us to do His will here on earth as is done in heaven, I guess it's only proper that we know what God's will is as regards worship or better still how it is rendered in heaven so we can do likewise on earth. Thank God the record of the apostle's revelation concerning worship in heaven can afford us a model to learn from.

> *'1 AFTER THIS I looked, and behold, a door standing open in heaven! And the first voice which I had heard addressing me like [the calling of] a war trumpet said, Come up here, and I will show you what must take place in the future. 2 At once*

I came under the [Holy] Spirit's power, and behold, a throne
stood in heaven, with One seated on the throne!'
'10 The twenty-four elders (the members of the heavenly
Sanhedrin) fall prostrate before Him Who is sitting on the
throne, and they worship Him Who lives forever and ever; and
they throw down their crowns before the throne, crying out, 11
Worthy are You, our Lord and God, to receive the glory and the
honor and dominion, for You created all things; by Your will
they were [brought into being] and were created . . .'
Revelation 4:1, 2; 10, 11

From the above worship experience in heaven it is obvious that during worship, a couple of things happen.

CONSCIOUSNESS OF THE KING

The Bible says that the apostle saw a throne. Now who sits upon a throne is the question. Obviously the throne depicts KINGSHIP authority, power and dominion.

If there is anything at all we can learn from this, it is the fact that, we first of all need to worship with an awareness of the King. Worshipping with this consciousness will influence the manner in which we comport ourselves in His presence. Time and again I have mentioned that if there are things we will not dare do in the presence of our earthly kings, there is absolutely no room for those things to even cross our minds whilst in God's presence.

FALLING DOWN BEFORE GOD

This depicts submission and complete loss of self-esteem. We considered the expression of lying prostrate before God earlier on. This expression generally says, 'You can do as you please with me' and portrays hitting rock bottom and says 'There is nowhere else to go except to you God'. It is an expression that shows obedience and note that what was recorded in the revelation of the worship of heaven to the apostle was not mere, empty or vain tradition. The four and twenty elders must have meant every single expression in their worship to God.

Bible says in **Revelations 1:17:**

'17 When I saw Him, I fell at His feet as if dead. But He laid His right hand on me and said, Do not be afraid! I am the First and the Last,'

Revelation 7:11, 12:

'11 And all the angels were standing round the throne and round the elders [of the heavenly Sanhedrin] and the four living creatures, and they fell prostrate before the throne and worshiped God. 12 Amen! (So be it!) they cried. Blessing and glory and majesty and splendor and wisdom and thanks and honor and power and might [be ascribed] to our God to the ages and ages (forever and ever, throughout the eternities of the eternities)! Amen! (So be it!).'

Psalms 72:11

'11 Yes, all kings shall fall down before Him, all nations shall serve Him.'

CASTING DOWN CROWNS

Crowns signify the enviable results of hard work. To know that the four and twenty elders cast their crowns before God tells me that, we must cast down all that we have acquired, lived for and achieved when we come before His throne in worship. It shows that God is worth more than all our achievements and we cannot hold on to all these things in His presence. If in worship we are unable to let go of our crowns we indirectly say to God that we are not willing to receive anything either. How can we receive when our hands are full and how can we hear in the midst of distractions?

1 Corinthians 6:20 teaches us that everything we have has been bought with a price:

> '20 *You were bought with a price [purchased with a preciousness and paid for, made His own]. So then, honor God and bring glory to Him in your body.'*

Again, Genesis teaches how Abraham laid aside the thought of Isaac being a gift. He could have held on to him possessively and refused to let go. You see, when we come before God's throne in worship we should be prepared to come with our all in all—our gifts, our wealth, our crowns, and all. Nothing can be withheld. After all, every good and perfect gift comes from God and aside that He is an all knowing God so what is it that you think you successfully hide from Him? Just as was taught Abraham, I am sure God is teaching us also, the truth that He does not demand the things that are dearest to us because He needs them so desperately (after all He provided them Himself in the first place). Rather He asks for them for our own good; to release us from the control they may have or already have on us.

ARTICULATION

In *verse 11 of Revelation 4*, the Bible records what the four and twenty elders were singing. That is to say that, the song they sung was audible.

I have been in praise and worship services where I have not been able to make out a single word of what the ministers were *singing.* I kept wondering to myself—if this is what happened in heaven as regards the worship of the four and twenty elders, we might have as well not had anything written for *Revelations 4-11*, because then, the apostle wouldn't have heard let alone recorded it. It is necessary that during our praise and worship we voice out our expressions to God clearly. Yes there are times that we may groan or sing in the language of the Spirit. But, according to the Bible, as urged by the apostle, we are to sing with our spirits by the Holy Spirit within us, and with our minds and understanding too. Either way, in worship, whether or not we sing with our understanding the important thing is for us to do it well.

'14 For if I pray in an [unknown] tongue, my spirit [by the Holy Spirit within me] prays, but my mind is unproductive [it bears no fruit and helps nobody]. 15 Then what am I to do? I will pray with my spirit [by the Holy Spirit that is within me], but I will also pray [intelligently] with my mind and understanding; I will sing with my spirit [by the Holy Spirit that is within me], but I will sing [intelligently] with my mind and understanding also.' 1 Corinthians 14:14-15

A WALK THROUGH THE TABERNACLE

There are certain experiences we never get to encounter in our approach to God's presence because we have not even expected such experiences as a result of ignorance. It is said that you cannot find something unless you know what you are looking for. At times we encounter certain experiences because we have known about them and have anticipated them. Hence if what we expect to experience does not manifest, we obtain an indication that something might have probably gone wrong.

Unfortunately, there are a lot of things we hardly pay attention to in worship, because we don't even know of their existence in the first place. As a result, we never get to enjoy the full experience of worship. A story is told of a young man who never attended a buffet dinner whilst on a two-week stay onboard a ship citing his lack of money to afford it as an excuse. After staying in his ignorance for two weeks, the ship docked and eventually he met a friend whilst disembarking, who asked why he had never showed up for the sumptuous daily buffet dinner everyone else had enjoyed. Sensing his ignorance, the friend explained to him that, the buffet was part of the package he had already paid for. Because this man had not known about it, he had exempted himself from the wonderful experience and starved himself every evening.

I suppose, a clearer perspective of the outlay of the tabernacle which eventually became the temple (and which our bodies are supposed to be anyway) can help us understand the purpose and significance of certain furniture that were placed therein at God's command, and furthermore enhances our understanding of the worship experience that we are called to.

In view of this, I yield to the Spirit of God as He directs me into certain truths I will share with you over the next few pages as we explore the outlay and furnishing of the tabernacle which was assembled according to God's instructions. You will realize the relevance such furnishing has on our present day worship as individuals and as a church. The Bible specifically mentions certain things that had to be done from generations to generations and which were therefore not abandoned when a more permanent place of worship (the Temple) was built, and which we cannot afford to ignore in our present day worship, considering that they must be even more relevant now than ever, since our bodies are the temple of God.

The tabernacle was portable or moveable so it was possible to dismantle the tabernacle when the Israelites were on the move and reassemble it whenever they camped again. Taking a closer look at the tabernacle I believe may bring out the picture better. We will come to understand that though in our present day we may not visibly see and tangibly touch some of the furniture that existed in the tabernacle and the temple of old, this furnishing still has a huge spiritual significance in our worship which we cannot afford to ignore.

It is important that we recognize and acknowledge these truths and work with or towards them in our lives of worship and it is my prayer that the following few pages, (regardless of your previous knowledge) will add meaning to your worship life.

Earlier in this book I mentioned that we worship God on His terms and not on ours. You must have realized that in the olden days whenever God decided to meet with His people, even the venue was chosen by Him. Right from the days of Adam and Eve, Adam had no idea about how the Garden of Eden (the place where God's presence touched the earth) came into existence. It was God Himself who planted the garden and put them there.

Then again with Moses at the burning bush, the man did not even know he was standing on Holy Ground. God had chosen where to meet with Moses, and there are other numerous examples that show that God determined even the venue where He would meet with His people.

Is it not an honor that God has now chosen our bodies to be the temple where He would want to meet with us? The specifications for building the tabernacle were from God's directives. I believe the importance of being careful to hear and obey God's directions when it comes to 'seemingly trivial' issues like where He desires that we worship Him need to be emphasized. As to when to worship, we know that our whole lives are supposed to be full of worship to God.

I have come to learn that the Tabernacle teaches the way to reach into God's divine presence. **Hebrews 9:1-9** indicates the way into the Most Holy place according to the pattern of the Tabernacle.

1 NOW EVEN the first covenant had its own rules and regulations for divine worship, and it had a sanctuary [but one] of this world. 2 For a tabernacle (tent) was erected, in the outer division or compartment of which were the lamp stand and the table with [its loaves of] the showbread set forth. [This portion] is called the Holy Place. 3 But [inside] beyond the second curtain or veil, [there stood another] tabernacle [division] known as the Holy of Holies. 4 It had the golden altar of incense and the ark (chest) of the covenant, covered over with wrought gold. This [ark] contained a golden jar which held the manna and the rod of Aaron that sprouted and the [two stone] slabs of the covenant [bearing the Ten Commandments]. 5 Above [the ark] and overshadowing the mercy seat were the representations of the cherubim [winged creatures which were the symbols] of glory. We cannot now go into detail about these things. 6 These arrangements having thus been made, the priests enter [habitually] into the outer division of the tabernacle in performance of their ritual acts of worship. 7 But into the second [division of the tabernacle] none but the high priest goes, and he only once a year, and never without taking a sacrifice of blood with him, which he offers for himself and for the errors and sins of ignorance and thoughtlessness which the people have committed. 8 By this the Holy Spirit points out that the way into the [true Holy of] Holies is not yet thrown open as long as the former [the outer portion of the] tabernacle remains a recognized institution and is still standing, 9 Seeing that that first [outer portion of the] tabernacle was a parable (a visible symbol or type or picture of the present age). In it gifts and sacrifices are offered, and yet are incapable of perfecting the conscience or of cleansing and renewing the inner man of the worshipper.' Hebrews 9:1-9

Then ***Hebrews 9:23-24*** again mentions that:

'23 By such means, therefore, it was necessary for the [earthly] copies of the heavenly things to be purified, but the actual heavenly things themselves [required far] better and nobler sacrifices than these. 24 For Christ (the Messiah) has not entered into a sanctuary made with [human] hands, only a copy and pattern and type of the true one, but [He has entered] into heaven itself, now to appear in the [very] presence of God on our behalf.'

I believe that it could not be any clearer—the fact that the way into true worship should be a 'copy' of the tabernacle.

As earlier stated, we don't stumble into the presence of God or drop into His Holy of Holies by mistake, and we cannot afford to do whatever we choose in His presence either.

The outlay of the tabernacle—the Outer Court, The Holy Place and The Holy Of Holies—could be a parallel to the nature of God Himself (as in The Father, Son and Holy Spirit) and also to the First, Second and Third Heavens and even further the nature of man (which consist of the body, soul and spirit).

Paul mentions in *2 Corinthians 12:2* that he was caught up in the Third heaven which therefore says to me that there is a first and second heaven as well.

> *'2 I know a man in Christ who fourteen years ago—whether in the body or out of the body I do not know, God knows-was caught up to the third heaven.' 2 Corinthians 12:2*

Note also that within the Tabernacle there were three kinds of light available, which were the natural light in the court yard, the artificial light in the holy place provided by the seven-branched lamp stand and the light provided by the supernatural presence of the glory of God, otherwise referred to as the *'shekinah'* (Hebrew), in the Holy of Holies.

In summarizing what we have so far discussed, we notice that there is:

► The Outer Court where there was Natural Light and which can be paralleled to the Father (the God Head) and also to the body of man.
► The Holy Place where there was Artificial Light, paralleled to the Son and also to the soul of man.

► The Most Holy Place where there was the Shakina Glory or the Supernatural Presence, paralleled to the Holy Spirit and also to our (man's) spirit.

Now, let's keep these three points in mind as we go have a walk about in the tabernacle!!!!

THE TABERNACLE'S LAYOUT SHOWING THE OUTER COURT

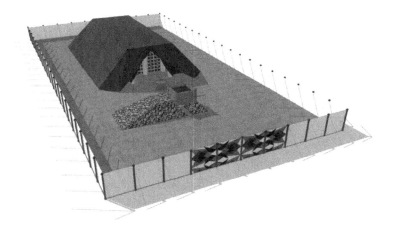

CHAPTER 19

THE TABERNACLE

THE tabernacle was like a church—more like a place to meet God. It was a structure built for worship by the Israelites according to God's own specifications and which became the centre of the Israelite community whilst they were in the wilderness. Whenever they pitched camp, the camping place for each tribe was determined in relation to the positioning of the tabernacle and I pray that the very presence of God determines where you pitch your camp in every aspect of your life. The Levites surrounded the tabernacle and the families of Moses and Aaron always camped on the east side in front of the entrance. Even whilst travelling, the tabernacle stayed in the centre, with six tribes proceeding and the other six following it. This was to consciously though 'symbolically guard' the presence of God.

POSITIONS WHERE THE TRIBES OF
ISRAEL PITCHED CAMP

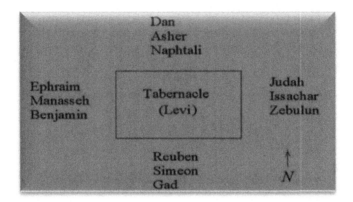

I suppose that in our daily lives of worship, considering that we carry the very presence of God in and with us, we need to 'consciously guard' this presence in our midst and as a people, allow this 'ark' to determine where we camp in every aspect of our lives. Physically, financially, martially, socially, academically, in our secular jobs, most importantly spiritually and in every other aspect of our lives, it is the presence of God that should determine our 'resting place'. And whilst on the move, through our life's journey, the presence of God needs to be right in the centre. That is to say it is the presence of God in our lives and in our midst that should determine where every decision concerning every aspect of our lives rests.

Considering that the resources used in building the tabernacle were uncommon and expensive there is no doubt about the fact that it was intended to be a very sacred gathering place. I believe it also indicates that anything related to God needs to be of the highest worth.

Note that, satisfying God's explicit directives for building the tabernacle required skills beyond those of Moses and Aaron. As a result, Bezalel and Oholiab who were the main architects, along with many skilled experts, all of whom probably learned their crafts in Egypt *(Exodus 31:1-11)* were consulted to lend their skills to the execution of God's directives as regards the building of the tabernacle.

*'1 AND THE Lord said to Moses, 2 See, I have called by name Bezalel son of Uri, the son of Hur, of the tribe of Judah. 3 And I have filled him with the Spirit of God, in wisdom and ability, in understanding and intelligence, and in knowledge, and in all kinds of craftsmanship, 4 To devise skillful works, to work in gold, and in silver, and in bronze, 5 And in cutting of stones for setting, and in carving of wood, to work in all kinds of craftsmanship. 6 And behold, I have appointed with him Aholiab son of Ahisamach, of the tribe of Dan; and to all who are wise hearted I have given wisdom and ability to make all that I have commanded you: 7 The Tent of Meeting, the ark of the Testimony, the mercy seat that is on it, all the furnishings of the tent—8 The table [of the showbread] and its utensils, the pure lamp stand with all its utensils, the altar of incense, 9 The altar of burnt offering with all its utensils, the laver and its base-10 The finely worked garments, the holy garments for Aaron the [high] priest and for his sons to minister as priests, 11 And the anointing oil and incense of sweet spices for the Holy Place. According to all that I have commanded you shall they do.' **Exodus 31:1-11**

I have come to understand that preparing a meeting place for God may place a demand on our God-given skills and in some cases the skills required may transcend the individual capabilities we've been blessed with at a particular point in time. This shows that it is very natural for us to encounter times when we may need the help of the 'Bezalels' and 'Oholiabs' of our time—men with skill. And that's another reason why sometimes we need praise leaders, lead worshippers, and instrumentalists who are skillful to be called upon to help prepare the congregations to meet with God. Again even as lead worshippers, it's important to note that there may come times when you (for one reason or the other) may not be able to execute your duties explicitly to glorify God due to the lack of a certain level of skill and it is in such times that you will need help from some other persons who God might have endowed with that required level of skill. In such times, please don't be proud or feel too big in your shoes to approach others for help. After all, if we all understand that it is not about us but about an ultimate aim of reaching and satisfying God Almighty then the issue of who did what and the laying claim to fame and human praise should never be thought of in our midst. It may be a church member's help, or an instrumentalist's help or the help of another minstrel that you may need to accomplish God's will. God knows your capabilities and knows the areas in which you lack certain skills as well, and He still called you into ministry. Don't be surprised then that He may lead you along certain paths where you may feel inadequate. It could be to train you and to bring the best out of you by cajoling you to develop your skills. On the other hand, it could also be because He knows that He has given grace to someone else around you, whose help you can solicit (if only you would lay aside pride) to accomplish your service in ministry. God must have known that Moses and Aaron were not as skillful as Bezalel and Oholiab (at least in a certain field of craftsmanship), yet He still gave directives to Moses to build the Tabernacle within which He would meet with His people. I believe if the two of them had strived to do it all by themselves just to gain some selfish human praise and fame they would have messed up big time and not attained the perfection that God desired. The fact that someone's help was solicited does not make that person a better person before God—so what is the problem?

Beyond skilled labor, however, the Israelites needed resources. Have you ever thought about the fact that it was impossible to have mined gold, bronze, and silver on a desert? Yet all these were used in beautifying the place where God was to meet with His people. Of course, the Israelites did not dig mines on the dessert—the people themselves contributed their resources (their gold, silver and jewelry). They gave so generously that they eventually had to be stopped from giving.

> '6 So Moses commanded and it was proclaimed in all the camp. Let no man or woman do anything more for the sanctuary offering. So the people were restrained from bringing, 7 For the stuff they had was sufficient to do all the work and more. . '
> **Exodus 36:6&7**

There is the need to realize that in spite of our efforts and God—given divine skill, there comes a time when we also need to sacrifice physical, tangible and fiscal resources. This is because God may ask us to find gold in the desert to prepare a place to meet with Him. In such times there is the need for us to sacrifice whatever we can so as to provide whatever God demands of us.

One other important thing, worthy of note is that fact that, whenever the tabernacle was dismantled and was to be moved, various families had specific jobs: the Kohathites transported the more sacred items, using the carrying poles.

'1 AND THE Lord said to Moses and Aaron, 2 Take a census of the Kohathite division among the sons of Levi, by their families, by their fathers' houses, 3 From thirty years old and up to fifty years old, all who can enter the service to do the work in the Tent of Meeting. 4 This shall be the responsibility of the sons of Kohath in the Tent of Meeting: the most holy things. 5 When the camp prepares to set forward, Aaron and his sons shall take down the veil [screening the Holy of Holies] and cover the ark of the Testimony with it, 6 And shall put on it the covering of dolphin or porpoise skin, and shall spread over that a cloth wholly of blue, and shall put in place the poles of the ark. 7 And upon the table of showbread they shall spread a cloth of blue and put on it the plates, the dishes for incense, the bowls, the flagons for the drink offering, and also the continual showbread. 8 And they shall spread over them a cloth of scarlet, and put over that a covering of dolphin or porpoise skin, and put in place the poles [for carrying]. 9 And they shall take a cloth of blue and cover the lamp stand for the light and its lamps, its snuffers, its ashtrays, and all the oil vessels from which it is supplied. 10 And they shall put the lamp stand and all its utensils within a covering of dolphin or porpoise skin and shall put it upon the frame [for carrying]. 11 And upon the golden [incense] altar they shall spread a cloth of blue, and cover it with a covering of dolphin or porpoise skin, and shall put in place its poles [for carrying]. 12 And they shall take all the utensils of the service with which they minister in the sanctuary, and put them in a cloth of blue, and cover them with a covering of dolphin or porpoise skin, and shall put them on the frame [for carrying]. 13 And they shall take away the ashes from the altar [of burnt offering] and spread a purple cloth over it. 14 And they shall

put upon it all its vessels and utensils with which they minister there, the fire pans, the flesh hooks or forks, the shovels, the basins, and all the vessels and utensils of the altar, and they shall spread over it all a covering of dolphin or porpoise skin, and shall put in its poles [for carrying]. 15

When Aaron and his sons have finished covering the sanctuary and all its furniture, as the camp sets out, after all that [is done but not before], the sons of Kohath shall come to carry them. But they shall not touch the holy things, lest they die. These are the things of the Tent of Meeting which the sons of Kohath are to carry. 16 And Eleazar son of Aaron the priest shall have charge of the oil for the light, the fragrant incense, the continual cereal offering, and the anointing oil, with the oversight of all the tabernacle and of all that is in it, of the sanctuary and its utensils. 17 And the Lord said to Moses and Aaron, 18 [Since] the tribe of the families of the Kohathites [are only Levites and not priests], do not [by exposing them to the sin of touching the most holy things] cut them off from among the Levites. 19 But deal thus with them that they may live and not die when they approach the most holy things: Aaron and his sons shall go in and appoint them each to his work and to his burden [to be carried on the march]. 20 But [the Kohathites] shall not go in to see the sanctuary [the Holy Place and the Holy of Holies] or its holy things, even for an instant, lest they die. '
Numbers 4:1-20

The Gershonites handled all the soft furnishing, the altar of sacrifice, and its accessories.

'21 And the Lord said to Moses, 22 Take a census of the sons of Gershon, by their fathers' houses, by their families. 23 From thirty years old and up to fifty years old you shall number them, all who enter for service to do the work in the Tent of Meeting. 24 This is the service of the families of the Gershonites, in serving and in bearing burdens [when on the march]: 25 And they shall carry the curtains of the tabernacle, and the Tent of Meeting, its covering, and the covering of dolphin or porpoise skin that is on top of it, and the hanging or screen for the door of the Tent of Meeting, 26 And the hangings of the court, and the hanging or screen for the entrance of the gate of the court which is around the tabernacle and the altar [of burnt offering], and their cords, and all the equipment for their service; whatever needs to be done with them, that they shall do. 27 Under the direction of Aaron and his sons shall be all the service of the sons of the Gershonites, in all they have to carry and in all they have to do; and you shall assign to their charge all that they are to carry [on the march]. 28 This is the service of the families of the sons of Gershon in the Tent of Meeting; and their work shall be under the direction of Ithamar son of Aaron, the [high] priest . . . '

Numbers 4:21-28

Whilst the Merarites were responsible for the hard furnishing, such as the frames, bars, and bases.

'29 As for the sons of Merari, you shall number them by their families and their fathers' houses; 30 From thirty years old up to fifty years old you shall number them, everyone who enters the service to do the work of the Tent of Meeting. 31 And this is

what they are assigned to carry and to guard [on the march],
according to all their service in the Tent of Meeting: the boards
or frames of the tabernacle, and its bars, and its pillars, and
its sockets or bases, 32 And the pillars of the court roundabout
with their sockets or bases, and pegs, and cords, with all their
equipment and all their accessories for service; and you shall
assign to them by name the articles which they are to carry
[on the march]. 33 This is the work of the families of the sons
of Merari, according to all their tasks in the Tent of Meeting,
under the direction of Ithamar son of Aaron, the [high] priest. '
Numbers 4:29-33

In carrying the presence of God in our churches, corporately and as individuals we need to appreciate that God desires an exceptionally high level of order. People need to understand and respect the fact that there are different responsibilities for different people as determined by God and these different responsibilities must be carried out with reverence. Note that it is not everyone and anyone who was to carry the hard furnishing, nor was everyone supposed to carry the soft furnishing; again it was not the strongest that were responsible for the poles. The key is that each one had a duty to perform as God desired. What is your God-given responsibility? Even in the Praise and Worship team, for some, their calling may be to pray for the team and the church, whilst for others, theirs may be to be lead vocalist and yet for others, theirs may be just to back the lead vocalists. Would it therefore surprise you if it turned out to be somebody's responsibility in the church or in the Praise and Worship Team, to ensure that the presence of God that you carry is preserved? If you acknowledge that as a possibility, then be careful not to get offended when someone plays their role by rebuking you occasionally. After all, they may just be 'carrying their hard furniture', or for that matter performing their duties.

As a corporate body (or a church), it is important that we play our roles in carrying the presence without trying to individually do everything all by ourselves. In fact, we don't even determine for ourselves what we want to do. We ask God what He will have us do. It is God who determines and delegates our duties. There is therefore the need for us to appreciate each other's duties and work hard to compliment each other's efforts in our bid to preserve God's presence in our midst. By so doing we will be able to eliminate every form of 'identity crisis'. Does it not alarm you that it was when Lucifer lost sight of and refused to play his role in heaven, that pride must have entered him, the consequence being an 'identity crisis' which eventually lead to his being thrown out of God's presence? I am sure that even up to date, many are being cast down from the presence of God as a result of pride. Don't take your eyes off the ball—just play your part and refuse to be distracted by any form of *'identity crises'*.

Regarding the building of the tabernacle, when all other items had been completely fitted every piece except the 'place of atonement' or the cover of the ark between the cherubim were anointed with special oil and set aside for their specific function. The climax of this was when the glory of the Lord filled the inner tent which teaches me that, should we be mindful of the manner in which we approach God, by setting ourselves apart, dedicating and sanctifying all that we come before God with, the obvious climax would be a tangible manifestation of His Glory.

'34 Then the cloud [the Shekinah, God's visible presence] covered the Tent of Meeting, and the glory of the Lord filled the tabernacle! 35 And Moses was not able to enter the Tent of Meeting because the cloud remained upon it, and the glory of the Lord filled the tabernacle. 36 In all their journeys, whenever the cloud was taken up from over the tabernacle, the Israelites went onward; 37 But if the cloud was not taken up, they did not journey on till the day that it was taken up. 38 For throughout all their journeys the cloud of the Lord was upon the tabernacle by day, and fire was in it by night, in the sight of all the house of Israel.' **Exodus 40:34-38**

Scripture says that He came to be present among His people, and thereafter the cloud by day and fire by night provided a reassurance of His presence and guidance. What gives you a reassurance of God's presence and guidance in your walk of worship? With this understanding, we can now take a closer look at the layout of the temple as was directed by God.

A CLOSER LOOK AT THE COURTYARD OUTLAY OF THE TABERNACLE

► The layout

The courtyard was the outermost part of the tabernacle and accommodated the *brazen altar* and *the laver* or wash basin—both significant and worth taking a closer look at.

Just as in the case of the tabernacle where natural light was encountered in the courts, when we approach God, we do so starting from our natural physical nature which entails our natural senses and knowledge. In the courts, we are entreated to praise God, which we do by lending the members of our body to such expressions as lifting up of hands and dancing amongst others, in acknowledgement of what the Father has done and will do for us.

BRAZEN ALTAR

Right within the courtyard stood the altar for burning sacrifices. Aside burning sacrifices, there was yet an additional significance of this altar. At the corners of the altar were carved horns overlaid with bronze. These horns may have been useful to tie up animals before sacrificing them, yet these horns had some other significance.

For protection, a person in Israel who felt rejection and neglect and a victim of injustice when being sought after could run to the altar and cling to the horns; and so long as this person held unto the horns of the brazen altar, he could not be harmed by anyone. Now, even in our modern churches, all manner of people with different experiences of neglect, injustice and rejection still run into the church (or to the altar for that matter) in search of solace and refuge.

The altar stood immediately inside the courtyard and was for burning sacrifices. As a prerequisite for entering into God's presence, sinners had to offer animal or grain sacrifices to demonstrate remorse for their sins. It was impossible for a sinful man to go into the presence of God and look upon His glory and live. Hence, sacrifices had to be offered for the cleansing of sins in those days to enable a progression to the next stage in the courtyard. However, just as people are exempted from reading certain courses, after considering their educational credentials when joining an educational institution (because it could be assumed that certain things have already been catered for), so are we who are born again, spirit-filled, Christ believing members of the universal church exempted from performing sacrifices on the *'Brazen Altar'* because of the one and only perfect sacrifice, Christ performed on our behalf, which has catered for all such grain and animal sacrifices.

That is why it is impossible for one to access the presence of God if they are not born again. As Christians therefore, knowing that Jesus Christ was sacrificed for our sins and has fully paid for our sins by performing that one perfect sacrifice, we need not perform these animal and grain sacrifices anymore. We however learn here that our whole worship experience therefore starts at the cross, where Jesus paid that one and perfect sacrifices on our behalf so we can bypass the brazen altar. Note however that, we can only bypass the brazen altar if we have truly accepted Christ as our personal Savior and Lord by acknowledging that one perfect sacrifice He offered on the cross. It is impossible therefore to ignore the CROSS. Having 'removed' the brazen altar (by performing the perfect sacrifice), the 'vacuum created by its removal' in the tabernacle setting is therefore now filled with the cross—our only bridge to the Holy place. So until we acknowledge and accept the sacrifice of the cross we may probably just stay in the courtyard—at best offering thanksgiving and praise.

With this in mind, we can now progress to the next stage within the tabernacle.

LAVER

Exodus 30:17-21

'17 And the Lord said to Moses, 18 You shall also make a laver or large basin of bronze, and its base of bronze, for washing; and you shall put it [outside in the court] between the Tent of

Meeting and the altar [of burnt offering], and you shall put water in it; 19 There Aaron and his sons shall wash their hands and their feet. 20 When they go into the Tent of Meeting, they shall wash with water, that they die not; or when they come near to the altar to minister, to burn an offering made by fire to the Lord, 21 So they shall wash their hands and their feet, lest they die; it shall be a perpetual statute for [Aaron] and his descendants throughout their generations . . .'

THE POSITION OF THE LAVER RELATIVE TO THE HOLY PLACE AND THE BRAZEN ALTAR

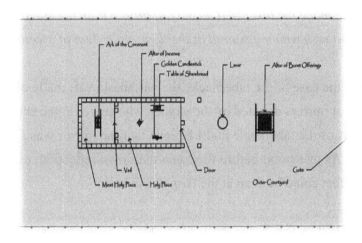

The laver or washbasin was set between the brazen altar and the inner tent of the tabernacle. By standing in front of the entrance to the inner tent, the washbasin protected the inner portions of the tabernacle from being tainted with dirt. God is holy, and He required that the priests 'clean up' before ministering in the tent of the tabernacle.

For me, it signifies the fact that, quite apart from having the atonement for sins, there is the need for each person to make an additional conscious effort to ensure their cleanliness before approaching the presence of God.

In Solomon's temple, a large laver called the *"molten sea"* was placed between the altar of burnt offerings in the courtyard and the entrance to the inner temple. This consisted of the large basin and the pedestal on which it sat. The pedestal was made of bronze or brass, melted and shaped from mirrors or highly polished metal given by Israelite women.

Exodus 38:8

'8 He made the laver and its base of bronze from the mirrors of the women who ministered at the door of the Tent of Meeting.'

Even in the case of the tabernacle, the washbasin was made of bronze and out of mirrors donated by the women who served at the entrance to the court of the tabernacle and I believe that the mirror was symbolic as well. As one stood before the basin their own reflection, especially of their feet could be seen at the base of the basin.

This could therefore be symbolic of the need to assess one's self. Again, seeing one's feet's reflection could serve as a reminder of where the person had trod with their feet before coming to God. In spite of the sacrifice that has been performed on our behalf by Christ Jesus, there are times that, as human as we are, we go astray and hence need this self assessment.

It is important to note that, attending upon the laver was compulsory, and its neglect before entering the Holy Place was punishable by death. For me this emphasizes the need for us to assess ourselves as we approach God to ensure that we don't defile His presence—we can't afford to take salvation for granted, go astray and expect that we can just stroll casually back into His presence. Note that so many things may represent 'spiritual dirt' in our day and we must 'clean up' before we step into the Holy Place. This unlike the sacrifice that Christ performed for us once and for all has to be done as frequently as we approach God's presence. Hence, though born again, as one stands before the entrance of the inner tent there is the need to ensure a right standing with God. There is the need for us to be clean, sanctified, pure, holy, tried and true so as not to carry filth into God's presence.

Lord Prepare me,
To be a Sanctuary; Pure and Holy, Tried and True;
With thanksgiving, I will be a living,
Sanctuary for You.

This mirror at the base of the laver could also be symbolic of the word of God which is likened to a mirror according to ***James 1:23***

'23 For if anyone only listens to the Word without obeying it and being a doer of it, he is like a man who looks carefully at his [own] natural face in a mirror; 24 For he thoughtfully observes himself, and then goes off and promptly forgets what he was like.'

If the word of God serves as a mirror in which our real spiritual nature is reflected, thereby revealing all our inadequacies, then it means that, in our bid to reach into the presence of God, there is the need to enrich ourselves with His Word, which will reflect our true nature in order that we 'clean up' wherever and whenever the need arises.

Again, water which was contained in the laver, (which was used for washing the hands and feet), could as well be symbolic of the Word of God, only this time, as a purifier. So as we approach the presence of God, there is the need to purify ourselves with the word of God.

> *Ephesians 5:25-27:*
> *'25 Husbands, love your wives, as Christ loved the church and gave Himself up for her, 26 So that He might sanctify her, having cleansed her by the washing of water with the Word, 27 That He might present the church to Himself in glorious splendor, without spot or wrinkle or any such things [that she might be holy and faultless].'*

Hence we see our true state as we look into the word of God which reflects our true nature at any point in time and furthermore purifying ourselves with the same Word in order to be accepted when we step into the Holy place.

CHAPTER 20

A CLOSER LOOK AT THE INNER TENT

THE HOLY PLACE

THE Holy Place was the first part of the inner tent of the tabernacle. The priests would enter here to carry out their daily routines on behalf of God's people. As mentioned earlier, in the olden days, the priests would perform worship on behalf of the people but in our present day we are a royal priesthood and have the inherent ability to perform worship ourselves by the Spirit of God. Now let us step into the holy place as a royal priesthood and a chosen people, to see the true significance of the furnishing there as well.

Inside the Holy Place were three special pieces of furniture.

▶ THE TABLE OF THE BREAD OF THE PRESENCE
▶ INCENSE ALTAR
▶ GOLDEN LAMPSTAND

THE TABLE OF THE BREAD OF THE PRESENCE

This bread consisted of twelve loaves made of the finest flour, as referred to in the following Scriptures:

> *'30 And you shall set the showbread (the bread of the Presence) on the table before Me always . . .'*
> **Exodus 25:30**

> *'32 Of their Kohathite kinsmen, some were to prepare the showbread every Sabbath.'*
> **1 Chronicles 9:32**

> *'7 And upon the table of showbread they shall spread a cloth of blue and put on it the plates, the dishes for incense, the bowls, the flagons for the drink offering, and also the continual showbread.'*
> **Numbers 4:7**

1 THEN DAVID went to Nob, to Ahimelech the priest; and Ahimelech was afraid at meeting David, and said to him, Why are you alone and no man with you? 2 David said to Ahimelech the priest, The king has charged me with a matter and has told me, Let no man know anything of the mission on which I send you and with what I have charged you. I have appointed the young men to a certain place. 3 Now what do you have on hand? Give me five loaves of bread, or whatever you may have. 4 And the priest answered David, There is no common bread on hand, but there is hallowed bread—if the young men have kept themselves at least from women. 5 And David told the priest, Truly women have been kept from us in these three days since I came out, and the food bags and utensils of the young men are clean, and although the bread will be used in a secular way, it will be set apart in the clean bags. 6 So the priest gave him holy bread, for there was no bread there but the showbread which was taken from before the Lord to put hot bread in its place the day when it was taken away.'

1 Samuel 21:1-6

They were flat and thin, and were placed in two rows of six each on a table in the Holy Place before the Lord and were changed every Sabbath.

'5 And you shall take fine flour and bake twelve cakes with it; two-tenths of an ephah shall be in each cake [of the showbread or bread of the Presence]. 6 And you shall set them in two rows, six in a row, upon the table of pure gold before the Lord. 7 You shall put pure frankincense [in a bowl or spoon] beside each row that it may be with the bread as a memorial portion,

an offering to be made by fire to the Lord. 8 Every Sabbath day Aaron shall set the showbread in order before the Lord continually; it is on behalf of the Israelites, an everlasting covenant. 9 And the bread shall be for Aaron and his sons, and they shall eat it in a sacred place, for it is for [Aaron] a most holy portion of the offerings to the Lord made by fire, a perpetual due [to the high priest].'
Leviticus 24:5-9

Each Sabbath, the twelve loaves of bread placed on this table had to be replaced with new ones and those that were removed were to be eaten by the priests only in the holy place.

'3 Now what do you have on hand? Give me five loaves of bread, or whatever you may have. 4 And the priest answered David, There is no common bread on hand, but there is hallowed bread-if the young men have kept themselves at least from women. 5 And David told the priest, truly women have been kept from us in these three days since I came out, and the food bags and utensils of the young men are clean, and although the bread will be used in a secular way, it will be set apart in the clean bags. 6 So the priest gave him holy bread, for there was no bread there but the showbread which was taken from before the Lord to put hot bread in its place the day when it was taken away.'
1 Samuel 21:3-6

'3 He said to them, have you not even read what David did when he was hungry, and those who accompanied him—4 How he went into the house of God and ate the loaves of the

showbread—which was not lawful for him to eat, nor for the
men who accompanied him, but for the priests only?'
Matthew 12:3-4

The number of loaves represented the twelve tribes of Israel, and also the entire spiritual Israel, (the true Israel) and placing them on the table symbolized the consecration of the entire Israel to the Lord, and their acceptance of God as their God.

The bread was arranged as directed by God Himself—in two rows of six. I have come to understand that, in approaching the Most Holy Place (the presence of God), there is the need for orderliness, according to God's instructions. We cannot do things anyhow and expect to reach into the presence of God. If he asks us to stay in two rows of six, that is what He means, that is what He demands, and that is what we must obey. No questions asked and no lackadaisical attitudes exhibited.

Actually the original translation of 'showbread is ' the bread of face' as seen in **Numbers 4:7**, and is also known as the 'continual' bread, indicating that it was continually before the face of the Lord. This indicates to me that in the Holy Place as we approach the presence of God, there is the need for us to consecrate ourselves to God entirely and continually.

Bread in scripture is indicative of strength. Remember that the Holy Place is a progression from the natural (in the courtyard where we dealt with our bodies) to the place where we now deal with the soul and how it relates to Christ. Therefore having laid the bread before God is indicative of us coming before God in total surrender of every strength in our entire soul (will, intellect and emotions) to God.

*Also Scripture says in **Psalms 104:14-15:***

> *'14 He causes vegetation to grow for the cattle, and all that the earth produces for man to cultivate, that he may bring forth food out of the earth—15 And wine that gladdens the heart of man, to make his face shine more than oil, and bread to support, refresh, and strengthen man's heart . . .'*
> ***Psalms 104:14-15***

Hence, as we surrender our strength to God, in the Holy Place, He in turn provides for all three aspects of the soul—wine speaks of our emotions, oil of our intellect and bread of our will.

Note also how in ***Joel 2:19*** God speaks of sending grain which is symbolic of the strength of the Word of God, Oil which is symbolic of the Holy Spirit and new wine which speaks of the joy of the Lord.

> *'19 Yes, the Lord answered and said to His people, Behold, I am sending you grain and juice [of the grape] and oil, and you shall be satisfied with them; and I will no more make you a reproach among the [heathen] nations'*
> ***Joel 2:19***

Now with the strengthening of our will therefore in the Holy Place, we are able to discern right from wrong and judge accurately.

> *'30 I am able to do nothing from Myself [independently, of My own accord—but only as I am taught by God and as I get His orders]. Even as I hear, I judge [I decide as I am bidden to decide. As the voice comes to Me, so I give a decision], and*

My judgment is right (just, righteous), because I do not seek or consult My own will [I have no desire to do what is pleasing to Myself, My own aim, My own purpose] but only the will and pleasure of the Father Who sent Me.'
John 5:30

It was the doing of God's will that gave Jesus strength or in other words the doing of God's will was His bread.

John 4:31-34 indicates what Jesus' food was.

'31 Meanwhile, the disciples urged Him saying, Rabbi, eat something. 32 But He assured them, I have food (nourishment) to eat of which you know nothing and have no idea. 33 So the disciples said one to another, has someone brought Him something to eat? 34 Jesus said to them, My food (nourishment) is to do the will (pleasure) of Him Who sent Me and to accomplish and completely finish His work.'

Again, in speaking of the showbread, Derek Prince once mentioned amongst other things that to make bread, the grain needs to be ground or beaten until very fine.

'28 Does one crush bread grain? No, he does not thresh it continuously. But when he has driven his cartwheel and his horses over it, he scatters it [tossing it up to the wind] without having crushed it.'
Isaiah 28:28

Thus in relation to the human will, there is the need for our human will to be bruised or beaten or better still, ground until it is smooth as flour and acceptable for God's use.

Furthermore, bread needs to be molded pointing to the fact that, in the Holy place as we approach God's most holy presence, our human will needs to be molded to suit God—the pattern being Christ Himself.

Interestingly, it is worth noting again that bread is always baked. In like manner then, our souls need to be 'baked' which indicates that our souls may have to pass through holy heat or holy fire of testing. We observe that as in the case of the Israelites, they did it symbolically every week. It is important for us I believe to lay ourselves bare before God on a regular basis, consecrating ourselves and our families to God.

GOLDEN LAMP STAND

THE SEVEN BRANCHED LAMP STANDS THAT GAVE LIGHT TO THE HOLY PLACE, DAY AND NIGHT

The stand for oil lamps or the lamp stand, otherwise called the *"candelabrum."*

Moses was commanded to make seven branches, one in the middle and three on each side-to hold the lamps.

> *'31 You shall make a lamp stand of pure gold. Of beaten and turned work shall the lamp stand be made, both its base and its shaft; its cups, its knobs, and its flowers shall be of one piece with it. 32 Six branches shall come out of the sides of it; three branches of the lamp stand out of the one side and three branches out of its other side; 33 Three cups made like almond blossoms, each with a knob and a flower on one branch, and three cups made like almond blossoms on the other branch with a knob and a flower; so for the six branches coming out of the lamp stand; 34 And on the [centre shaft] itself you shall [make] four cups like almond blossoms with their knobs and their flowers. 35 Also make a knob [on the shaft] under each pair of the six branches going out from the lamp stand and one piece with it; 36 Their knobs and their branches shall be of one piece with it; the whole of it one beaten work of pure gold. 37 And you shall make the lamps of the [lamp stand] to include a seventh one [at the top of the shaft]. [The priests] shall set up the [seven] lamps of it so they may give light in front of it. 38 Its snuffers and its ashtrays shall be of pure gold. 39 Use a talent of pure gold for it, including all these utensils.'*
> *Exodus 25:31-39*

These burned only the purest olive oil, and the stand was hammered from purest gold. The branches of the lamp stand were shaped like almond blossoms with buds and petals and snuffers and trays for trimming. The refilling of the lamps was done regularly. It is worth understanding that the tabernacle was a tent without windows, and thus, light was needed. The light provided here was artificial and was supplied by the candlestick, which, however, served as a symbol of the church or God's people. It can also symbolize the knowledge of God. It is worth noting that the light here was not the sun or of any natural source (common to everyone). It was artificial light supplied with specially prepared oil. *The knowledge of God* is in truth neither natural nor common to all men; It is over and above the natural. Let me therefore quickly mention that there is the need for the church universal, through the knowledge of God to emit an uncommon light to the world.

It is the light of God through His word that lightens up our intellect, emotions and our will (our soul). In the Holy Place therefore, as we encounter His Word, He affords us the illumination by way of spiritual enlightenment in our daily walk. That is not common or natural

Again we read of the eye as a lamp of the body and also as the knowledge of right and wrong.

> *'22 The eye is the lamp of the body. So if your eye is sound, your entire body will be full of light. 23 But if your eye is unsound, your whole body will be full of darkness. If then the very light in you [your conscience] is darkened, how dense is that darkness!* **Matthew 6:22-23**

> *'33 No one after lighting a lamp puts it in a cellar or crypt or under a bushel measure, but on a lamp stand, that those who are coming in may see the light. 34 Your eye is the lamp*

of your body; when your eye (your conscience) is sound and fulfilling its office, your whole body is full of light; but when it is not sound and is not fulfilling its office, your body is full of darkness. 35 Be careful, therefore, that the light that is in you is not darkness. 36 If then your entire body is illuminated, having no part dark, it will be wholly bright [with light], as when a lamp with its bright rays gives you light.' **Luke 11:33-36**

The Bible again speaks of Christ as the Light of the World

'12 Once more Jesus addressed the crowd. He said, I am the Light of the world. He who follows Me will not be walking in the dark, but will have the Light which is Life.' **John 8:12**

We are also warned to pay attention to the prophetic word as a light shining in the dark.

'19 And we have the prophetic word [made] firmer still. You will do well to pay close attention to it as to a lamp shining in a dismal (squalid and dark) place, until the day breaks through [the gloom] and the Morning Star rises (comes into being) in your hearts.' **2 Peter 1:19**

'23 For the commandment is a lamp, and the whole teaching [of the law] is light, and reproofs of discipline are the way of life,' **Proverbs 6:23**

Note that God and the spirit of man are also symbolized as lamps in *2 Samuel 22:29:*

'29 For You, O Lord, are my Lamp; the Lord lightens my darkness.' **2 Samuel 22:29**

'27 The spirit of man [that factor in human personality which proceeds immediately from God] is the lamp of the Lord, searching all his innermost parts.' **Proverbs 20:27**

While in **Proverbs 13:9** "lamp" is synonymous with the essence of life itself.

'9 The light of the [uncompromisingly] righteous [is within him—it grows brighter and] rejoices, but the lamp of the wicked [furnishes only a derived, temporary light and] shall be put out shortly.' **Proverbs 13:9**

From all the aforementioned Scriptures therefore, the lamp stand could be likened to the human intellect (or knowledge) which is enlightened by the purest olive oil which is symbolic of the Holy Spirit. Meaning that our intellect as part of our human soul needs to be fuelled and called to be dependent on the Holy Spirit as we draw near to God for enlightenment. In fact, every thought has to be brought into captivity and the obedience of Christ which can only be done via the illumination of the Word of God which is Christ Himself.

Note also that the lamp stand required daily attention, to keep burning efficiently and thus had to be refueled regularly. Can I suggest therefore that in a bid to get into the Most Holy Place in our worship, we will encounter the golden lamp stand in the Holy Place which will demand our regular attention—This symbolizes the knowledge of God, Christ as the Light of the World, the true teaching that shines like light in the dark, and in fact the essence of life itself.

One definitely cannot afford to remain the same after encountering the golden lamp stand and attending to it as the case may be. You now see why He says no one can enter into the Kingdom of God except through Him. To get into the presence of God, one will have to pass through the Holy Place where the artificial light (Christ) is.

INCENSE ALTAR

The Golden Incense Altar—located in the Holy place of the tabernacle just outside the Holy of Holies

*'1 AND YOU shall make an altar to burn incense upon; of acacia wood you shall make it. 2 A cubit shall be its length and a cubit its breadth; its top shall be square and it shall be two cubits high. Its horns shall be of one piece with it. 3 And you shall overlay it with pure gold, its top and its sides roundabout and its horns, and you shall make a crown (a rim or molding) of gold around it. 4 You shall make two golden rings under the rim of it, on the two ribs on the two opposite sides of it; and they shall be holders for the poles with which to carry it. 5 And you shall make the poles of acacia wood, overlaid with gold. 6 You shall put the altar [of incense] in front and outside of the veil that screens the ark of the Testimony, before the mercy seat that is over the Testimony (the Law, the tables of stone), where I will meet with you. 7 And Aaron shall burn on it incense of sweet spices; every morning when he trims and fills the lamps he shall burn it. 8 And when Aaron lights the lamps in the evening, he shall burn it, a perpetual incense before the Lord throughout your generations. 9 You shall offer no unholy incense on the altar nor burnt sacrifice nor cereal offering; and you shall pour no libation (drink offering) on it. 10 Aaron shall make atonement upon the horns of it once a year; with the blood of the sin offering of atonement once in the year shall he make atonement upon and for it throughout your generations. It is most holy to the Lord.' **Exodus 30:1-10**

The altar of incense was the tallest object in the Holy Place. It was two cubits high as compared to everything else which was one and a half cubits high and gave off a whiff pleasurable to God.

According to God's instructions, only special incense made by a special formula, (which was not to be copied or burnt under any other condition) was to be burnt on this altar, symbolizing the fact that there is true worship that cannot under any circumstance be offered to any other but God.

The New Testament does not demand that Christians offer physical incense but it is worth noting the significance of the burning of this precious substance.

Incense also represented prayer in the olden days, as is still the case in some churches. Now unlike the brazen altar in the courtyard, this altar was not used for animal sacrifices.

If we consider the fire in the golden altar to represent our zeal, passion and purity, then comes the revelation of the requirement of having to ensure that our sacrifices and prayers are consumed in these aforementioned elements.

Therefore as we stand in the Holy Place just on the other side of the Most Holy Place (behind the veil and just on the other side of the ark—the presence of God) we must let off an odor pleasing to God, as our prayers are consumed (burned) in purity, sincerity, intensity and passion. As in the burning of incense on the altar of incense, our prayers must be pleasing to God.

Note that it was difficult work to extract the fragrant juices, and costly as well to transport them from afar off, hence this special incense was very expensive and precious, and made a befitting offering to God as can be seen from *Malachi 1:11*:

'11 For from the rising of the sun to its setting My name shall be great among the nations, and in every place incense shall be offered to My name, and indeed a pure offering; for My name shall be great among the nations, says the Lord of hosts . . .'
Malachi 1:11

Incense offerings also provided a tangible (or smell-able) sense of God's holiness in the tabernacle's inner tent and the smoke rising to the sky symbolized the prayers of the people.

'2 Let my prayer be set forth as incense before You, the lifting up of my hands as the evening sacrifice.' **Psalms 141:2**

'10 And all the throng of people were praying outside [in the court] at the hour of incense [burning].' **Luke 1:10**

'8 And when He had taken the scroll, the four living creatures and the twenty-four elders [of the heavenly Sanhedrin] prostrated themselves before the Lamb. Each was holding a harp (lute or guitar), and they had golden bowls full of incense (fragrant spices and gums for burning), which are the prayers of God's people (the saints).' **Revelations 5:8**

'3 And another angel came and stood over the altar. He had a golden censer, and he was given very much incense (fragrant spices and gums which exhale perfume when burned), that he might mingle it with the prayers of all the people of God (the saints) upon the golden altar before the throne. 4 And the smoke of the incense (the perfume) arose in the presence of God, with

the prayers of the people of God (the saints), from the hand of the angel.' **Revelations 8:3-4**

At the same time, the smoke in the temple could symbolize the presence of God, just as it had once been portrayed by the cloud in the wilderness.

'18 Mount Sinai was wrapped in smoke, for the Lord descended upon it in fire; its smoke ascended like that of a furnace, and the whole mountain quaked greatly . . . ' **Exodus 19:18**

'9 When Moses entered the tent, the pillar of cloud would descend and stand at the door of the tent, and the Lord would talk with Moses. 10 And all the people saw the pillar of cloud stand at the tent door, and all the people rose up and worshiped, every man at his tent door.' **Exodus 33:9-10**

'25 And the Lord came down in the cloud and spoke to him, and took of the Spirit that was upon him and put It upon the seventy elders; and when the Spirit rested upon them, they prophesied [sounding forth the praises of God and declaring His will]. Then they did so no more.' **Numbers 11:25**

Again, together with the rising sun, the smoke provided a powerful symbol of the glory of the Lord.

'1 IN THE year that King Uzziah died, [in a vision] I saw the Lord sitting upon a throne, high and lifted up, and the skirts of His train filled the [most holy part of the] temple. 2 Above Him stood the seraphim; each had six wings: with two [each]

covered his [own] face, and with two [each] covered his feet, and with two [each] flew. 3 And one cried to another and said, Holy, holy, holy is the Lord of hosts; the whole earth is full of His glory! 4 And the foundations of the thresholds shook at the voice of him who cried, and the house was filled with smoke. 5 Then said I, Woe is me! For I am undone and ruined, because I am a man of unclean lips, and I dwell in the midst of a people of unclean lips; for my eyes have seen the King, the Lord of hosts! 6 Then flew one of the seraphim [heavenly beings] to me, having a live coal in his hand which he had taken with tongs from off the altar; 7 And with it he touched my mouth and said, Behold, this has touched your lips; your iniquity and guilt are taken away, and your sin is completely atoned for and forgiven . . . '
Isaiah 6:1-7

In the New Testament also, the Christian's testimony about Christ is compared to the offering of incense.

'14 But thanks be to God, Who in Christ always leads us in triumph [as trophies of Christ's victory] and through us spreads and makes evident the fragrance of the knowledge of God everywhere, 15 For we are the sweet fragrance of Christ [which exhales] unto God, [discernible alike] among those who are being saved and among those who are perishing. '
2 Corinthians 2:14-15

Likewise, money from the Philippians came to Paul in the form of an incense sacrifice—an expensive expression of love and devotion.

'18 But I have [your full payment] and more; I have everything
I need and am amply supplied, now that I have received from
Epaphroditus the gifts you sent me. [They are the] fragrant
odor of an offering and sacrifice which God welcomes and in
which He delights.'
Philippians 4:18

Actually, incense seemed to sanctify and accompany the prayers of the saints into the presence of God which says to me that as we stand in the holy place and attend upon the altar of incense, our prayers and a sweet smelling sacrifices, precious and befitting for God, are consumed in our passion and intensity of worship.

We bear the ultimate testimony about Christ as we give off our very best (our most costly worship).

Whatever we offer here needs to be pure and sanctified, costly, pure, intense and passionate and should exclude sweet talk. Note that in **Leviticus 2:11** God specifically mentioned that He did not want any honey on the offerings of the Lord made by fire.

Scripture teaches us that, once a year, the horns of the golden altar of incense had to be purified with the blood of the propitiatory sacrifice on the Day of Atonement—an indication of the fact that it is only by Christ's Blood that we gain access into God's presence and not sweet elements.

In the olden days, in attending upon the golden altar of incense, one would almost be standing in His very presence, since the Holy Place was directly on the other side of the ark separated by just the veil.

245

Now, at the crucifixion of Jesus, this veil was ripped in two which suggests to me that, after the one and only perfect sacrifice was made on our behalf, we now have direct access into the Holy of Holies.

It was only the priests that could enter the Holy Place, so you can imagine how this whole spectacle that has been described was kept away from the eyes of the entire Israelite community, (since the furthest they could get was the outside of the inner tent beyond which the priests and the High priest would enter the Holy Place to perform these duties on their behalf).

However we (who are Christians) are a royal priesthood and a chosen generation as specified by the Bible and so we are able to enter into the Holy Place as priests. Not only that, but after entering into the Holy Place, unlike in the days of old when it was only the High Priest who was allowed into the Most Holy Place, through the one and only perfect sacrifice we now have a direct, and 'unlimited' access into the Most Holy Place where the very presence of God (which was in those days represented by the ark) rests. Is it not amazing that after so long a time subsequent to Adam and Eve being driven away from the Garden of Eden (the place where God's presence touched the earth) that we are now able to come freely once again into His presence?

So now we have access into the Holy Of Holies, the Most Holy Place where we can find the ark of God which was symbolic of the presence of God, with our bodies, our souls (will, intellect and emotions) and our spirits well prepared and pleasing to God.

CHAPTER 21

A CLOSER LOOK AT THE MOST HOLY PLACE & THE ARK OF THE COVENANT

THE Ark of the Covenant was the most important piece of furniture in the wilderness tabernacle. It represented God's presence with humanity. It was portable like everything else in the tabernacle with long wooden poles covered with gold passing through gold rings at each lower corner.

THE ARK OF THE COVENANT

'*4 It had the golden altar of incense and the ark (chest) of the covenant, covered over with wrought gold. This [ark] contained a golden jar which held the manna and the rod of Aaron that sprouted and the [two stone] slabs of the covenant [bearing the Ten Commandments].*'
Hebrews 9:4

The Ark of the Covenant contained:

▶ A CONTAINER FOR THE TWO TABLETS OF THE COVENANT GIVEN TO MOSES
▶ A POT OF MANNA
▶ AARON'S ROD THAT SPROUTED

A CONTAINER FOR THE TWO TABLETS OF THE COVENANT GIVEN TO MOSES

This was then covered with the atonement cover above which and between the two golden Cherubims, the Lord would speak.

> *'16 And you shall put inside the ark the Testimony [the Ten Commandments] which I will give you.'*
> ***Exodus 25:16***

▶ *The Tablets Also Called The 'Testimony'*

After Moses broke the tablets of the Ten Commandments that God gave him on the mountain, the second one which was written with God's finger was to be hidden in the ark. That is why the ark was sometimes called the "ark of the testimony." By this the Israelites were reminded constantly of the Holy Law of God it contained and the need for them to follow God's will as enshrined in His 'covenant'.

In our present day, with us being temples of God who carry His presence, the Word of God should be hidden in us as well. I suppose that is why in *Hebrews 8:8-10*, God pledges to put His laws into our minds, and write them in our hearts.

For me, this implies that when we get into the Most Holy Place our lives need to be turned around and affected by the will of God as shown in His Word which we encounter. Hence, it cannot be overemphasized that in His presence, we are bound to encounter God's word and will for our lives.

A POT OF MANNA & AARON'S ROD THAT SPROUTED & THE TABLETS OF THE TEN COMMANDMENTS

▶ *The Pot of Manna*

Manna was the miraculous food provided by God

> '*33 And Moses said to Aaron, Take a pot and put an omer of manna in it, and lay it up before the Lord, to be kept throughout your generations.' Exodus 16:33*

God made sure that throughout the wilderness experience He provided for them each day's manna. Note that no one was supposed to keep the manna for the next day; and those who did suffered the consequences. The manna got infested with worms and stank.

> '*19 Moses said, Let none of it be left until morning. 20 But they did not listen to Moses; some of them left of it until morning, and it bred worms, became foul, and stank; and Moses was angry with them.' Exodus 16:19-20*

> '*48 I am the Bread of Life [that gives life—the Living Bread]. 49 Your forefathers ate the manna in the wilderness, and [yet] they died. 50 [But] this is the Bread that comes down from heaven, so that [any] one may eat of it and never die.' John 6:48-50*

And then in *Revelations 2:17* he says:

> '*17 He who is able to hear, let him listen to and heed what the Spirit says to the assemblies (churches). To him who overcomes (conquers), I will give to eat of the manna that is hidden, and I will give him a white stone with a new name engraved on the stone, which no one knows or understands except he who receives it.'*

251

Therefore, in the presence of God, we feed on Christ, our manna via our spiritual communion with Him.

The Golden Pot of Manna I believe portrayed God's ability to provide for the Israelites their daily needs and in our present day as well, as we go before Him in worship, we must have an expectation of encountering God's provision. Thus, when we reach into God's Most Holy Place and encounter His presence, we must experience His provision regardless of our dry wilderness experience.

Aaron's Rod That Sprouted

> '10 And the Lord told Moses, Put Aaron's rod back before the Testimony [in the ark], to be kept as a [warning] sign for the rebels; and you shall make an end of their murmurings against Me, lest they die.' **Numbers 17:10**

This rod signified God's authority being paramount over all other authority. You will remember that in those days the people had risen against Moses and Aaron claiming to be holy too and accusing them of lording themselves over them. They were in a way fighting over the priesthood and authority. As a result, God had to prove to them who He had chosen to be in authority in order to settle the controversy. Therefore He asked for the rods from each house to be placed in the tabernacle of witness.

> '1 AND THE Lord said to Moses, 2 Speak to the Israelites and get from them rods or staves, one for each father's house, from all their leaders according to their father's houses, twelve rods. Write every man's name on his rod. 3 And you shall write

Aaron's name on the rod of Levi [his great-grandfather]. For there shall be one rod for the head of each father's house. 4 You shall lay them up in the Tent of Meeting before [the ark of] the Testimony, where I meet with you. 5 And the rod of the man whom I choose shall bud, and I will make to cease from Me the murmurings of the Israelites, which they murmur against you.

*6 And Moses spoke to the Israelites, and every one of their leaders gave him a rod or staff, one for each leader according to their fathers' houses, twelve rods, and the rod of Aaron was among their rods. 7 And Moses deposited the rods before the Lord in the Tent of the Testimony. 8 And the next day Moses went into the Tent of the Testimony, and behold, the rod of Aaron for the house of Levi had sprouted and brought forth buds and produced blossoms and yielded [ripe] almonds. 9 Moses brought out all the rods from before the Lord to all the Israelites; and they looked, and each man took his rod. 10 And the Lord told Moses, Put Aaron's rod back before the Testimony [in the ark], to be kept as a [warning] sign for the rebels; and you shall make an end of their murmurings against Me, lest they die. 11 And Moses did so; as the Lord commanded him, so he did. 12 The Israelites said to Moses, Behold, we perish, we are undone, all undone! 13 Everyone who comes near, who comes near the tabernacle of the Lord, dies or shall die! Are we all to perish?' **Numbers 17***

Undoubtedly, God proved that His authority was supreme and that He would dictate the terms.

Aaron's rod budded, which was indicative of life. When a plant buds, it is enough indication of the plant's ability to continue germination.

Again, the Bible says it blossomed. As a plant blossoms, the whole world can see it, so in saying that Aaron's rod blossomed, it was an indication of becoming a showpiece. Then Bible says that it bore ripe almonds. That is to say that it became fruitful supernaturally and over such a short period as well. Again, it's worth noting that, that it was almond fruit that it bore. It is believed that the almond plant is the first to bud and blossom after winter, when all other plants are still laying dormant. Now what does all this tell me? I am convinced that in the Holy of Holies, when we encounter the ark (which is His very presence) in which rests 'the rod of Aaron' which budded, blossomed and bore ripe almond fruit, regardless of the authorities that team up to fight against us and create controversy in a bid to overthrow us from our God-appointed positions; God's authority will surpass them all and vindicate us. We will bud, (show evidence of life) in operating our God-given gifts and ministries and blossom (become a showpiece to the whole world). Furthermore, we will bear the first fruits, when all others are dormant and unwilling to come out (when they are all still 'icy' from the wintery and dry seasons). As a result of encountering God's presence, we will be fruitful and bare ripe fruit and with supernatural speed as well. In the Holy of Holies therefore no authority can stand the authority of God and in His presence, we come alive (show signs of life). We also blossom as a showpiece to the world and become fruitful in ministry and in operating our God-given gifts.

THE LID OF THE ARK WAS CALLED THE "MERCY SEAT" OR "PLACE OF MERCY

'17 And you shall make a mercy seat (a covering) of pure gold, two cubits and a half long and a cubit and a half wide.' **Exodus 25:17**

This was a piece of gold fitting over the top of the ark and it held its own importance. Once a year, the High Priest made atonement for the people of Israel. He would sprinkle the mercy seat with the blood of bulls and goats:

'2 The Lord said to Moses, Tell Aaron your brother he must not come at all times into the Holy of Holies within the veil before the mercy seat upon the ark, lest he die; for I will appear in the cloud on the mercy seat. 3 But Aaron shall come into the holy enclosure in this way: with a young bull for a sin offering and a ram for a burnt offering. 4 He shall put on the holy linen undergarment, and he shall have the linen breeches upon his body, and be girded with the linen girdle or sash, and with the linen turban or mitre shall he be attired; these are the holy garments; he shall bathe his body in water and then put them on. 5 He shall take [at the expense] of the congregation of the Israelites two male goats for a sin offering and one ram for a

burnt offering. *6 And Aaron shall present the bull as the sin offering for himself and make atonement for himself and for his house [the other priests]. 7 He shall take the two goats and present them before the Lord at the door of the Tent of Meeting. 8 Aaron shall cast lots on the two goats—one lot for the Lord, the other lot for Azazel or removal. 9 And Aaron shall bring the goat on which the Lord's lot fell and offer him as a sin offering. 10 But the goat on which the lot fell for Azazel or removal shall be presented alive before the Lord to make atonement over him, that he may be let go into the wilderness for Azazel (for dismissal). 11 Aaron shall present the bull as the sin offering for his own sins and shall make atonement for himself and for his house [the other priests], and shall kill the bull as the sin offering for himself. 12 He shall take a censer full of burning coals of fire from off the [bronze] altar before the Lord, and his two hands full of sweet incense beaten small, and bring it within the veil [into the Holy of Holies], 13 And put the incense on the fire [in the censer] before the Lord, that the cloud of the incense may cover the mercy seat that is upon [the ark of] the Testimony, lest he die. 14 He shall take of the bull's blood and sprinkle it with his finger on the front [the east side] of the mercy seat, and before the mercy seat he shall sprinkle of the blood with his finger seven times. 15 Then shall he kill the goat of the sin offering that is for [the sins of] the people and bring its blood within the veil [into the Holy of Holies] and do with that blood as he did with the blood of the bull, and sprinkle it on the mercy seat and before the mercy seat. 16 Thus he shall make atonement for the Holy Place because of the uncleanness of the Israelites and because of their transgressions, even all their sins; and so shall he do for the Tent of Meeting,*

that remains among them in the midst of their uncleanness.'
Leviticus 16:2-16

In fact, the English expression "mercy seat" is related to the word "atone." The lid was called a "seat" because the Lord was considered as enthroned between two cherubims (winged creatures) and that's why it is sometimes referred to as the seat of atonement as well.

> *'1 THE LORD reigns, let the peoples tremble [with reverential fear]! He sits [enthroned] above the cherubim, let the earth quake!'*
> *Psalms 99:1*

The Lord spoke to Moses from between the cherubim:

> *'89 And when Moses went into the Tent of Meeting to speak with the Lord, he heard the voice speaking to him from above the mercy seat that was upon the ark of the Testimony from between the two cherubim; and He spoke to [Moses].'*
> *Numbers 7:89*

Symbolically therefore, I can say that God has made enough provision and arrangements to meet with His people any time we seek Him in His Most Holy Place where He is enthroned—which is the secret place of the Most High.

Provided we appreciate, acknowledge and honor the symbolic connotations at each stage along the way from the Court Yard via the Holy Place to the Most Holy Place, we can rest assured that we would have done the right thing to position us in the right place to hear Him speak in His majesty.

Even more than ever you should now understand why in sincere worship, the gift of prophecy is usually born. After all, when God is enthroned and we are in the right place to hear Him speak directly to us, then we can in turn speak forth His mind when He affords us the honor by grace. I am sure that the clarity of God calling out to Samuel must have been enhanced symbolically due to His closeness to the Ark of God. In like manner, I trust that if we are rightly positioned, we are bound to hear the voice of the Most High.

At this point, I have no words, worthy of describing the ultimate experience which can be so intimately experienced by anyone who will learn to do the right thing in preparing to meet with God.

CHAPTER 22

DON'T DARE!!!

MOST often, we consciously or unconsciously take God and for that matter His presence for granted. This chapter reveals how dangerous it is to take the presence of God for granted and sounds a warning to desist from certain actions which may defy God. In as much as His presence is so loving, sweet and essential, we must also realize that His presence can be deadly as well if we take Him for granted and misbehave in His Presence.

WE CANNOT AFFORD TO MARK ABOUT WITH THE ARK WHICH IS GOD'S PRESENCE

The ark in its day was seen as a visible sign that the invisible God was dwelling in Israel's midst. Hence as we come into the Holy Of Holies we need to discover a tangible sign of the Invisible God.

In any case this ark had a devastating and often 'deadly holiness'. Hence, it's important to know that we can as a church be corporately punished for disrespecting the presence of God. Do you want proof?

The people of Beth-shemesh were severely punished after they had treated the ark with contempt.

> *'19 And the Lord slew some of the men of Beth-shemesh because they had looked into the ark of the Lord; He slew seventy men of them, and the people mourned because the Lord had made a great slaughter among them . . .'* **1 Samuel 6:19**

Don't get it twisted—individually too we stand to be punished, regardless of our intentions, if we attempt to touch God's presence in an unprepared and rush state. Remember that the man Uzzah was killed by the Lord when he touched the Ark with his hand to keep it from tumbling to the ground from the cart.

> *'6 And when they came to Nacon's threshing floor, Uzzah put out his hand to the ark of God and took hold of it, for the oxen stumbled and shook it. 7 And the anger of the Lord was kindled against Uzzah; and God smote him there for touching the ark, and he died there by the ark of God. 8 David was grieved and offended because the Lord had broken forth upon Uzzah, and that place is called Perez-uzzah [the breaking forth upon Uzzah] to this day. 9 David was afraid of the Lord that day and said, How can the ark of the Lord come to me?'*
> **2 Samuel 6:6-9**

The ark was 'dangerous' to touch. It was the very symbol of God's presence. No wonder, God commanded that the ark be placed in the Holy of Holies, where it was to be separated from the rest of the tabernacle (later the temple) by a heavy veil.

'31 And make a veil of blue, purple, and scarlet [stuff] and fine twined linen, skillfully worked with cherubim on it. 32 You shall hang it on four pillars of acacia wood overlaid with gold, with gold hooks, on four sockets of silver. 33 And you shall hang the veil from the clasps and bring the ark of the Testimony into place within the veil; and the veil shall separate for you the Holy Place from the Most Holy Place.' Exodus 26:31-33

'3 But [inside] beyond the second curtain or veil, [there stood another] tabernacle [division] known as the Holy of Holies. 4 It had the golden altar of incense and the ark (chest) of the covenant, covered over with wrought gold. This [ark] contained a golden jar which held the manna and the rod of Aaron that sprouted and the [two stone] slabs of the covenant [bearing the Ten Commandments]. 5 Above [the ark] and overshadowing the mercy seat were the representations of the cherubim [winged creatures which were the symbols] of glory. We cannot now go into detail about these things.' Hebrews 9:3-5

No sinful person could look upon the glory of God above the ark and live.

'1 AFTER THE death of Aaron's two sons, when they drew near before the Lord [offered false fire] and died, 2 The Lord said to Moses, Tell Aaron your brother he must not come at all times

*into the Holy of Holies within the veil before the mercy seat upon the ark, lest he die; for I will appear in the cloud on the mercy seat.' **Leviticus 16:1&2***

Now if the ark signified the very presence of God and it was unthinkable to mess around with the ark, then in our day as well, it is extremely unthinkable to mark around when we go before God in worship. Beloved, we can't fool around with His presence.

SIGNIFICANT ROLES PLAYED BY THE ARK

Clearly, the ark or for that matter the presence of God played a significant number of roles in the lives of the Israelites and undoubtedly still plays momentous roles in our lives today.

In The Crossing of The Jordan

'13 When the soles of the feet of the priests who bear the ark of the Lord of all the earth shall rest in the Jordan, the waters of the Jordan coming down from above shall be cut off and they shall stand in one heap. 14 So when the people set out from their tents to pass over the Jordan, with the priests bearing the ark of the covenant before the people, 15 And when those who bore the ark had come to the Jordan and the feet of the priests bearing the ark were in the brink of the water—for the Jordan overflows all its banks throughout the time of harvest—16 Then the waters which came down from above stood and rose up in a heap far off, at Adam, the city that is beside Zarethan; and those flowing down toward the Sea of the Arabah, the Salt [Dead] Sea, were wholly cut off. And the people passed over opposite Jericho. 17 And while all Israel passed over on dry

*ground, the priests who bore the ark of the covenant of the Lord stood firm on dry ground in the midst of the Jordan, until all the nation finished passing over the Jordan.' **Joshua 3:13-17***

*'9 And Joshua set up twelve stones in the midst of the Jordan in the place where the feet of the priests bearing the ark of the covenant had stood. And they are there to this day. 10 For the priests who bore the ark stood in the midst of the Jordan until everything was finished that the Lord commanded Joshua to tell the people, according to all that Moses had commanded Joshua. The people passed over in haste.' **Joshua 4:9-10***

The presence of God within you is destined to do your enemies in, trap them and kill them if that is what it takes to prevent them from getting to you. That same thing that your enemies think will prevent you from escaping from them will make way for the presence of God which you are supposed to be carrying to pass through with you and there after shut behind you to trap the enemy.

► In The Conquest of Jericho

'6 So Joshua son of Nun called the priests and said to them, Take up the ark of the covenant and let seven priests bear seven trumpets of rams' horns before the ark of the Lord. 7 He said to the people, Go on! March around the enclosure, and let the armed men pass on before the ark of the Lord. 8 When Joshua had spoken to the people, the seven priests bearing the seven trumpets of rams' horns passed on before the Lord and blew the trumpets, and the ark of the covenant of the Lord followed them. 9 The armed men went before the priests who blew the trumpets, and the rear guard came after the ark, the priests

*blowing the trumpets as they went. 10 But Joshua commanded the people, You shall not shout or let your voice be heard, nor shall any word proceed out of your mouth until the day I tell you to shout. Then you shall shout! 11 So he caused the ark of the Lord to go around the city once; and they came into the camp and lodged in the camp.' **Joshua 6:6-11***

Those thick and high walls that your enemies seem to have fortified themselves with will come crumbling down to expose them so that you can have access to them to utterly destroy them, because of the presence of God which you carry

▶ In the life of the Israelites in their New Land

*'33 And all Israel, sojourner as well as he who was born among them, with their elders, officers, and judges, stood on either side of the ark before the Levitical priests who carried the ark of the covenant of the Lord, half of them in front of Mount Gerizim and half of them in front of Mount Ebal, as Moses the servant of the Lord had commanded before that they should bless the Israelites.' **Joshua 8:33***

*'27 And the Israelites inquired of the Lord—for the ark of the covenant of God was there [at Bethel] in those days,' **Judges 20:27***

In those new grounds that you are taking or are yet to take, His presence is so pivotal to your survival—be it in your new marriage, new job, new school or in whatever new you find yourself doing.

GOD'S PRESENCE HAS NO MAGICAL CONNOTATIONS AND SHOULD NOT BE TREATED AS SUCH

There is no suggestion of gullible or magical use of the ark. Instead, the ark signified awe. It contained God's 'testimony' and the pledge of His presence.

Religious life in Israel had hit rock bottom in the days of Eli and his sons (at the end of the period of the judges). Now, though the ark was still treasured, it was seen by some to poses some magical power which could conjure automatic victory whenever they needed it. When losing a battle with the Philistines, the Israelites hurried the ark to the battlefield hoping it would work some magic for them.

'1 AND the word of [the Lord through] Samuel came to all Israel. Now Israel went out to battle against the Philistines and encamped beside Ebenezer; the Philistines encamped at Aphek. 2 The Philistines drew up against Israel, and when the battle spread, Israel was smitten by the Philistines, who slew about 4,000 men on the battlefield. 3 When the troops had come into the camp, the elders of Israel said, Why has the Lord smitten us today before the Philistines? Let us bring the ark of the covenant of the Lord here from Shiloh that He may come among us and save us from the power of our enemies. 4 So the people sent to Shiloh and brought from there the ark of the covenant of the Lord of hosts, Who dwells above the cherubim. And the two sons of Eli, Hophni and Phinehas, were with the ark of the covenant of God. 5 And when the ark of the covenant of the Lord came into the camp, all Israel shouted with a great shout, so that the earth resounded. 6 And when the Philistines heard the noise of

the shout, they said, What does this great shout in the camp of the Hebrews mean? When they understood that the ark of the Lord had come into the camp, 7 The Philistines were afraid, for they said, God has come into the camp. And they said, Woe to us! For such a thing has not happened before. 8 Woe to us! Who shall deliver us out of the hand of these mighty gods? These are the gods that smote the Egyptians with every kind of plague in the wilderness. 9 Be strong, and acquit yourselves like men, O you Philistines, that you may not become servants to the Hebrews, as they have been to you; behave yourselves like men, and fight! 10 And the Philistines fought; Israel was smitten and they fled every man to his own home. There was a very great slaughter; for 30,000 foot soldiers of Israel fell. '
1 Samuel 4:1-10

The Lord would not tolerate such an obvious abuse of the ark. He allowed it to be captured by the uncircumcised Philistines who inflicted defeat on Israel and visited death on the house of the high priest Eli.

Do we sometimes try to hurry the very presence of God unto our battlefields rather than do the right thing? If we do, then this I trust should be enough caution.

*'11 And the ark of God was taken, and the two sons of Eli, Hophni and Phinehas, were slain. [Foretold in **1Sam. 2:34**.]*
1 Samuel 4:11

In any case in ***1 Samuel 4:13-22:***
'13 When he arrived, Eli was sitting by the road watching, for his heart trembled for the ark of God. When the man told the

news in the city, all the city [people] cried out. 14 When Eli heard the noise of the crying, he said, What is this uproar? And the man came hastily and told Eli. 15 Now Eli was 98 years old; his eyes were dim so that he could not see. 16 The man said to Eli, I have come from the battle; I fled from the battle today. Eli said, How did it go, my son? 17 The messenger replied, Israel fled before the Philistines, and there has been a great slaughter among the people. Also your two sons, Hophni and Phinehas, are dead, and the ark of God is captured. 18 And when he mentioned the ark of God, Eli fell off the seat backward by the side of the gate. His neck was broken and he died, for he was an old man and heavy. He had judged Israel forty years. 19 Now his daughter-in-law, Phinehas' wife, was with child, about to be delivered. And when she heard that the ark of God was captured and that her father-in-law and her husband were dead, she bowed herself and gave birth, for her pains came upon her. 20 And about the time of her death the women attending her said to her, Fear not, for you have borne a son. But she did not answer or notice. 21 And she named the child Ichabod, saying, The glory is departed from Israel!—because the ark of God had been captured and because of her father-in-law and her husband. 22 She said, The glory is gone from Israel, for the ark of God has been taken.' 1 Samuel 4:13-22

That is to tell us that God will in no way allow an obvious misuse of His Presence and should we do that, the result could be fatal (to say the least). At the same time, God defended the honor of the ark when it was offered to Dagon, the god of the Philistines. The account of the efforts of the pagan Philistines to get rid of the ark is so funny.

'6 But the hand of the Lord was heavy upon the people of Ashdod, and He caused [mice to spring up and there was] very deadly destruction and He smote the people with [very painful] tumors or boils, both Ashdod and its territory.' **1 Samuel 5:6**

This story dramatically illustrated that the Holy Ark could neither be treated gullibly by God's people nor mocked by his enemies. Thus we need to be mindful of the way and manner in which we treat the presence of God, knowing that even though God will not allow His presence to be mocked, He will also not tolerate us taking the presence for granted and have us use it as though it were a magical charm of some sort.

▶ The Difference must be Obvious

After an encounter with God in worship, a difference in our lives should be noticeable, hence if our whole lives are supposed to be lives of worship, then in every aspect of our lives, and wherever we find ourselves, our continual encounter with God should make us conspicuous and the difference should be seen. At the end of *Exodus 34* Moses descends from Mount Sinai after such a powerful encounter with God and the Bible tells us how radiant his face was—such that he had to wear a veil to cover his face because the people were afraid to look at him. Yet the Bible says in *verse 34* that whenever he went into God's presence he removed the veil until he came out. That is to say that nothing was allowed to obscure the gaze upon God when he went into God's' presence. I still affirm that there should be a perceptible change in our lives as a church and as individuals as we continually encounter God's presence. As a matter of fact, the greater the revelation we have in God's presence, the greater the transformation should be.

Secondly, when we go before the Lord in worship we must make a careful effort to remove anything that would hinder unconditional

access into His presence. Note that Moses removed his veil anytime he went before God and more so, *2 Corinthians 3:18* teaches that we are also capable of being uncovered worshippers.

> '*18 And all of us, as with unveiled face, [because we] continued to behold [in the Word of God] as in a mirror the glory of the Lord, are constantly being transfigured into His very own image in ever increasing splendor and from one degree of glory to another; [for this comes] from the Lord [Who is] the Spirit.*'

CHAPTER 23

DON'T DOUSE THE
FLAME OF THE SPIRIT!

IF you have had the opportunity to read a little bit of basic science you might know how the fire extinguisher works. I know that there are different types of fire extinguishers and depending on the type of fire and what might have caused a particular fire; the appropriate extinguisher may be chosen to quench it. Now the main aim of using a fire extinguisher is to cut off one or more of the things that the fire needs to keep burning (oxygen, fuel or heat). So the idea is to cut off any of these elements or at best all three.

Hence one may choose to cut off heat by cooling the fire with water or any other cool liquid that is not inflammable to dampen the fire.

Another option would be to cut off oxygen supply. I remember a simple experiment we used to do in college whilst I was still a science student.

You simply light a candle and whilst the flame is burning you cover the burning candle with a beaker which obviously cuts off oxygen supply thereby causing the flame to go out, which proves that whenever oxygen supply is completely cut off, a flame will go out.

Again, fuel that may be needed to burn a flame could range from inflammable substances like petrol through to cloth or ordinary fire wood (anything that would help combustion actually). That is why usually during fire outbreaks, when the fire service personnel are called in they would as a matter of urgency want to remove anything that can burn easily out of the way of the fire.

In worship I can say that we experience the Holy Spirit 'burning' in us to make us fit and worthy of our encounter with God. The Holy Spirit is really very important in our lives of worship and thinking of the Holy Spirit as the 'burning flame of fire', we can see clearly that there is the possibility of quenching this Holy fire in our lives by eliminating any of the aforementioned which otherwise would have helped the burning process. Now, whenever we quench the Holy Spirit which burns in our lives, we damage our lives of worship.

It is clear from *Philippians 3:3* that we worship God by the Spirit of God.

'3 For we [Christians] are the true circumcision, who worship God in spirit and by the Spirit of God and exult and glory and pride ourselves in Jesus Christ, and put no confidence or dependence [on what we are] in the flesh and on outward privileges and physical advantages and external appearances.'
Philippians 3:3

Hence, if we quench the Spirit of God, then we quench our worship as well.

> *'30 And do not grieve the Holy Spirit of God [do not offend or vex or sadden Him], by Whom you were sealed (marked, branded as God's own, secured) for the day of redemption (of final deliverance through Christ from evil and the consequences of sin).'*
>
> **Ephesians 4:30**

It is the bitterness, anger and concentration on the physical advantages and external appearances, as well as our investing of confidence in, or our dependence on carnality amongst other sins that the Holy Spirit cannot cohabit with. All these are hereby collectively represented by the beaker that will cut off the Holy Spirit who as per this analogy is the 'oxygen' that keeps your worship burning. Hence if you are able to rid your life of all these sins you can at least be assured of one element that will ensure that your flame of worship is burning, that is your oxygen supply—the Holy Spirit.

Again, another element for combustion is fuel as mentioned earlier. The deeper the revelation of God we have, the better we are able to worship Him. For this analogy therefore the revelation of God is seen as the 'fuel' that is needed to keep the flame of worship burning. Now the good thing is that regardless of how advanced we are in our Christian lives, God through His Word is able to reveal extraordinarily new things to us. The truth is that, there is always a new level of revelation that God is ready to open up to us. Hence there is always a generous amount of fuel at our disposal. Let us add more fuel to our flame of worship rather than 'starve' our flame of 'fuel' that is abundant in the word of God.

Lastly, it is important to know that the pressures and trials of this world are capable of cooling us off spiritually. Eventually, after being cold for a while we begin to lose trust and deceive ourselves with such excuses as—we will bounce back on track when things get better. The truth may be hard to take but the truth says that the true worshipper always trusts, always hopes and always perseveres.

> '7 *Love bears up under anything and everything that comes, is ever ready to believe the best of every person, its hopes are fadeless under all circumstances, and it endures everything [without weakening].'*
> **1 Corinthians 13:7**

There is a problem with trying to quench all types of fire with water. There are certain fires you can quench with water and there are others you cannot. Why? Fires that can be quenched with water are those which have fuel that can mix with the water, thereby allowing the water to dampen the fuel and consequently put it out.

In instances where the fire is caused by a fuel, like petrol; that cannot mix with water, the less dense substance which is the petrol as in this example will float on the water and spread, and thus cause the fire also to spread. What I am driving at is that, if the water or the dampening liquid can mix with the fuel then the fire can be extinguished but when the two cannot mix, then one will float over the other depending on which is less dense—and rather cause the fuel to float and spread and consequently cause the fire to spread also.

Now what I am saying here is that when the trials, temptations, strives and problems of life appear, we do not have to mix with them because if we do, then they will dampen our flame of worship, cool us off and ultimately put out the flame all together. If we will refuse to mix with the carnal dampening elements of this life, then the fuel which we have mentioned as the revelation of God will float and the fire or flame of worship will be spread even wilder.

CHAPTER 24

SOME POWERFUL WORSHIP MINISTERS OR MINSTRELS AND THEIR SONGS OF WORSHIP

NOW, let's meditate on some worship songs of some personalities recorded in the Bible.

MOSES' PRAYER OF WORSHIP

'1 THEN MOSES and the Israelites sang this song to the Lord, saying, I will sing to the Lord, for He has triumphed gloriously; the horse and his rider or its chariot has He thrown into the sea. 2 The Lord is my Strength and my Song, and He has become my Salvation; this is my God, and I will praise Him, my father's God, and I will exalt Him. 3 The Lord is a Man of War; the Lord is His name. 4 Pharaoh's chariots and his host has He cast into the sea; his chosen captains also are sunk in the Red Sea. 5 The floods cover them; they sank in the depths [clad in mail] like

a stone. 6 Your right hand, O Lord, is glorious in power; Your right hand, O Lord, shatters the enemy. 7 In the greatness of Your majesty You overthrow those rising against You. You send forth Your fury; it consumes them like stubble. 8 With the blast of Your nostrils the waters piled up, the floods stood fixed in a heap, the deeps congealed in the heart of the sea. 9 The enemy said, I will pursue, I will overtake, I will divide the spoil; my desire shall be satisfied upon them; I will draw my sword, my hand shall destroy them.

10 You [Lord] blew with Your wind, the sea covered them; [clad in mail] they sank as lead in the mighty waters. 11 Who is like You, O Lord, among the gods? Who is like You, glorious in holiness, awesome in splendor, doing wonders? 12 You stretched out Your right hand, the earth's [sea] swallowed them.

13 You in Your mercy and loving-kindness have led forth the people whom You have redeemed; You have guided them in Your strength to Your holy habitation.' Exodus 15:1-13

THE MAGNIFICENT (MARY)

'46 And Mary said, My soul magnifies and extols the Lord, 47 And my spirit rejoices in God my Savior, 48 For He has looked upon the low station and humiliation of His handmaiden. For behold, from now on all generations [of all ages] will call me blessed and declare me happy and to be envied! 49 For He who is almighty has done great things for me—and holy is His name [to be venerated in His purity, majesty and glory]! 50 And His mercy (His compassion and kindness toward the miserable and afflicted) is on those who fear Him with godly reverence, from generation to generation and age to age. 51 He has shown strength and made might with His arm; He has scattered the

proud and haughty in and by the imagination and purpose and designs of their hearts. 52 He has put down the mighty from their thrones and exalted those of low degree. 53 He has filled and satisfied the hungry with good things, and the rich He has sent away empty-handed [without a gift]. 54 He has laid hold on His servant Israel [to help him, to espouse his cause], in remembrance of His mercy, 55 Even as He promised to our forefathers, to Abraham and to his descendants forever.'

Luke 1:46-55

HANNAH'S SONG

'1 HANNAH PRAYED, and said, My heart exults and triumphs in the Lord; my horn (my strength) is lifted up in the Lord. My mouth is no longer silent, for it is opened wide over my enemies, because I rejoice in Your salvation. 2 There is none holy like the Lord, there is none besides You; there is no Rock like our God. 3 Talk no more so very proudly; let not arrogance go forth from your mouth, for the Lord is a God of knowledge, and by Him actions are weighed. 4 The bows of the mighty are broken, and those who stumbled are girded with strength. 5 Those who were full have hired themselves out for bread, but those who were hungry have ceased to hunger. The barren has borne seven, but she who has many children languishes and is forlorn. 6 The Lord slays and makes alive; He brings down to Sheol and raises up. 7 The Lord makes poor and makes rich; He brings low and He lifts up. 8 He raises up the poor out of the dust and lifts up the needy from the ash heap, to make them sit with nobles and inherit the throne of glory. For the pillars of the earth are the Lord's, and He has set the world upon them. 9 He will guard the feet of His godly ones, but the wicked shall

be silenced and perish in darkness; for by strength shall no man prevail. 10 The adversaries of the Lord shall be broken to pieces; against them will He thunder in heaven. The Lord will judge [all peoples] to the ends of the earth; and He will give strength to His king (King) and exalt the power of His anointed (Anointed His Christ).'

1 Samuel 2:1-10

CHAPTER 25

CORPORATE WORSHIP

IN as much as God has given each person the ability to worship Him (individually), it is also important that we come together to offer corporate worship to God. The Bible says that praise awaits God in Zion (which is the assembly of the saints). As believers, we are encouraged not to forsake the assembly of the saints. In this chapter we will get to learn more to enhance our corporate worship.

BENEFITS OF CORPORATE WORSHIP

Direction and precision in hearing God's voice:

> '*2 And many nations shall come and say, Come, let us go up to the mountain of the Lord, to the house of the God of Jacob, that He may teach us His ways, and we may walk in His paths. For the law shall go forth out of Zion and the word of the Lord from Jerusalem.*'
>
> **Micah 4:2**

Public or corporate worship gives God's people an important opportunity to hear His Word proclaimed and to learn about God and His ways.

I presume the best place to operate any gadget will be in the habitation of the inventor. That way if anything should go wrong you are sure to hear the voice of the inventor and you can rest assured that his directions will be the best to adhere to. I am by no means reducing human beings to ordinary gadgets. I am just laying a foundation with this illustration. I am sure that as human beings created by God and in His own image, the best place for us to dwell is in His presence in a life of worship. That way we *can hear Him more clearly, love Him more dearly and follow Him more nearly, day by day*, knowing that when He metes out instructions in our time of need or 'malfunction', they will be just right.

I can tell you for a fact that the further away we stray from Him the less we will hear Him and understand His paths.

DELIVERY OF OUR MUCH AWAITED ANSWERS

God meets with his people in a powerful way when they worship him together.

> *'1 WHEN SOLOMON had finished praying, the fire came down from heaven and consumed the burnt offering and the sacrifices, and the glory of the Lord filled the house.'*
> *2 Chronicles 7:1*

▶ The Immeasurable Benefits of a Life of Worship

The benefits of worshipping God are immeasurable. Again, with reference to Abraham and his sacrificing of Isaac we notice that,

Abraham might not have gained momentarily, but his reward was more precious than he could ever ask for. In case you are wondering what his reward was, God Himself has it tucked away so nicely in *Genesis 15:1* where He says:

> *'1 AFTER these things, the word of the Lord came to Abram in a vision, saying, Fear not, Abram, I am your Shield, your abundant compensation, and your reward shall be exceedingly great . . .'*

Can you imagine what would have happened if Abraham had held back. I think he would have lost out on this great reward, and for me, just the thought of God Himself being my shield and exceedingly great reward makes me feel good, and presents me with more than good reason to worship Him.

CHAPTER 26

UNDERSTANDING YOUR CALL TO SERVICE

PRAISE LEADERS & LEAD WORSHIPPERS' ELIGIBILITY FOR SERVICE

In 1 Chronicles 15:12-22 King David affords us an illustration of the type of preparation that is expected of us in ushering in the presence of God.

If you believe that you have been called to minister in the office of a praise leader and a lead worshipper it is my prayer that you confirm your eligibility for service by considering these five core criteria listed below as indicated in *1 Chronicles 15:12-22.*

1. **Sanctification:** Have you set yourself apart from sin and dedicated yourself to the things of God? *(1 Chronicles 15:12).*

2. **Knowledgeable:** Are you knowledgeable in the things of God? In the first attempt to carry the Ark of God into Jerusalem the lack of knowledge cost a man his life. *(1 Chronicles 15:13).*

3. **Willingness:** Are you willing to carry the weight and responsibility of doing the work that comes with being in the presence of God? *(1 Chronicles 15:15).*

4. **Recognition of Your Positions as One of Service as well as One of an Appointment:** Do you realize that you are not able to choose which position you want? Neither are you able to reject the God—approved assignments given you by your God-approved leaders? *(1 Chronicles 15:16).*

5. **Skillfulness:** Are you skillful? Do you realize that skill sets a high standard of excellence and quality for others to follow? *(1 Chronicles 15:22).*

God in His own wisdom established order and structures in the church. It also pleased Him to establish gifts and offices as well. Now, these offices and gifts differ from each other and more so, each has its own commensurate amount of GRACE to ensure credible, excellent and exhaustive execution of duties associated the particular offices as pleases God.

> *'18 But as it is, God has placed and arranged the limbs and organs in the body, each [particular one] of them, just as He wished and saw fit and with the best adaptation.'*
> *1 Corinthians 12:18*

'27 Now you [collectively] are Christ's body and [individually] you are members of it, each part severally and distinct [each with his own place and function]. 28 So God has appointed some in the church [for His own use]: first apostles (special messengers); second prophets (inspired preachers and expounders); third teachers; then wonder-workers; then those with ability to heal the sick; helpers; administrators; [speakers in] different (unknown) tongues.'
1 Corinthians 12:27-28

Each person has their own peculiar gift and time within which to operate these gifts depending on when God provides the grace. It is thus dangerous to start operating gifts which are not God-given, and even where they are God-given, it is still dangerous to start operating them ahead of God's own appointed time. Many have crushed, landed real hard and ruined what could have been a blessing for themselves and the body of Christ as a whole, just because they either went ahead of God's plan or forced themselves into operating gifts they had not been called to. Even when given the same gift as someone else it is worth understanding that there are still varying levels and roles of operation.

'4 For as in one physical body we have many parts (organs, members) and all of these parts do not have the same function or use,'
Romans 12:4

Michael Essien and Didier Drogba may both be gifted to play soccer. Even though they may be playing the same team (Chelsea FC) now, they still have different roles on the field of play.

Now, the fact that one scores more goals than the other does not solely and necessarily make the goal-poacher a better player than his colleague who does not score as many goals. My point exactly is that, rather than seeking popularity, fame and attention for ourselves in whichever area we are called to serve, it is important to concentrate on the reason why we were brought 'on board' in the first place and to concentrate on playing our roles effectively and to the best of our God given ability. We can't afford to attempt jumping into other people's roles when we have not been called to serve in those capacities.

When we lose our focus in this regard, we end up ruining the whole body of Christ alongside ruining ourselves. If Peter Czech (the goalkeeper of Chelsea FC) should for instance abandon his goal post all the time in a bid to score goals, because he feels Drogba is enjoying some enviable amount of fame, you can imagine what the result will be. First of all, he might never even score a goal since that is not his specialty, and secondly he might have exposed the whole team to their opponents' counter onslaught which could be thankfully exploited to the detriment of the whole Chelsea FC team and its fans. I am sure that should Czech ever put up such behavior, it will lead to his early exit from the first team if not the entire team on the grounds of incompetence.

Again, with such a behavior you can envisage how disappointed the team's cheering fans would be. Meanwhile, if he had stayed at post he might have made some daring and decisive saves which would have on the other hand helped the team better and won him the much desired admiration of the fans.

Similarly, you can picture how much damage we cause the body of Christ, when we jump into roles that have not been assigned to us.

Don't forget what the Bible says concerning the existence of a great cloud of witnesses. When we irresponsibly abandon the reasons for our calling, we end up disappointing our team (the Church), ourselves and our fans (the great cloud of witnesses that compass about us). Essien (a Chelsea FC player) may not personally make out a single supporter in the stands from the field of play but I am sure each time he steps on the field of play he knows very well that someone is in the stands cheering him on. Similarly, from my field of play, I may not make them out but you know what? I know for a fact that there is a great cloud of witnesses that compass about me and I cannot afford to let them down!!!

Which gift do you operate as a lead worshiper of a praise leader?

'1 THEREFORE THEN, since we are surrounded by so great a cloud of witnesses [who have borne testimony to the Truth], let us strip off and throw aside every encumbrance (unnecessary weight) and that sin which so readily (deftly and cleverly) clings to and entangles us, and let us run with patient endurance and steady and active persistence the appointed course of the race that is set before us,' **Hebrews 12:1**

'6 Having gifts (faculties, talents, qualities) that differ according to the grace given us, let us use them: [He whose gift is] prophecy, [let him prophesy] according to the proportion of his faith; 7 [He whose gift is] practical service, let him give himself to serving; he who teaches, to his teaching; 8 He who exhorts (encourages), to his exhortation; he who contributes, let him do it in simplicity and liberality; he who gives aid and superintends, with zeal and singleness of mind; he who does

acts of mercy, with genuine cheerfulness and joyful eagerness.'
Romans 12:6-8

Now concentrating on the gift of HELP (as mentioned in the scripture above as he who gives aid) it is important to note that, the one who HELPS does not completely take over but rather supports, furthers, contributes to or facilitates an already continuing process. If I asked you to help me build a house, it probably would mean that I am prepared and must have started working at building the house. Now depending on my deficiency, I might then solicit for your help.

If I said, "Please help me get to London", I must have made some necessary arrangements or probably set some arrangements in motion before soliciting for your help. So then, what I may be asking for is for you to come in and offer me some aid to enable me accomplish my aim. Note that I asked for aid and so when you agree to come on board you do so to help, and not to take over completely.

On the other hand and even more importantly, since I solicited for your aid I am expected to corporate with you to get the goal accomplished and not to leave it all to you. I have on occasions heard people complain about situations where they have been asked to help others accomplish certain tasks and in the process of lending their help, the one who solicited for the help had left the entire burden on them. T rust me; it is not a pleasant experience.

It is also important to mention that after lending the help you were asked for, the normal expectation will be for you to take your leave when your work is done. It's not pleasant either when the person you solicited help from, comes in and begins to throw their weight about, bossing over you and taking over everything. It could even be worse when such 'helpers' (even if they had done a good job), still stuck around after their work was done and there was no further need for their service. Worst of all however is when they still stick around when they did not even give the kind of help needed from them in the first place.

Please do not overstay your welcome as a praise leader or a lead worshipper. It can be extremely irritating for the congregation if you do. It's like remaining in a foreign country well after the expiry of your leave. Now you have a picture of how irksome you can easily be. As a praise leader or a lead worshipper your duty is to **help** bring people into God's Presence. So then **your gift** is to aid the congregation before which you stand. Hence, ideally, you are to facilitate an already initiated and probably ongoing process, after which you are supposed to take your leave.

YOUR OFFICE AS A PRAISE LEADER OR A LEAD WORSHIPPER:

IS AN OFFICE OF DIVINE CALLING

That is to say that one cannot just assume the office of a lead worshipper or for that matter a praise leader. You should be called to this honorable office if not, frustration and ruin will creep up on you and eventually engulf you. You must have a God-given ability to help by way of leading people into God's presence, and until God Himself calls you to occupy such a position, I can only wonder where else you can attain the ability and grace to operate this gift. Without such divinely called leaders, the full potential of Worship may not be attained.

Saying that the office of a praise leader or lead worshipper is a divine call does not mean that individually we cannot praise or worship God or that even on individual basis one will always need a lead worshipper or praise leader to praise and worship God. That is not what I mean. Everyone has the ability to worship God individually, but the point is that it is not everyone who can effectively help bring others into the presence of God (as is expected of those called to serve in the office of a praise leader or a lead worshipper). Most people may be able to drive themselves and maybe a few others around in their saloon cars, yet not everyone has the ability to drive a commercial bus full of passengers on a long journey.

CANNOT BE TAKEN LIGHTLY

The office should be held with a serious sense of leadership, responsibility and duty. In the Old Testament days a singer was admitted to the Levitical choir at the age of thirty, following a five-year apprenticeship.

'3 The Levites thirty years old and upward numbered, man by man, 38,000,'
1 Chronicles 23:3

Five years was a relatively short time, considering the amount of material these singers had to memorize and the ritual they had to master. It is even purported that they actually started training from childhood. While others performed other duties connected to the sacred service, the singers were excused from all other duties because they were on duty day and night.

'33 These are the singers, heads of the fathers' houses of the Levites, dwelling in the temple chambers, free from other service because they were on duty day and night.' **1 Chronicles 9:33**

Skill was and still is a significant part of (temple) worship, and they devoted their entire life to the development of their musical ability. I cannot overemphasize how vital it is for us to acknowledge the importance, seriousness and dedication we need to attach to this office.

WORSHIPPING ON BEHALF OF THE PEOPLE— AN OT (Old Testament) PHENOMENON

In the olden days, the High Priest performed worship on behalf of the congregation, but now it is not the case. We have the ability to go before God individually and corporately in worship. Thus, it is wrong to think that in your position as a lead worshipper you are to perform worship on behalf of the people. Yours in that office is just to aid the people attain a certain level where they can reach out to God with their God-given ability to worship Him (at which time their spirits are able to intimately communicate with the Spirit of God), at which point they must be allowed to worship.

For this reason, it is imperative to be sensitive enough to know when the people you are helping have attained that level (you were called in to aid them attain) and then back off gradually into the background, allowing them to share sweet fellowship with God as His Spirit leads. At this point, you must just avail yourself to be led by the Spirit to fellowship with God too.

Again, remember that you have been asked in your office to help the congregation reach into God's presence. Though as an individual, you may be 'sharp' enough in your spirit to reach out and fellowship with God easily, not everyone in the congregation may have matured to your level and so it may take relatively more time for them to be brought to that 'level' (into His presence). For this reason, you need to be sensitive enough. Please do not rush the congregation. Be cautious not to drag them along or push them. Stay with them and gently help them. If you attempt to hurry them you may lose them in the process in which case you would have failed in your duty. You should emulate the good Shepherd, who in Isaiah is said to be gentle with His flock caring for those who carry their young.

SUSTAIN OR PRESERVE A SIMPLE UNCONTAMINATED HEART

Usually what tends to be the greatest challenge for lead worshippers and praise leaders is the ability to preserve a simple uncontaminated heart of worship in the public domain. As a minister, it is vital to note that the difficult challenge of keeping an uncontaminated heart comes 'in the fields' where no one is around and more so, when we have been entrusted with public office. Our public persona; (how we comport ourselves), should be of very high regard to us.

'19 But the firm foundation of (laid by) God stands, sure and unshaken, bearing this seal (inscription): The Lord knows those who are His, and, Let everyone who names [himself by] the name of the Lord give up all iniquity and stand aloof from it.'
2 Timothy 2:19

YOU ARE EXPENDABLE

This may be easy to understand yet very hard to accept especially when you find yourself on the wrong side. As a servant, you are expendable when you refuse to do as God demands of you. If you refuse to serve in your God-given office, God will not force you.

He will never mess with your free will. All He may do in such circumstances may be to raise others who are willing to be obedient to Him which will eventually render you a liability rather than the asset you were destined to be in the house of God. Usually, it is when God has raised others to take up the mantle which people have lost through their own pride, disobedience and neglect of duty, that you find them disgruntled and complaining. God is able to choose anyone at all. If even Lucifer could lose his position in heaven, you should know by now that you are replaceable as a lead worshipper—don't deceive yourself.

NOT GIVEN TO SHOWMANSHIP

Your gift was not given for showmanship. When David danced, it was not to show off; neither was it some effect of an adrenalin rush; it was actually an overflow of the abundance of love in his heart for God.

> '45 The upright (honorable, intrinsically good) man out of the good treasure [stored] in his heart produces what is upright (honorable and intrinsically good), and the evil man out of the evil storehouse brings forth that which is depraved (wicked and intrinsically evil); for out of the abundance (overflow) of the heart his mouth speaks.'
> **Luke 6:45**

295

It is significant to note that what once might have been a pure act or expression of love to God can become a mere performance on stage, if we are not mindful. Our actions in God's presence I believe are not seen through their mere appearances but rather via the heart with which we minister unto God, hence there is the need for us to guard against the subtle element of 'performance' creeping up on us. As a lead worshipper the fact that you have the privilege of helping others reach God in His majesty and splendor should humble you and be seen as such an honor rather than cause you to concern yourself with cheap human popularity.

As a matter of fact, it is an offence to distract attention from God. You know deep down in your heart whether or not you are performing on stage when you stand before the congregation. You know very well whether you are pointing people to God or you are pointing to yourself (which should never happen). If you are simply 'performing' in order to point attention to yourself, then you are in other words trying to rob God of or share in His glory which is extremely dangerous. Now there is a distinction you need to understand. Having won the victory, He is enjoying the glory. Now in His glory, we are allowed to participate in the celebration of the victory (which is to triumph). That is different from sharing in or robbing God of His Glory. The Glory is His. He may give you a share of His power and authority to do His work, but understand that the Glory thereafter is His and should be accordingly directed to Him. Even when men mistakenly direct it to you, you should be quick to redirect it to God. Did you not know that He says He will share His glory with no man?

A STRONG AND LASTING RELATIONSHIP WITH HIM

In worshipping God we need to have a strong and lasting relationship with Him. *1 Corinthians 2:9 ff*

In our life of worship there is the all important need for us to care for the spiritual things of God and in so doing, do the right things. There has been much debate as to why Abel's sacrifice was acceptable before God whilst that of Cain was rejected but without taking sides as to what the reasons were, all I know and stick by is the fact that Abel according to the Bible did the right thing as mentioned in Hebrews. In your life as true worshippers just seek to do the right things and I believe your sacrifice before God in praise and worship will be acceptable.

SOME THINGS AND / OR SOME PEOPLE IN OUR LIVES MUST 'DIE'

In a bid to see God more clearly it is crucial that some things or people in our lives 'die'. The Bible says that in the year King Uziah died, the prophet Isaiah had a revelation of the Lord. Remember that the man had been a prophet for years, known as a genuine God anointed prophet for that matter. Does it mean that he did not have a revelation of God all those years prior to the death of King Uziah? I don't think so. Rather, I believe that this was a whole different dimension of revelation; a new and special revelation that he attained in the year the king passed on. As we come before God in worship, there are some characters in our lives, behaviors and people that may have to die off. The time they die off may just be a reference point for us to say that in the year that they passed on, we had a brand new revelation of God. Beloved, some things must happen for us to have a reference point for a greater revelation of God!!!

More so, the King at a time was disrespecting God and the things of God and pride had engulfed him. Beloved, anything or anyone that tries to exalt itself or themselves above God or the attention due God must die in order for you to have a new and better revelation of God in your life of worship. This could be pride, friends, behavior, relatives, relationships or other passions that exalt themselves above God or the things of God. Like King Uzziah, they must die for you to have a clearer revelation and a more intimate relationship with God (in worship). **(Isaiah 6:1)**

CHAPTER 27

SOME CHARACTERISTICS OF A LEAD WORSHIPPER

SOMETIMES we want to be sure about certain people and to be confident that these ones who we look up to are genuinely called by God. T o this extent, it is prudent to assess whether such persons who stand before us saddled with the responsibility of helping us reach into the presence of God are true lead worshippers. In this chapter we will consider a few of the many unique characteristics of true lead worshippers.

ANOINTED AND EQUIPPED

Holding this office goes way beyond just calling out songs to being a blessing unto others, such that people you minister to are evidently blessed by your God-given gift. Obviously such blessings are not experienced as a result of your own achievements but rather as a result of the grace of God upon your life which refreshes people. The Bible says we are blessed in order to be a blessing unto others.

ANOINTING

In the Old Testament, vessels and tools for ministry were sanctified or anointed with oil for specific ministries. This anointing signified a supernatural enablement or equipment for the Grace to function. Without the anointing, minstrels become concert men and women just performing on stage and consequently upsetting God. One of the qualities of a lead worshipper is to be anointed of God for service.

EQUIPPING

Lead worshippers are to equip themselves through personal discipline to become sharp in ministry and leadership. They need to be creative and always desiring to excel in ministry.

As aforementioned, in the Old Testament the Levites' skills were an important part of temple worship, and they devoted almost all if not their entire lives to the development of their musical ability. I make reference to the Levites in the old testament because in their time the singers and musicians responsible for temple worship were chosen from the tribe of Levi.

'1 ALSO DAVID and the chiefs of the host [of the Lord] separated to the [temple] service some of the sons of Asaph, Heman, and Jeduthun, who should prophesy [being inspired] with lyres, harps, and cymbals. The list of the musicians according to their service was:'

*'7 So the number of them [who led the remainder of the 4,000],
with their kinsmen who were **specially trained in songs for the
Lord, all who were talented singers**, was 288.'* **Chronicles
25:1&7**

As lead worshippers it is important we dedicate our lives to the
development of our skills by equipping ourselves though training. In
your calling there is the need for you to dedicate your life to development
as Timothy was admonished as a teacher in *2 Timothy 2:15:*

*'15 **Study and be eager** and do your utmost to present yourself
to God **approved (tested by trial)**, a workman who has **no cause
to be ashamed, correctly analyzing and accurately dividing
[rightly handling and skillfully teaching]** the Word of Truth.'*

COORDINATOR
As earlier mentioned, worship in our day, is not performed on behalf
of the congregation rather as a lead worshipper, the service expected
of you is to aid by way of **guidance and coordination by the Holy
Spirit.** Since you are saddled with the responsibility of coordinating the
musicians, the team you are working with and the congregation so that
everyone can worship God appropriately, it is important that you do
not hijack the service. I have come across lead worshippers who hijack
services as though it is all about them.

There are some people who just don't heed to any promptings
whatsoever and think they are the ultimate ones in control. Even when
prompted about time, it is then that they want to 'sing their last song'.
They act as though they are an authority unto themselves and refuse
any form of control whatsoever. When you behave in this manner, you

only cause confusion and cause the congregation to lose concentration which I don't think is of God. When this happens, you may realize that a previously yielding and participating congregation eventually loses concentration, sometimes depicted by their sitting down, fidgeting or doing other things. Note that I am not by any means imputing that people cannot worship God in certain postures. I am referring to the attitude of some ministers which cause the loss of concentration. You might be quick to blame the loss of concentration with its consequences such as non participation on the congregation but before passing on the blame ask yourself who caused it?

If through our journey to spiritual maturity, we have fallen victim to this attitude, we can thank God that we can now do the right thing, rather than lead others into it.

'1 AND [Jesus] said to His disciples, Temptations (snares, traps set to entice to sin) are sure to come, but woe to him by or through whom they come!' **Luke 17:1**

THE PROPHETIC MINISTRY

The prophetic ministry is more often released strongly out of the spirit of worship. I can remember that when I first operated in this ministry by the grace that was and has been afforded me, it was out of a strong spirit of worship. I had spoken the mind of God concerning certain situations and had honestly, forgotten all about it until a time when some of the things I had uttered under the direction and unction of the Holy Spirit started to manifest. As one of the few who were privileged to hear about some of these manifestations, I just marveled. Upon expressing my amazement about what God had done, a dear sister in Christ (Jackie) drew my attention to the fact that God had spoken about the situation through me during a worship service previously. I seriously had not even considered it and so it has been with many others who have been blessed with the prophetic unction. They will tell you that this office is closely related to a spirit of worship. If you can show me a true prophet of God I can readily point to you a true worshipper. There is a close bond between the spirit of worship and prophecy.

From the Bible, we learn that:

a) King David was referred to as the sweet Psalmist of Israel and some of his Psalms were prophetic.

b) Asaph who also wrote some of the Psalms operated in the prophetic ministry.

c) In *2 Kings 3:14-16* we notice how closely the ministry of prophecy is linked to song ministration.

> '*14 And Elisha said, As the Lord of hosts lives, before Whom I stand, surely, were it not that I respect the presence of Jehoshaphat king of Judah, I would neither look at you nor see you [King Joram]. 15 But now bring me a minstrel. And while the minstrel played, the hand and power of the Lord came upon [Elisha]. 16 And he said, Thus says the Lord: Make this [dry] brook bed full of trenches.' 2 Kings 3:14-16*

'God-inspired and originated' music can be used as a means to calm the spirit and to tune in to God. As mentioned, when King Joram went to enquire of the Lord from Elisha the power of music was used to aid him tune into God.

> '*1 ALSO DAVID and the chiefs of the host [of the Lord] separated to the [temple] service some of the sons of Asaph,*

Heman, and Jeduthun, who should prophesy [being inspired] with lyres, harps, and cymbals. The list of the musicians according to their service was: 2 Of the sons of Asaph: Zaccur, Joseph, Nethaniah, and Asharelah, the sons of Asaph under the direction of Asaph, who prophesied (witnessed and testified under divine inspiration) in keeping with the king's order. 3 Of the sons of Jeduthun: Gedaliah, Zeri, Jeshaiah, Shimei, Hashabiah, and Mattithiah, six in all, under the direction of their father Jeduthun, who witnessed and prophesied under divine inspiration with the lyre in thanksgiving and praise to the Lord. 4 Of Heman: the sons of Heman: Bukkiah, Mattaniah, Uzziel, Shebuel, Jerimoth, Hananiah, Hanani, Eliathah, Giddalti, Romamti-ezer, Joshbekashah, Mallothi, Hothir, and Mahazioth. 5 All these were the sons of Heman the king's seer [his mediator] in the words and things of God to exalt Him; for God gave to Heman fourteen sons and three daughters, 6 All of whom were [in the choir] under the direction of their father for song in the house of the Lord, with cymbals, harps, and lyres, for the service of the house of God. Asaph, Jeduthun, and Heman were under the order of the king. 7 So the number of them [who led the remainder of the 4,000], with their kinsmen who were specially trained in songs for the Lord, all who were talented singers, was 288.' 1 Chronicles 25:1-7

'2 While they were worshipping the Lord and fasting, the Holy Spirit said, Separate now for Me Barnabas and Saul for the work to which I have called them. 3 Then after fasting and praying, they put their hands on them and sent them away.'

Take note of how a key missionary was birthed in the atmosphere of prayer, fasting and worship. That is not to say that if you are a lead worshipper and God has not granted you the prophetic ministry your gift is not authentic. Just wait on your gift and God will raise you in the prophetic in His own time if need be (in His eyes). He will provide the grace when the time is right. NOT all lead worshippers are prophets or are supposed to be prophets anyway.

The office of the prophet is a unique calling of honor and I must stress that the fact that God might have used a person in that capacity at a point does not necessarily make the person a prophet. For instance, though I may have sometimes received prophetic messages and words of discernment, I have never held myself up as a prophet. I recognize that, though God uses me in that capacity occasionally, it doesn't necessarily make me a prophet. Praise leaders and lead worshippers should thus be mindful of jumping into the office of a prophet just because God might have used them in that capacity on certain occasions. If God has called you to be a prophet, by all means yes, you can hold yourself up as such. All I am putting across is the fact that in deep worship God may speak through you if there is something He would want you to say to His children, but when that happens be careful not to immediately start calling yourself a prophet or prophetess. If I was hungry and so went into the kitchen to fix myself something to eat (a duty my house help would usually perform for me), would that make me the house help? I don't think so. Again, if all the president's spokespersons were engaged on assignments and he had a very important speech to be delivered on his behalf and a minister was called upon to deliver the speech on his behalf, would that automatically make the minister one of the president's official spokespersons? No! Well if you thought it did, then I can only wonder what you will say of the ass whose mouth the Lord opened to speak to Balaam in *Numbers 22:28*? I am certain, you will not say that it made, the ass a senior prophet?

KNOWLEDGEABLE

As a lead worshipper, in as much as you make the effort to sharpen and develop your skills, there is also the need for you to be in tune and informed as regards all aspects of the areas you are to coordinate. There should be a natural burning desire within you to excel, which will ultimately drive you to learn. I am quick to chip in however that, though the amount of knowledge you are able to amass will be enhanced by the effort you put in to sharpen your skill and grow spiritually, you can never and should never attempt to replace the Holy Spirit with the knowledge you might have acquired regardless how liberal it is.

Subject all things that you do and have been taught as a lead worshipper to the Spirit of God and be sensitive to His promptings in order to discern the direction in which God wants you to go.

'21 And your ears will hear a word behind you, saying, This is the way; walk in it, when you turn to the right hand and when you turn to the left.'
Isaiah 30:21

DEVELOPS MUSCIANSHIP

Since music is important in enhancing worship, it is vital that we develop skills in music. I am sure you would refuse to board an aircraft if someone whispered into your ears just before boarding, that the pilot was inexperienced. If you work in a particular field it is anticipated that you will at least have a fair idea or working—knowledge of the resources you will be expected to use in executing your duties. In like manner, it is necessary for us to develop our musicianship since we use music in our line of duty as lead worshippers and praise leaders. Music, I guess you know by now, is an essential ingredient that enhances our worship to God and hence to offer worship effectively in our honorable office as coordinators of music, there is the need for us to develop musicianship.

I have occasionally heard some lead worshippers pass comments like they will 'worship anyhow even if the instruments were not working' and that if there was no music **it did not matter**. Don't get me wrong, I am not saying you cannot worship God in the absence of instruments—of course we can, **but to say that the absence of instruments does not matter** is a bit unjustified. Music does matter!!! And when available, it enhances worship which I am convinced pleases God.

PERSONAL COMMITMENT

Lead worshippers need to live a personal life of holiness. Actually, lead worshippers' ability to function effectively in their God appointed office is directly influenced by their life style. This entails personal holiness and continual spiritual growth. Anybody called into this divine office should be set apart and needs to live as such.

In the Old T estament High Priests were supposed to demonstrate holiness, sanctification and devotion by wearing their priestly garments.

Exodus 28: 1-3; 36-38

'1 FROM AMONG the Israelites take your brother Aaron and his sons with him, that he may minister to Me in the priest's

office, even Aaron, Nadab and Abihu, Eleazar and Ithamar, Aaron's sons. 2 And you shall make for Aaron your brother sacred garments [appointed official dress set apart for special holy services] for honor and for beauty. 3 Tell all who are expert, whom I have endowed with skill and good judgment, that they shall make Aaron's garments to sanctify him for My priesthood.'
Exodus 28:1-3

'36 And you shall make a plate of pure gold and engrave on it, like the engravings of a signet, HOLY TO THE LORD. 37 You shall fasten it on the front of the turban with a blue cord. 38 It shall be upon Aaron's forehead, that Aaron may take upon himself and bear [any] iniquity [connected with] the holy things which the Israelites shall give and dedicate; and it shall always be upon his forehead, that they may be accepted before the Lord [in the priest's person].'
Exodus 28:36-38

Aaron would only be acknowledged before God if his commitment to holiness was put on his forehead and made evident to the whole world.

This principle can also be seen in the New Testament where Jesus admonishes us to live like Him in ***Matthew 11:29:***

'29 Take My yoke upon you and learn of Me, for I am gentle (meek) and humble (lowly) in heart, and you will find rest (relief and ease and refreshment and recreation and blessed quiet) for your souls.'

In our day therefore, we need to live a life evidently worthy of our calling.

BRINGS ALONG

A lead worshipper aids the congregation to move into the spirit of worship. Once that is done and everyone is in the position to touch God the work is done and ideally the lead worshipper should allow the congregation to carry on with it, whilst keeping an eye on those who may have fallen by due to weariness in order to help them get back in line. However, this duty of bringing every one along should be executed by God's enablement. It is sensible to know that people are of different levels of spiritual maturity and understanding and that people also encounter varying experiences before attending services. For this reason, you cannot expect everyone to flow at the same pace. As a lead worshipper you do not have to drive, drag nor push the congregation. Your duty is to gently help them by God's enablement. If we aspire to be Christ-like then it is in order that we take after Him as well. Isaiah speaking of the Lord says in *Isaiah 40:11* that He will:

> *'11 . . . feed His flock like a shepherd: He will gather the lambs in His arm, He will carry them in His bosom and will gently lead those that have their young.'*

In the church a lead worshipper needs to come to the understanding that due to different experiences and circumstances members encounter before services, some may be as weak, tender and vulnerable as lambs. There may probably be others who could be weary, frustrated and drained. But note the manner in which the Lord deals with all these manner of people. He does not rush, bully, nor push them about by some antics but rather what He does is to '. . . *gather the lambs in His arm, He will carry them in His bosom and will gently lead those that have their young.'*

That suggests a gentle varying and creative approach in the execution of our duty as lead worshippers. Never leave the flock behind. Stick with them and help them for after all, that is your duty, that is your gift, and that is why you are in that privileged position in the first place.

SKILLFULNESS AND CREATIVITY

A lead worshipper needs to be skillful and creative.

'3 Sing to Him a new song; play skillfully [on the strings] with a loud and joyful sound.'
Psalms 33:3

'17 Saul told his servants, Find me a man who plays well and bring him to me.'
1 Samuel 16:17

Does it mean anything to you, that when Saul sought for a musician he did not just ask for any one at all (which was an option available to him anyway)? Rather, he asked for someone who could **play well**—someone **who could play with skill**. It is important then that worshippers and musicians settle for nothing less than the highest possible level of skill. Make sure however to subject creativity and skill to the Holy Spirit's direction.

SENSITIVITY TO THE HOLY GHOST

As children of God, in the execution of our duties it is paramount that we avail ourselves to His direction which makes it pivotal to our ministry, that we remain sensitive to the directions and promptings of the Holy Spirit.

'For all who are led by the Spirit of God are sons of God.'
Romans 8:14

'26 But the Comforter (Counselor, Helper, Intercessor, Advocate, Strengthener, Standby), the Holy Spirit, Whom the Father will send in My name [in My place, to represent Me and act on My behalf], He will teach you all things. And He will cause you to recall (will remind you of, bring to your remembrance) everything I have told you.' **John 14:26**

If we stay sensitive to the Holy Spirit we can be assured that we will be guided into all truth and be brought into illumination which ultimately glorifies the Father.

We don't perform tricks to access God's presence. Spiritual things, just don't work that way. The fact that God enjoyed your worship at a particular time during which a certain sequence of songs were ministered does not mean He necessarily wants to hear the same sequence of songs today as well. Even as mortal beings we sometimes get tired of listening to that same CD in our cars or stereos, not because the songs are not 'anointed' or 'powerful' but because it just gets a little monotonous over time. In any case as mentioned earlier on, worship is not to be done 'our way'. It is God who calls the shots. We worship on His terms. That is why at times as a lead worshipper you might have organized a song list yet immediately you start to minister, you are prompted to minister some different songs all together. It is important to note that it is not about you as a lead worshipper or the songs you enjoy but rather it's all about the intimate fellowship God wants to share. So the mere fact that you might have prepared a certain list does not mean that it should be used by all means. Be sensitive to the Spirit of God. That is one way to be effective in your calling.

I have been in some very orderly worship services and I have also been in others during which it seemed as though everything had just gone completely off—instrumentalists in their own world, the team in theirs and the lead worshippers in theirs as well. The question I am tempted to ask in such haphazard worship sessions is whether the ministration was with skill and sensitivity to the Lord? If so, how could everything have gone so wrong when God loves order and the lead worshipper was supposedly yielding to the directions of an Excellent Spirit?

I have always maintained that there should be extreme harmony and orderliness in our worship to God.

PREFER TO REMAIN ANONYMOUS

Let's consider the widow's mite in *Luke 21:1-4*. In *verse 3* Jesus declared that the woman had put in more than all the others. The fact remains that it is really not the amount per se that matters but rather how much it costs us and the heart with which we sacrifice as previously discussed.

True worshippers don't mind being undetected since they know that it is not about them but about God (the one whom they render worship to). True worshippers crave not after the attention of the world. For the true worshipper, it is the attention of God which is most important. As in the case of this widow, she did not mind going unnoticed but her sacrifice attracted the attention of the most important person present because of what and the manner in which she sacrificed. Do you mind going unnoticed in the eyes of men or is there a part of you that wants to be recognized? In that vein, you should probably ask yourself whether you want to be served or you want to serve. I know that if the right Spirit is within you, then you most definitely will not crave for worldly attention. You should know what you are doing and who you are doing it for. That way, whether human beings notice it or not will not matter at all. Our worship should be aimed at an audience of ONE—GOD!

The lead worshipper ideally should simply encourage and help others worship God and possibly stay unnoticed. Note that there is a need for you to set an example for others to follow. To draw attention to yourself is dangerous.

Can you imagine yourself in the presence of the most holy God, with the whole of heaven worshipping God as described in Revelations? The elders bowing as low as they can, the angels lying prostrate before God, casting down their crowns, the Seraphim covering their faces. Then in the midst of such a sublime and holy atmosphere, stands one person tall above everyone else (you) even more conspicuous due to the fact that everyone else has bowed down, and all you keep doing is showing off some unholy spiritual gymnastics.

I read somewhere that in the design of a boat or a ship for that matter, that which is below the waterline must always outweigh that which is above the waterline if not, come the least of winds or waves, and the boat will capsize.

Now, things may seem alright (above the waterline) on the outside, having acquired a few skills with the instruments and your vocals you may have a sweet voice that may allow you to modulate and hit some crazy notes but God is concerned with what happens below the 'waterline'. Below the 'waterline' lies what we like to do when no one else is there to see us, how much we throw ourselves into praise and worship when it is not us on stage, and even when it is us on stage, the things that run through our minds when things are 'going well'—In such times, is it a self congratulation feeling of and pure fulfillment or a spirit of true worship? You know yourself better and so I leave your self assessment to your own conscience.

God is concerned with what lies below what human eyes can see. If that is strong and heavy enough to outweigh the visible, then you will not be tossed about when the storms blow.

CAUTION

PRAISE AND WORSHIP SHOULDN'T BE TREATED WITH CONTEMPT

Have you been in church services where praise and worship teams have been rushed to get the praise and worship over and done with, in order to make way for something else even though the congregation was in deep, meaningful and sweet worship? Have you experienced times when it were as though praise and worship session were such a waste of time, and worship teams where bullied offstage by either a pastor or an MC, cutting short a great time of communion with God and in the process committing grievous 'spiritual abortions' as my brother in ministry, Albert chooses to call it?. How it baffles me that in these same churches, in times when probably a main speaker for an occasion has for some peculiar reason been held up, these same praise and worship teams are then called upon to fill in the gap. Or it is then and only then that there are extended praise or worship sessions. Beloved, I am not imputing that praise and worship in those times is sin. Neither am I saying that it is not worth worshipping or praising God in such times. In fact, I would not turn down any opportunity available to praise and worship God in church. My problem is why worship should be looked down upon and used as a *stopgap*. There are some who perceive worship as just a mere prelude to a sermon but for me, it is important that we attach a great deal of due respect and reverence to our worship and refrain from using it as a mere temporary solution or prologue to some other activity.

Imagine that you had gone to pick up someone from the airport and upon arrival you were told that for some reason the flight had delayed. Would you then decide to drive over to the 'Jubilee House' (as in the case of Ghana) or the White House (as in the case of America) to visit the president just because it was around the corner and convenient for you to while away the time with him whilst waiting for your visitor? Yet that's how we treat God sometimes. Think about it.

CHAPTER 28

HOW TO SHARPEN YOUR GIFT

IT is important that we learn how to sharpen our ability to use our gifts in order to attain maximum benefit for God's purposes and glory, the church, the world in general and ourselves in particular. In this regard, this chapter will treat a few of the many ways by which we can sharpen our gifts for mutual and maximum benefit.

USEFUL WAYS TO ENHANCE OUR PREPARATION

Ensure Congregation Is In Right Standing With God

Before attempting to approach The Most Holy Place, the great prophet Samuel, was in no unjustified haste and as such made no attempt to restore the ark to its rightful place after it was returned to Israel. He allowed it to remain in Kirjath jearim *(1 Samuel 6:21; 1 Samuel 7:2).*

'21 And they sent messengers to the inhabitants of Kirjathjearim, saying, The Philistines have brought again the ark of the LORD; come ye down, and fetch it up to you.' 1 Samuel 6:21

'2 And it came to pass, while the ark abode in Kirjathjearim, that the time was long; for it was twenty years: and all the house of Israel lamented after the LORD.' 1 Samuel 7:2

First of all, Samuel had to get Israel to obey God's covenant before the Ark of the Covenant could be of any use. Please don't be in a hurry to restore the ark (God's presence) before the congregation is ready to receive His presence. Be sure that the people are in the right standing with God, upright and ready.

Update Song Lists

I believe that God has something new for us every time. The Bible says the manna that some stored with the intention of eating the following day, had by morning bred worms and stank.

'Moses said, Let none of it be left until morning. 20 But they did not listen to Moses; some of them left of it until morning, and it bred worms, became foul, and stank; and Moses was angry with them.' Exodus 16:19-20

If we are not obedient to God and His promptings and decide to keep our song lists for longer periods than we are asked to, we can be sure that they will breed worms and they will stink. Would it surprise you then that there might have been times when our ostensible worship might have stunk before God?

It would help if we avoided unnecessary repetitions. Praise and for that matter worship too need to be up to date. Unfortunately, in some settings because the same things have been done over and over again, they have been reduced to mere tradition and have become so obsolete. The Bible encourages us to be creative in our praise and worship rather than to stick to our old ways—refusing to be flexible. The time has come for us to yield to the directives of the Holy Spirit.

Plan

It is necessary to plan ahead according to defined themes. If you know the theme that is being treated by the church in a particular period it could be helpful to plan around it. For instance, you could stick with love songs, or songs that speak of God's greatness and good works, or probably songs about His Blood, or the Cross. This helps you to condition the hearts and minds of members of the congregation in a certain orderly manner. In all that, there is the need to be sensitive to the promptings of God. Even with your choice of songs to minister, as you plan and pray, most importantly, be sensitive to the directions of the Lord. Even after settling on a song list, as you minister still be sensitive for you might never know when God would demand an alteration. Be flexible. There have been occasions when instrumentalists and probably some projector operators have walked up to me to ask what happened during worship. Why? Because I must have veered off the list we might have settled on or the list I might have handed over to them before service. I always don't have an explanation other than to say it was God, and this is one more reason why instrumentalists as well, need to be in tune and sensitive to the directions and promptings of the Holy Spirit. That way they can always 'flow' along smoothly.

Encourage Congregation to Meditate

You would find it useful at times, as God directs, to share a little from the word of God before launching into praise and worship. This may condition the minds of the congregation and help them understand worship better. It may also encourage them to meditate and do the right thing. Even in between songs as God directs, there may be the need to encourage the congregation to come along with you so as to attain a level at which they can freely worship. However, please don't preach a whole sermon before and after every song. You will only be a distraction by so doing.

Try Not To Use Up More Time Than The Congregation Is Accustomed To

Unless specifically led by God, whether you are a visitor or a local, whether it is your first or last time of leading praise or charged with the duties of a lead worshipper, please do not use up more time than you have been apportioned or than the congregation is used to. You can ask if you are a visitor, to be given an idea of the time the local church is used to. Remember our little talk about hijacking a service? If given the opportunity and the honor to discharge your duties in such an office over a period of time and there is the God—directed need to increase the time for praise and worship, please build on gradually. Don't just jump on one occasion from say ten minutes to an hour. That would be tantamount to gross insensitivity. In all of this, still remember to be sensitive to God's Spirit.

Boldly Deal With Problems

As a lead worshipper and a praise leader, you should be the first to know that certain behaviors, attitudes and conducts cannot be countenanced and accepted in God's presence. You should know that distracting behaviors, unedifying prophecies, show of casual attitudes and disrespect for God's presence is unacceptable. In your position you should be able to deal with these to ensure that no one stops you or the church from attaining your goal (which is to revere and worship the Almighty God).

This though should be done in love, and unless really gross and extremely distractive I would suggest you call the culprits to the side, say after service, and rebuke them rather than shouting out their names during service. That could even be more distractive and embarrassing. If such acts are checked effectively it will help attain the depth in worship as expected of everyone.

If you were in a boat and one person decided to knock a hole through the base of the boat and you decided to look on unconcerned, you should know that when water eventually enters the boat, everyone (yourself inclusive) will be exposed to the risk or danger of drowning. So you see why you can't afford to look on as selfish and immature individuals either deliberately or unknowingly by their actions or inactions expose everyone else to drown spiritually.

Let God Be Your Focus and Exalt the Trinity

There are times that we may tend to forget that we serve a Trinity God. In worshipping God make sure that you do acknowledge a Trinity God—God the Father, God the Son and God the Holy Spirit. It is important that we focus on God and not part of God. Get the focus right.

Rehearse With the Team and Work as Such

This is one area I must admit I struggled with a lot to overcome in ministry. I used to wonder why I had to rehearse what I wanted to give God with anyone else. Again, there were times I wouldn't be sure anyway what God required of me to offer as a sacrifice until the last moment. I used to ask myself, "What if I had rehearsed with the team and at the last moment God redirected me to do something else?" Then what? Again, I used to have this sinful selfish attitude in me. I really can't say for sure what it was but for want of a better expression I would say it might have been my ego. I wanted to be the only one to know what songs would follow next and then 'drop' them one after the other as a 'surprise' of some sort. But if you have in the past or still feel same, please repent. First of all, you cannot surprise God, even if you tried your best and secondly it is not about you and your surprises, it is about God. It might even change in the long run, but what do you stand to lose anyway if you rehearse with the team and the instrumentalists who are going to work with you anyway. Can you imagine a project manager who would not reveal to his foreman or construction team what they were building? Consider a project manager working with a team which did not know whether it was a two-storey building or a skyscraper they were building and all the team would do would be to report in the morning and just follow the manager perform particular tasks each day. I don't think such a project manager would be doing his team and himself any good. When we share we even stand a better chance of learning from our experienced team as well. Medical doctors will tell you they sometimes learn from their experienced and competent nurses. That doesn't necessarily make nurses better than doctors. Imagine a doctor going into the operation theatre with a team of medical staff to perform a surgery without letting anyone know what kind of case it was. What then can be expected of them when the patient goes under the knife? Yet truly, how often do members of praise and worship teams (instrumentalists inclusive) know the theme the lead worshipper or praise leader has chosen for a particular service, let alone the songs to be ministered? Yet the whole team is dragged to duty blindly with the expectation that they will give off their best. Can you imagine the irony?

By preparing everyone on your team and attaining oneness of mind, understanding and consensus, I am certain without researching for a sermon on 'oneness of mind' that you almost definitely (all other things being spiritually correct) will get the best out of everyone on your team. To work with a team which cannot flow with you, understand you, nor tell what next to expect could be spiritually suicidal. Come to think of it, choirs rehearse, sometimes months ahead of programs or services, with everyone knowing what they are going to minister at particular function and still they are able to minister powerfully (all other things being spiritually correct). Where then from all the selfishness and self-centeredness?

Step Down When Necessary
It is not about you as a person my dear. There are things that you and I know can hinder the proper execution of your duties as a praise leader or a lead worshipper. Whenever you are convicted of any of them please immediately hand over to someone in the team who is better prepared and deal with it. That is another reason why everyone on the team needs to be prepared, in season and out of season. You may be ill-prepared, it could be your thoughts that are not right or it could be some form of sin that may be hindering your ministration. I beg you by

the mercies of God, whenever you are convicted of whatever you know is not acceptable before God, please hand over and sort it out first if not you will drive a bunch of innocent souls astray and be rest assured that God will demand an answer from you at an appointed time. I am not referring to those silly guilt games that the enemy plays with our minds at times. If you fell one way or the other and you have truly repented of your sin and have prayed to God and asked for forgiveness, just believe that you have been forgiven and disregard any guilt games the enemy will try to play on you whilst you minister. Rebuke him and he will flee and just minister to God. I recommended that you hand over when what you are convicted of is sin you have not confessed, prayed about and asked for forgiveness for.

Again, should there be the need to hand over, I am not asking that you announce your departure. You can do it quietly and seamlessly without being noticed, in which case the person taking over will have to flawlessly continue without publicity. That is why you are a team, remember? Again, if you have been rehearsing as a team and you are of one mind and understanding, this should not be a problem at all. During such a change over where necessary a lot will also rest on the instrumentalists who will need to skillfully 'bridge' the changeover. The fact that you started to minister does not necessarily mean that you should be the one to end. If you are a good team player, spiritually matured and with the right understanding of your God-given gift in ministry you should not have a problem at all with someone starting and handing over to you for one reason or the other. On the other hand also, you should not find it problematic handing over to someone on your team if the need be. If only we would listen more attentively and be sensitive enough to the Holy Spirit, we may just hear the Spirit of God prompt us to hand over the microphone occasionally. There have been occasions when I have just handed over the microphone so discreetly and the congregation had thought it was part of the 'original plan' yet those I had handed over to most often had come over to ask why I had put them on the spot.

CONCLUSION

IN conclusion, may I emphasize that the terms of our covenant with God in our present day, are far more superior to those of the Old Testament and hence we cannot afford to be lax in our approach to worshipping Him.

The Bible urges us to show forth, express or demonstrate the excellencies of The One who called us out of darkness into His marvelous light and we must be prepared to lend our all in all to such demonstrations (in our bodies, soul and spirit) as in the case of David who in *Psalms 103* tasked all that was within him to bless the Lord God Almighty.

Our praises must be readily available to God. In *Psalms 65:1* the Psalmist declares that praise awaits God in Zion (which is the gathering of the saints). In our congregations, we need to prepare our praise to await God Almighty. When children of God gather in His presence, their praises should not be prepared for any other human being, object, virgin, saint, person (living or dead, priest, pastor, bishop or pope) aside God. The practice in some churches where songs of praises are showered on to martyrs, deceased persons, virgins and all manner of demons should cease in view of the fact that the Bible says that our praise must await only God in Zion, where the children of God gather.

Protestants, the Charismatic and Pentecostals also cannot continue to fall victim to the unacceptable practice of offering God—deserving praise to others aside God.

Frankly, many people often indulge in certain things just to milk their own selfish antagonistic ambitions rather than making God the focus when they gather to worship. How many times have we not replaced songs which God might have Himself inspired and prompted us to minister with those that we felt were popular even though not necessarily God-inspired? Have many not often made the tune and manner of songs more important than the matter of them? I am by no means belittling the importance of skill and excellence in music. Brethren, if we should concentrate on just the music and neglect the real essence of our worship to God, then we would have missed the mark. Instrumentalists especially need to understand that, in spite of the fact that their place in worship is vital, God's house is not an opera house full of ordinary audiences. Church is not a place where people gather to amuse themselves and display their prowess in musical talents. Church should see a gathering of participating worshippers who truly understand what worship is all about. Church folk need to understand the 'SOS' of worship. In praise and worship, God should be *Our Subject, Our Object and Our Source.*

We are called to worship and not just to do what worshippers do. If I fixed a broken down vehicle and got it to move, I might have done what mechanics do but that would not necessarily make me a mechanic. In like manner, if I delivered a speech on behalf of a president, I might have done what that president would have usually done but that would not make me a president. With this understanding, may I suggest to you that the true worshipper is not necessarily the one who does what worshippers do but the one who worships in spirit and in truth, prompted by faith and who is yielded to the Holy Spirit to do the right thing.

The true worshipper's experience with God cannot be taken lightly. As we approach God's 'dangerous' holiness, it is imperative that we heed to God's demand for sanctification, given to Moses for His children in *Exodus 19:10*.

It is also essential that we observe Jacob's call unto his household (as recorded in *Genesis 35:2*) to put away all the strange gods amongst them and act accordingly, if we really want to enjoy a true worship experience.

Again, as we approach God in worship, there is the need for us to be obedient to His commands and to ensure that we do not offer 'strange fire' before Him in disobedience as Nadab and Abihu, the sons of Aaron did (*Leviticus 10:1*). If we disobey God, we could suffer the same consequence of naughtiness (death) as seen in *Numbers 3:4*.

Furthermore, it is important to note that we cannot approach God's Holy Presence irresponsibly. That would be tantamount to committing 'spiritual suicide'. In *Exodus 30:18-21*, God instructed Aaron and his sons to wash their hands and feet at the laver before entering the tabernacle in order that they do not die. Brethren, if we attempt to defile the presence of God, the penalty could be dreadful.

David asks in **Psalms 24:3:**

> 'Who it is that, will ascend into the hill of the Lord or stand in the Holy place and then intimates that it is the one who has clean hands, a pure heart and who has not lifted up his soul (feelings, intellect and will) unto vanity nor sworn deceitfully.

In **Psalms 15,** David further mentions that the one who qualifies to stand in the presence of the Lord is the one who walks uprightly and in righteousness and who speaks the truth in his heart. He says it is the one who does not slander with his tongue nor take up a reproach against his neighbor. Amongst other qualities, David mentions that the one fit to stand in God's presence is he who does no evil to his friend and despises troublemakers: the one who honors those who fear Jehovah and who does not take reward against the innocent.

Such should be the nature of a true worshipper.

I trust that these love notes from God concerning a subject that brings Him pleasure, though not exhaustive, must have refreshed and possibly added a little more to your understanding of what praise and worship is due the Lord God Almighty. Let us all strive to do His will on earth as is done in heaven as regards rendering unto Him our reasonable service and worship.

God richly bless you and may you reap a full reward for your **REASONABLE SERVICE.**

BIBLIOGRAPHY

▶ GOSSETT, Don, *There Is Dynamite In Praise*, ©1974, Published by Whitaker House, 30 Hunt Valley Circle, New Kensington, PA 15068.

▶ HAYFORD, Jackie, *The Heart Of Praise*, ©2005, Published by Regal Books, Ventura, California, USA.

▶ REDMAN, Matt, *The Unquenchable Worshipper*, ©2001, Published by Regal Books, Ventura, California, USA.

▶ YOUSSEF, Michael, *Empowered By Praise*, ©2002, Published by WATERBROOK PRESS, 2375 Telstar Drive, Suite 160, Colorado Springs, Colorado 80920.